Bugging In
by
David E Crossley

© Copyright 2013   David E Crossley

ISBN-978-1-291-26685-6

All rights reserved. No part of this publication may be reproduced, stored in a retrieval system, or transmitted, in any form or by any means, electronic, mechanical, photocopying, recording, or otherwise, without the written prior permission of the author.

Index

Introduction	4
Bug In Basics	9
For what do you need to prepare?	13
Power	21
Shelter	55
Light	69
Warmth	81
Cooling	102
Food	109
Cooking and Preserving	143
Water	163
Hygiene	181
Health and medical care	188
Safety and security	207
Communications	237
Entertainment and Education	245
Finances	248
Bug In kit and supplies	255
Bugging In task list	269

New products, ideas and information 272

Summary 275

Acknowledgements 276

Reading list and links 277

About the author 278

Introduction

This morning I was having a cup of coffee and chatting with a neighbour. John and his wife Mary are part of our local network. He is a shooter, a caravanner, fisherman, canal boat owner. Mary brings us spare eggs from their hens and we give them some of our jam or homebrew in return.

The recent petrol shortage threat and warnings of a return to bad weather had prompted a question from John's brother, Donald, who has always been dismissive of any Prepping type stuff but who has been quieter about it after being caught out last winter. He asked what he could put together as an emergency kit. He doesn't want to talk about the apocalypse, nor to spend a fortune, isn't interested in Bugging Out or military gear. He just wants a box of stuff he can shove in the cupboard under the stairs and forget about unless he needs it, if he and his wife, Jane, are caught at home by bad weather and at the same time are hit by a power cut as they were last year. This is in addition to a couple of cans of diesel that, on the recommendation of the PM, he now has in the garage for his car. He reckons 3 days supplies should be enough and still believes that any more than that is a waste of money and space.

Donald's question was a surprise but good news to John; because he had always thought that if an emergency arose his brother would be on his doorstep by next morning at the latest. At least now John will have a breathing space and there is a mindset on which he thinks he might be able to gradually build, especially since he suspects that Jane would secretly like to be stocked up as a hedge against rising prices.

After some discussion, John and I decided that anything in the kit had to be: independent of mains utilities, easy to use, safe even for someone who has never used it before, not reliant on consumables that will deteriorate e.g. disposable batteries, and good at any time of year in even the worst of weather i.e. indoors only. Donald and Jane will have all the usual household hardware such as pots and pans, cutlery, bedding, etc. but the kit should not rely on them having any consumables on hand.

His brother's house is a modern bungalow, all electric, on mains water/drainage, no gas or open fires, but does have good double glazing, and cavity wall and loft insulation. It is in a small village in Argyle, so in the given timescale is unlikely to be affected by rioting or looting.

For **warmth** we chose a small portable gas heater, based on the fact that it is compact, safe, easy to use, reasonably efficient, and inexpensive. For 3 days we added a dozen gas cylinders.

For **cooking** we decided a gas stove would best fit the specification.

We could have chosen a smaller camping-type model but this is very stable, again easy to use, and works with the same cartridges as the heater. For 3 days 3 cylinders should be more than enough but we specified 6 to allow some spares for both this and the heater. We also listed a disposable lighter in case the built-in igniter didn't work for any reason. For safety we decided that gas rather than liquid or solid fuel was undoubtedly the way to go.

For Light, safety was again a major consideration, so no liquid fuel or candles. We discussed solar lights, maybe normally placed around the garden, but because of concentration on an event in winter with poor recharging by solar, and wanting to avoid batteries that might be dud when needed, we went for dynamo lights.

2 wind-up lanterns

1 wind-up torch

For food we decided the best route was mainly tins or dry foods due to longevity, familiarity, and resistance to vermin, and bearing in mind that there is no intention to carry them anywhere but they will be kept in a clip-top box. Jane's tin opener is wall mounted and electric so we included a simple mechanical opener. John knows the eating habits of his brother and sister-in-law well enough and the choices were his. Your tastes might vary! I did ask if we should include alcohol but John doesn't believe there is any chance of them running short of that!

The menu includes:

Breakfast

3 tins 'all day breakfast'

1 pkt Ryvita

1 jar jam

3 sachets instant coffee (from John's stocks)

3 tea bags

1 pkt milk powder

12 sachets sugar (from burger place)

Main meal

3 tins meat – Stewed steak, Haggis, Chicken in sweet and sour sauce

2 tins potatoes

1 Pkt easy cook rice

3 tins peas

6 sachets salt, 3 pepper, (from burger place)

3 tins sponge desert

3 tins custard

3 sachets instant coffee (from John's stocks)

3 tea bags

12 sachets sugar (from burger place)

Milk powder from same pkt used for breakfast

Lunch or supper

3 tins condensed soup – differing flavours

Ryvita and jam from breakfast supplies

6 sachets instant hot chocolate in various flavours

1 tin of assorted biscuits

For **Water** we chose containers because there is no fresh surface water nearby and the users have no garden water butts, (only a small lawn and some edging plants) so:

6 1-gallon containers still water

Health and hygiene requirements are fairly self-explanatory, though Donald will probably question the need for the facemasks and gloves.

2 toilet rolls

1 pkt waste bin liners

3 bin liners

1 bar soap

1 tube toothpaste

1 small first aid kit (Asda £1 inc. variety of plasters, etc)

1 box tissues

1 pkt paracetamol

1 bottle hand sanitiser

1 bottle disinfectant

1 pkt disposable cleaning cloths

6 disposable facemasks

6 pairs disposable gloves

Both Donald and his wife are ardent readers but for information and entertainment we included a wind-up radio. To keep down costs this is built into the same unit as the torch.

And that was it. It's a bare minimum but it meets the requirements of the users and provides a couple of extras as a sound base on which to build. Total cost (late 2012) should be just over £90 if you shop around.

If you are taking your first steps into Prepping you might want to start with a similar kit to the one above. All of the items work but if any is not to your preference for any reason there are plenty of alternatives, though they might be more expensive. The kit covers the basics of warmth, light, food, water, health and hygiene, information and entertainment for routine short-duration emergencies such as: power cuts; a frozen or burst mains water pipe; running out of money near the end of the month; a bad cold, diarrhoea, or a pulled muscle that makes it difficult to get out of the house for a few days; or even an unexpected visitor when your cupboards are nearly bare. It will all fit into a couple of 35ltr boxes so it doesn't take up much space, it can be stored discretely, and if ever necessary it is easily transferred to a car for bugging out, though there are other things you would want to take as well in that case.

You might not want to stop at that level though, and for those concerned about the longer term there is far more that you can do. There are a wide range of potential Bug In situations, from staying warm, comfortable and in touch with the world even though the snow piles up outside and frozen, over-heavy power lines break, to keeping your family fed during a personal or national financial crisis, to shutting out the violence and germs while a pandemic rages through the country and panicking or avaricious people make the streets unsafe to travel.

Bug In Basics

Firstly, to put the rest of this book into context, I want to define my meaning of Bugging In. Bugging In is where an individual or group is confined to the limits of their residence without face to face contact with anyone from outside.

The residence could be a 7th floor flat, a suburban semi and its garden, or a remote farm on the moors. The group could be a single person, a family, or a survivalist collective. The isolation might be self-inflicted or forced on them by conditions outside the residence and its immediate surroundings.

One of the good things about Bugging In is that it doesn't much matter what the cause might be. Whether it is a snowstorm or a pandemic, once the decision is made the things you are going to need are much the same, and useful in many other circumstances too.

There certainly could be differences, especially early in a situation. In some cases the power might stay on for quite a while, when in others it is lost almost immediately. Loss of power is often an early and widespread feature of an emergency and in our modern world the one that is most disruptive. Yet because our infrastructure is normally reliable, cuts are rare and usually short-lived, so few people actually prepare for them to last for long and many don't prepare at all.

In some cases the conditions could prevent any threat from rioters, looters or ordinary thieves because they have to stay inside too but no relief water supplies can be delivered either. Or perhaps anything that comes from outside must be decontaminated before allowing it onto the property.

In the end, the basics of life are unvarying and to be properly prepared you should be able to survive without any mains utilities or help from official organisations. The most important question then becomes, 'for how long?'

In the Introduction to this book I wrote about Donald and Jane. Donald had decided that he needed to be ready for interruption of normal services lasting three days. That was based on his experience of bad weather and intermittent, if sometimes extended, power cuts which had substantially disrupted his family's activities for that period of time. The fact that those conditions could have persisted for a fortnight didn't really strike true with him. Three days was the worst he had experienced so three days was all he needed to prepare for.

By coincidence three days precisely matches the time recommended by government agencies in the USA for which families should be prepared to look after themselves in an emergency. This has lead to promotion of the now-familiar '72 hour kit', that being the time the authorities there say that they need before they can respond and get help to people affected by a disaster. Unfortunately, experience has shown that the victims might have to wait quite a lot longer than that before rescue or relief arrives but even if that is the case three days worth of preps is better than none.

I consider, and recommend, that a more realistic minimum time frame is two weeks. That takes into account the wide variety of differing situations that might arise but I emphasise that it is a *minimum* and after you reach that level it is prudent to extend it considerably.

Three months worth of preps should actually cover the vast majority of crises that might occur but if you factor in things like becoming unemployed, or wars and other events that could interrupt supply of oil and other trade, rapidly driving prices for food and other essentials to unprecedented levels, then stocking for a year is not unreasonable. If the disruptions then persist you have a strong base of support while you adapt, perhaps by developing a garden or whatever other measures are needed.

People who are working towards long-term self sufficiency and supplying their needs from their own produce rather than simply using stores go further and work to build a 2 or 3 year storage plan. That takes into account the possibility of a crop failure or loss of their animals to disease and a need to fall back on stores until the next harvest, or the next generation of animals is born.

How do you know what you need to include in your stores? My suggestion, which matches that of other people with experience in this field, is to keep all your shopping lists or till receipts from a month's worth of shopping. If you do not routinely buy in bulk, that should give you a good indication of the items you normally use up over that period. You then need to highlight each of the products that you could not consume before they would deteriorate to the point you had to throw them away if you had no mains power; mainly things such as dairy products, fresh fish or meat, or vegetables you keep in the refrigerator or freezer. Now decide which of those items are essential, which are desirable, and which are luxuries. For all the essentials, most of the desirables, and a few of the luxuries, you must then identify alternatives with long shelf lives.

This will give you an initial list of items of which you should build a stock. When you have decided how long your stock must last when in daily use, the totals from the receipts will also guide you in how much of each you need to buy.

As you read through this book you will realise that there are things not in your usual shopping list that you should add because of the changed circumstances inherent in an emergency situation - you might need a lot more batteries or salt for example - but other information on alternative power and food sources or preservation might change some items or reduce the quantities needed. Don't worry about it; if you use your receipts and the lists at the end of the book as a guide to building an initial reserve, then you can adapt and refine that as you learn what does and what doesn't work for your family and situation.

There are a couple of ways to develop your store, depending primarily on what you can afford. If you have the cash or credit to buy in bulk from a cash-and-carry store you can in fact make considerable savings. Remember, for the most part we are talking about the sort of consumables you use every day, so if nothing does happen you have simply bought in advance and can then rotate your stocks, having saved a lot of money in the process.

If you are on a tighter budget then you can gradually build up by taking advantage of 2-for-1 promotions and the like. Shopping on the basis of 'one to use and one for the stash' of a different item each week, whenever you can afford it, will both quickly build your stash and ensure that you are storing things your family like to eat or use now, while costing little more than you would normally spend. Take care with the offers though; shoppers regularly report that what is promoted as a saving if you buy a bigger pack can actually work out more expensive than buying the same items individually. It pays to work it out!

Before buying to put in your store, you might also want to compare 'own brand' items against those from better known makers. Sometimes the cheaper item is as good, or better, than that from the 'name' provider and sometimes it's not, especially with supermarket 'value' range products. We have tried baked beans and rice pudding from a couple of the value ranges and found they were disgusting, with virtually no bulk and a thin, weak flavoured liquid. Other items were as good as their premium range.

Food plays an important role in preserving morale during times of stress and discomfort; you don't want to waste storage or detract from its value by offering meals that people find unpleasant. For the same reason, try to include a few treats in your stores; they can go a long way to raising the mood when times seem particularly dark.

However, whether you are thinking about food or any other aspect of prepping, your choices will be much more efficient if they are properly informed by a sound knowledge of the subject. There are many aspects to survival while Bugging In and although every member of a group should have a grasp of the basics of all of them no individual can know everything. Each person within a family or a group must therefore have their roles and responsibilities. These should be based on their abilities and where possible their interests so that they will enjoy developing their knowledge and skills in these areas and achieve a higher level as a result.

When you really get into it, Prepping and the choices it involves become a normal way of life. The mindset can be usefully developed even at a young age. One member of Ludlow Survivors Group recently wrote that their 5 year old daughter's responsibility every Friday is to check that the torches kept in each room are working correctly and showing no sign of needing new batteries; a job she loves to do. At much the same age I used to set out the paper, sticks, and matches ready for my dad to light the fire and then watch fascinated as he did so. I gradually moved on to laying the fire and then to lighting it, though only while under supervision.

Prepping might seem like a modern phenomenon to many readers but nothing could be further from the truth, we have just given it a new name. I think we were lucky enough to enjoy some good times until recently and most people have forgotten, or never experienced, the need. When I was growing up, not long after the Second World War, the shortages and utility failures were still fresh in my parents' minds and though money was tight they did what they could to be ready for any problems we might face. I suppose I inherited that mindset.

We are not the first generation of Preppers but someone mocking what we do is a modern oddity. In fact people NOT putting aside for hard times when they could or NOT being ready to support themselves, rather than relying on others, has been thought of as foolishness throughout most of history. Now, if people put anything aside it is money, and if they take out any form of insurance that is also intended to pay money. Unfortunately, a stash of cash isn't always the answer; ask anyone who has lived in a country where the economy and banks collapsed or a disaster meant some necessities were not available at any price.

If you are reading this book then you clearly see the folly of not being prepared and self reliant. In times often beset by natural and man-made challenges, climate change, terrorists, global recession, official resources ever reduced by austerity measures, and so much more, the ability to look after yourself and your loved ones, without relying on outside help that might never come, is worth it for the peace of mind alone.

For what do you need to prepare?

If you want your preparations (hereafter referred to as preps) to be as efficient and effective as they should be, you first need to establish what you need to prepare for, and which threats have the highest priority because of likelihood and potential impact on you and your family.

Businesses and government agencies do this all the time in the guise of 'risk assessment and analysis'. Following the same procedure for prepping will help to ensure you are ready for the highest priorities first and that you don't waste time, money, and effort concentrating on things that should really be left until later or might not be needed at all.

Many people fall into the trap of doing things in the wrong order because they first address the subjects they most enjoy and are interested in; which would be fine, except it could leave you unprepared for something serious that would require you to Bug In when you have spent all your time and cash on camping gear for Bugging Out.

To follow the correct process, you have to go through a sequence of steps:

1) Identify potential dangers

2) Specify their possible effects

3) Evaluate the risk and threat levels

4) Prioritise dangers

5) Decide what measures you need to take to eliminate or minimise dangers

6) Plan how you are going to implement those measures

7) Put the plans into action

8) Test your results, then correct any omissions or failures

9) Review the risk and threat levels in light of the results of your actions

10) Re-prioritise as appropriate and move on to the next step in your preps

Identify potential dangers

This step simply consists of making a list of those things that potentially pose a threat to your survival.

The government posts information on what risks it considers being of highest priority, and how it arrived at that decision, on the website for the National Risk Register of Civil Emergencies, updated every two years.

http://www.cabinetoffice.gov.uk/resource-library/national-risk-register

That list includes:

Pandemic Influenza

Coastal flooding

Catastrophic terrorist attacks inc. suicide bombs, guns and grenades, CBR (Chemical Biological Radiological) attacks, cyber attacks, highjacking

Severe effusive volcanic eruptions abroad e.g. Iceland

Severe space weather inc. solar flares, coronal mass ejections, and solar energetic particle events

Severe weather inc. storms and gales, low temperatures and heavy snow, heat waves, and drought

Animal diseases

Major industrial accidents inc. fire, contamination – chemical or radiation release

Technical failure inc. electricity, water and sewerage, gas, telecommunications, fuel, marine pollution

Major transport accidents inc. rail, maritime, road and rail

Disruptive industrial action

Public disorder inc. riots

For your own list you might include all of those but add things like:

House fire

Local flooding

Earthquake

Subsidence and erosion

Global/national/personal financial collapse

Resource collapse e.g. Peak Oil, crop failures

Some of these, such as a house fire, or contamination from an industrial accident, might mean you need the guidance in Bugging Out, the companion volume to this book. Some, such as pandemic, riots, or severe air pollution from a volcanic eruption, would make it safer to Bug In. Local flooding might go either way, with you needing to Bug Out if your house is inundated but Bug In if the waters aren't in your home but block the roads in and out of your area.

Consider them all at this stage of the process but in this book we will deal with the detailed measures for those situations that prompt you to Bug In.

Specify their possible effects

Having made your list you then need to consider the potential effects of each event. Again, don't rule anything out at this stage. For example:

National financial collapse could result in: bank closures, loss of your savings, demand for payment of outstanding loans or mortgage with possible eviction if you can't pay; closure of credit and debit card systems with shops demanding cash only in payment; shortages of imported food stuffs, fuel, and other essentials; unemployment due to failure of your employer's business; riots; police, rubbish collectors, firemen, hospital staff and other public employees not working because they're not being paid, leading to increased crime, disease, and deaths; and all the other effects currently being regularly experienced in southern Europe and that others that have suffered in similar events elsewhere.

Evaluate the risk and threat levels

In Risk Management the terms risk and threat have different meanings. Risk relates to the likelihood of something happening, whereas Threat specifies the potential impact or consequences.

Often these are shown diagrammatically using a grid system with Risk on one axis and Threat on the other. The axes might be numbered from 0-5 or 10, or pretty much anything you prefer. You can decide on your own levels and their potential impact on you but for example:

Risk	Threat

5	Unavoidable and imminent	Severe	Death, disabling or disfiguring injury or illness, loss of home, bankruptcy
4	Probable in the near future	High	Injury, illness, poverty
3	Probable but time frame unknown	Medium	Downgrade to lifestyle, stress
2	Possible but not probable	Medium low	Financial loss, personal disadvantage, family troubles
1	Highly unlikely	Low	Inconvenience
0	Inconceivable	Zero	No noticeable effect

To calculate the over-all level of danger, you enter a particular event or effect in a box that reflects your decision as to how likely it is and what the probable impact would be. You then multiply the numbers to calculate the level for that Event. For example you might consider that flooding of your house wouldn't be fatal but you aren't insured for it so the impact would be serious, so you allocate the threat level as 4 out of 5 but since you live half way up a well drained hill and nowhere near water the Risk is 0, so the calculated level is 4 x 0, which is still 0. You have now considered that danger but can put it near the bottom your list of things about which you need to worry or do anything.

If, on the other hand, you live in a flat above a shop that rioters recently tried to rob and when they couldn't get in they tried to set it on fire, and you believe it might happen again before too long, you might put the Risk as a 4 and the threat as a 4, for a total score of 16 out of 25, which is 64%.

The table might look like this:

Threat						
5						
4	Flooding				Arson	
3				Unemployment		
2						
1						
0						
	0	1	2	3	4	5
				Risk		

With my categorisation of potential effects, any threat level very near to or greater than 40% is something you should consider tackling and anything over 50% should be on your priority list.

The more information you have, the greater the validity your rating will probably be. So if you don't 'think' a pandemic in the UK is very likely, but that is just an opinion, research the subject in the library, or online, or by talking to people who are 'in the know' before making your decision rather than risk making a serious mistake on the basis of guesswork and cynicism.

Prioritise dangers

After you have analysed the various hazards you included in your list you should have a rating for each of them. Now is the time to prioritise that list.

Logically, the higher the rating the higher the priority and the sooner you should look to taking the measures needed to lower the risk and its impact. However, if some ratings are very close you might want to look at those with higher risk i.e. probability, before those with a higher potential impact but which are less likely. It simply makes sense that if you have realised a threat is an almost daily danger for you because of your lifestyle, that you should deal with that first.

You also have to be realistic. There will inevitably be life factors, such as your bank balance, that you have to take into consideration. An item might be high on your priority list but dealing with it in the most effective way is something you just can't afford right now. Nevertheless, although you might not be able to eliminate the risk, you might be able to lower it or reduce the impact, using less expensive measures. With a lower risk and threat level it should then be further down the priority ratings, giving you time to investigate other ways to deal with it more effectively.

Decide what measures you need to take

There are five ways to counter danger:

1) Prevent it – stop the risk from materialising e.g. move to somewhere that isn't near a target for looters or arsonists

2) Reduce it – either reduce the likelihood of the risk or the impact if it does occur e.g. if you are in an area prone to flooding, install flood protection barriers to keep water out, and/or rearrange your living arrangements to put most of your expensive and vulnerable possessions upstairs, etc

3) Accept it – understand the risk and potential consequences but choose not to do anything about them
4) Transfer it – Make the impact somebody else's problem e.g. take out insurance
5) Plan for it – make a plan of what to do if the risk does materialise e.g. house fire = Bug Out.

In many cases your plan of action will include several of those counters. For example you might take steps to reduce the likelihood and potential impact, but have a plan of what to do as part of that, and have insurance so that if you don't manage to save everything some of the impact is transferred.

There are many factors that might come into play in deciding these things, including but not limited to: your health and fitness and that of other family members; types of transport available to you; whether you have a place to go if you do Bug Out; how well you can prepare and stock up for bugging in; your skills and help on which you can confidently rely.

When you have made those judgements you will have a much better idea of the circumstances and context in which you will need to apply the measures covered in this book or in Bugging Out.

Plan how you are going to implement those measures

Once you have identified what you need to and can do, you need a plan of how to do it.

If developing skills is needed you might look for a training course, or decide that reading a book and then practising what you have learnt is a better way for you.

If you need to buy supplies you might decide to save up, buy on credit, or gradually build your stock by buying a few extras on each shopping trip

The important thing is to make a realistic plan that you can actually achieve and then ...

Put your plan into action

The previous stages are essential to identify what you need to do, how and when, but until you actually do something about it none of what you have learnt and decided means anything.

Take the first step: buy that extra can of beans and put it in your store; go into the garden and make a rocket stove from some old bricks; cut up a can to make a candle lantern.

Then take the next step in your plan and keep moving forwards. You aren't going to achieve everything in a day but everything you do takes you that bit closer to safety and survival.

Test your results, then correct any omissions or failures

After you have completed the previous stages in this process, built up your stockpile, skills and knowledge base, there is an understandable temptation to congratulate yourself then sit back and relax in the warm glow of comfort and security.

Unfortunately there is something still missing; at this stage you don't know if any of your plans and preps will actually work!

Having got to this point you now need to test yourself and your gear to ensure things will function as you expect. Unless a real Event happens and provides the best test of all, then you will have to run a simulation.

For a Bug In situation; one Friday night turn off the mains supplies to your home and live for the weekend using only your preps. Better still, take a holiday and live it for the longer period.

This is when you find out that your prized solar-charged lamp is bright enough to let you walk around without bumping into the furniture but not to read Friday's paper, or that you use more water than you expected, or that you couldn't really face eating tinned chilli and tortillas every day!

There are some preps you are not going to be able to test realistically at home. Your options for many medical procedures are limited, for example, so you might want to take a suitable course where the instructor will have the appropriate equipment to ensure your CPR would work on a real casualty.

What ever method you use, make the rest as realistic as possible to the situation you want to simulate and don't cheat! Make notes of what works and what doesn't, what plans you need to change, what extra or different resources you need, and what knowledge or skills you need to build, and then address those things as soon as you can.

Review the risk and threat levels in light of your test results

Even when you are satisfied that your preps are as good as you can reasonably make them, you are still not finished. Things change. Your preps will have changed the risk and certainly the threat levels of some hazards. Aging or injury can affect your ability in various activities. Things that were once a minor risk become increasingly likely as the national or global situation changes.

Constant vigilance and regular reassessment are always needed to prevent your plans and preps becoming outdated and ineffective.

Re-prioritise and move on to the next step in your preps

As your assessment of hazards does change, either because you have prepped effectively or the risk or threat has increased, so their place in your priority list will also change. Be adaptable.

A high level of planning and preps will always provide a firm base on which to build your response, so the risk of having to start any prep from scratch is low, and so should be the threat it presents to you. That doesn't mean, though, that you can't improve your skills, add a wind turbine to your off-grid power system, or make friends with someone who has skills that you lack, and then invite them into your Prepper group.

Every little thing you can do raises the level of your preps and the security and comfort in which will be able to face any emergency.

Power

Before starting to write this chapter I decided to walk around our house to make a quick list of the items that use mains power and that we use on a daily or regular basis. I shouldn't have been surprised at how long the list became but I must admit I was. At the start of each chapter after this I'll include a reminder of those items from the list that are relevant to that need.

Household devices that use mains electricity

Air Purifiers	Fans	Bedside Clocks
Radios	Bedside Lamps	Overhead lights
Toothbrush	Boiler/central heating	Shower
Razor	Hair drier	Electric fire
Computers	Cable modem	Back up drive
Printer	Label printer	TV
Cable TV box	Table/standard Lamps	Telephone
Mobile phone chargers	Battery chargers	Toaster
Kettle	Fridge	Ovens
Microwave	Bread maker	Mincer
Food mixers	Blender	Deep fat fryer
Ice cream maker	Freezer	Dehydrator
Airers	Vacuum cleaners	Iron
Washing machine	Tumble drier	Dishwasher
Nebuliser	Steam machine	Back massager
Exercise machines	Sewing machine	Power Drill
Games machine	Door bell	Emergency lights (rechargeable)
Alarm system	External security lights	Security cameras

Mains Gas

Cooker hob, Boiler

Since these items are used as a part of our normal routine, when preparing for a Bug In situation that might feature a loss of mains power we had to identify which were utilities and which were luxuries and how we were going to power those we considered essential or what we could use instead for the rest. We did that some time ago, but it is surprising how little extras creep back into your lives.

It is certainly an important exercise at the start of prepping, and one at which I suggest all of you have a go, and occasionally review. Most of you will have many items similar to our own; some of you might have more.

Some of our items, such as the ice cream maker and the back massager are definitely luxuries used only occasionally and can be ignored for an emergency. Some we can easily replace with non-electric alternatives; the electric razor and toothbrush are good examples. Some can be replaced by non-electric versions, but not without a loss of efficiency and convenience. And some, such as the freezer and computers need an alternative source of electrical supply if their use is to continue.

The greediest user of electricity is the generation of heat. Unless you are resource-rich that rules out using alternative power generation for cooking, boiling kettles, or heating your home. On the other side of the coin, solar powered/charged lighting with long-life high-efficiency LED lamps, is an extremely efficient and low-draw use of electrical power, plus it can provide brighter and better quality illumination than most of the alternatives and will go on doing so for years without burning any fuel or wearing out any moving parts.

Power generation is, however, expensive. It doesn't matter what type of device you use it is going to cost you. The higher the output, the more costly it will be. So for example you might be able to buy a 650w two-stroke generator for around £60 but an 1800w diesel version will cost £3-400. A 100w solar panel will cost around £400 but if you want 1000w you must multiply that cost by ten.

Then you have to figure in running costs. A generator needs fuel and regular maintenance. Solar panels require neither but are more expensive per watt initially, need appropriate wiring and electronics and to be connected to a bank of batteries that will need to be maintained and replaced every seven to ten years, on average.

The sensible thing to do, therefore, is to minimise the amount of electricity you need to generate, so as to cut down both initial and on-going costs. To do that you can eliminate the use of some items completely; cut down the amount of use of those you do need; or find a non-electric alternative. However, if you choose the latter route you should also think about the cost of the alternative. You might, for example, decide to use candles instead of solar powered lighting because a box of candles is cheaper, but candles need to be replaced constantly as they burn whereas a few solar charged lights will go on working for years and so might be the better choice in the long term.

When you are looking at the alternatives for a long Bug In you must also consider whether one type of item will last for as long as you need it, and whether replacements are likely to be available. A generator is a wonderful piece of equipment for many power-down emergencies, but it is only useful for as long as you have fuel for it. Paraffin for lamps simply burns away. Solar panels often remain in service for over 20 years, but the batteries they are used to charge only have a life expectancy of one third to one half of that.

Having deliberated carefully, you might decide that a generator is worthwhile, because the main thing for which you need it is to power your freezer. You have calculated that you can store enough fuel to run the generator for a few hours per day, until you will have used the entire contents of the freezer, and the outlay compared against the monetary and nourishment value of the frozen food that would be lost without power makes buying one cost-effective. After that, if you can get fuel, you can use the genny occasionally for power tools or the like but it will have served its main purpose.

There are many options, and I suggest you read all the following chapters before starting to buy. In each of them I will provide information on the various ways to provide on-going facilities for the relevant purposes. For the rest of this chapter, I will review the alternative sources of power you could use for those items that will only run on electricity.

Generators

Generators are available to provide power at every level from running an electric hedge cutter or power tools on an allotment to keeping a farm, hospital or manufacturing plant functional when the mains go down.

You can buy a model that runs on two-stroke petrol/oil mix, four-stroke petrol, diesel, or Propane gas, and some are convertible. The larger types, known as Stand-by generators, are usually fixed in place and wired into the mains supply. Some have a sensor capability that will cause them to start automatically when the mains supply fails and the circuits will switch over to them within seconds, as soon as they are up to running speed. Others are manual; you have to start them yourself and select the source by turning a switch.

There are also lighter versions designed to be portable. Some are big enough that they are mounted on a trailer or trolley; some are small and light enough to be carried by one hand. These smaller types are often referred to as 'suitcase' generators, though the comparison is to size and their having a single handle rather than appearance.

Generally the most reliable and durable generators are designed to run on diesel fuel, but have the advantage that they will also burn domestic heating oil, aviation fuel, or a diesel/cooking oil or cooking oil/paraffin mix. Their disadvantages are that they tend to be larger and heavier than petrol types and are often correspondingly expensive.

Portable petrol/Propane convertible versions are well thought of by caravanners and boat owners, most of who agree that those made by Honda are particularly good, but many market stall holders use cheaper models and say that for light use they are adequate. Cheap two-stroke generators have the reputation of being most troublesome.

We have a 2Kw diesel model for use at the house but we also have a 2Kw portable petrol/Propane type which serves as a back-up or for use at our caravan, which is stored at one of our Bug Out locations on a farm. Although the farm has various generators and alternative energy sources, we like to have our own available in case we have to move on from there.

You should select what is right for your uses, or you might decide against a generator and go for one or more of the alternatives if that will be adequate for your needs.

Diesel

2GF

The picture above shows a fairly typical portable diesel generator. They produce standard UK domestic 230v 50 Hz supply and have either electric or manual (pull cord) starting. A 2Kw model will use a half to one litre of fuel per hour, so total running time depends on tank capacity. They might weigh up to 80Kg, so their being 'portable' is debateable for many people. They usually have at least 2 mains sockets, though some only have one, and some have connectors for caravan type cables and 12v leads as well. Noise level when running at full power is around 80dB.

Different makes and models differ in about every part of that specification so it pays to shop around, look at several, and try to move them.

A feature of generators that many people don't consider is that they run best and most reliably under 60-75% load and constantly running them on

24

lower than that can cause damage. This is another good reason (apart from cost) to calculate how much power output you will actually use and not buy a generator that is substantially bigger than you need.

Petrol/Propane

This is the Honda EU20i portable petrol generator, which can also be converted to run on Liquid Petroleum Gas (LPG)

It produces 2Kw at 230v 50Hz AC, or 12v DC, up to 8 amps

Fuel tank capacity is 4.1 litres which will give a running time of up to 10 hours.

Length is 510mm, Width 290mm, Height 425mm Dry weight is 21Kg.

Noise level is very low at only 52dB

This is a high class generator built to last but the price reflects that at just over £1000. In part you are certainly paying for the Honda reputation when you buy but it is well founded.

Similar models with compatible features are available from different manufacturers, such as this one from Clarke, for much less money. Hyundai and other manufacturers are also on the market for £400 upwards. Most are a bit thirstier and noisier than the Honda but over all they are not a bad buy considering the price difference.

Two-stroke

If you want a really cheap generator for occasional light use then you might be satisfied with a two-stroke,

This one is fairly typical of the breed, producing either the usual domestic voltage or 12v DC but only up to 850w maximum power and 720w constant output. It is quite cheap to run, giving over 8 hours from the 4ltr capacity tank, though you do have to add the small cost of 2-stroke mix oil to that. Reviews on this model are quite good; it is noisier than the 2Kw Honda but about the same as the Clarke. Weight is about 18Kilos and cost around £90. Two-stroke engines can be difficult to start after they have been sitting unused for a while and are not renowned for their longevity or reliability, but they are cheap so you get what you pay for.

The two main disadvantages of generators are the need for fuel and the noise they make. Fuel for running engines does not keep well in storage. Petrol can deteriorate with 3-6 months and diesel within a year, to the point where they will no longer run the generator or a car. You can extend the life by adding a stabiliser – Sta-bil is currently the most popular – and petrol will then keep for a couple of years and diesel for three or more if they don't get too hot. Propane will last almost indefinitely. However much you store it won't last forever but make the most of it while you can.

Of them all diesel is safest to store but the amount that you are allowed to store of any of these fuels is limited by law. You should ensure that any stocks you do keep are stored where they are safe from fire, secure from theft, and ventilated to allow dispersal of any vapour or gas that does leak. Ensure containers for diesel and petrol are clearly marked with the contents; spray painting the handles of petrol cans red and diesel black is fairly standard. Put metal cans on a pallet to reduce the chance of rust and protect the sides and top from rain or contact with any wall or other surface that might be damp. Have appropriate fire extinguishers nearby.

Noise is mainly a security concern in that it will attract the greedy or jealous who will want whatever benefits you have that they lack. They might initially be attracted to the generator but realising you have one they will inevitably start to wonder what else you might have that they would like (and of which, in their mind, they entitled to a share).

Because of the poisonous emissions, a generator must not be run within an inhabited building but although you won't get total silence, a noise-reducing box and a buried exhaust outside the building can quieten things considerably. When mains power is out and fuel is in short supply background noise will be noticeably lacking, but even so, normal working hours will remain the most active for the majority of people and will be when any noise you do make will be least noticeable, so confine your generator running to these times whenever possible.

Anyone who has lived in a country that has been through a major emergency which features power failure and fuel shortages will tell you that generators and fuel are high up in the list of things that quickly become desirable, and therefore valuable (more about other things on that list in the chapter on Finances). If you have them they need to be used efficiently and effectively, treasured and protected.

Alternative energy

Other than a generator, the main alternative source of electrical power for use during a cut is a battery. If you are like most people you will have lots of small personal items, such as radios, torches, CD players, games machines, etc. that run on them. If you are a Prepper then you will certainly realise the need to keep in a good stock of both disposable and rechargeable batteries in whatever sizes you use.

However, for many uses these small cells are too limited in the power they will store and what you need are large lead acid 12volt leisure batteries, possibly in a properly organised bank and with various equipment required for safe recharging and use. In a page or two after this you will find a diagram for the items needed for off grid power. That diagram features a box at the top specifying various charging devices such as solar panels. However, if you consider that any power cuts are likely to be of fairly short duration you can have the rest of the system but without these alternative power sources.

You could instead have the battery bank connected to the mains via a 'smart' battery charger that will reduce mains 240v supply to 12-14v for charging the batteries. It will also perform the functions of the charge regulator, by monitoring the state of the batteries, allowing what is necessary through to maintain the charge while preventing over-charging, and prevent damage to the system by feed back. This system can be configured to kick in automatically if mains power is cut, so that it functions as an Uninterruptible Power Supply (UPS) or you can have a manual switch to bring it into play.

If the mains failure is prolonged and you have a generator you could then simply change the charger from the mains socket to the generator and use that to recharge your batteries. Many large organisations such as hospitals and offices have a system similar to this but with a huge battery bank, generator and fuel stocks.

If you want longer-term power generation without having to worry about a continuing fuel supply, then you have to turn to alternative energy sources. For small scale use that means Photovoltaic (solar) panels, wind turbines, or water turbines.

One major difference between these sources and a generator is that the alternatives are not usually intended to provide power directly to the device that will make use of it. Instead, the power generated is passed through a voltage regulator to a bank of batteries. The power from this battery bank is then either routed directly to 12v devices or through an Inverter that converts it to 240v to run equipment that would usually be plugged into the mains.

That is basically all you need in a simple system. A panel or turbine generates the power; the regulator monitors the state of charge of the batteries and allows power to flow from the generating device as it is required, then stops the flow when the battery is fully charged. It also ensures that power does not flow back the wrong way and damage the panels/turbine; the batteries store the power; when a device demands power the inverter converts the flow from the batteries to the correct voltage and current; and the device operates as it should. For safety in a larger system you should also have various combiners, fuses or breakers, and power meters in the circuit.

One thing to be aware of when buying equipment for a system: most panels and turbines are designed to put out 12volts DC, but for commercial use 24v and 48v components are also available. Many articulated lorries and other large vehicles are fitted with 24v systems. 48v systems are more efficient but less common and normally used for emergency power or remote locations by large companies or organisations. For the remainder of this book I will stick with 12v systems because those are the most frequently used for our purposes and have the widest selection of gear available; just watch out for equipment in the other voltages if you decide to buy.

WAV

OK, I have been using some terms, particularly 'power', interchangeably to try and simplify things but now it is time to get a bit technical. In electricity, Power is measured in Watts, Current is measured in Amps, and Voltage is measured in Volts.

Don't worry about that too much for now but in the next section, in relation to how long it will take a battery to recharge, we will use a formula: $W = A \times V$

Where W = Watts, A = Amps and V = Volts

We will also consider the variations on that formula: $A = W/V$ and $V = W/A$ (The techies among us are now groaning and muttering about PIV and throwing in R for good measure. Just settle geeks, and bear with us, OK?)

Now let's look at a whole system for off-grid power and its various components.

Solar panels

More properly referred to as Photovoltaic (PV) panels these are appearing everywhere now. They are available as tiny accessories on phones, or even watches, as pocket-sized devices for charging personal electronic equipment, on lights for the garden and pumps for the fish pond, for leaving on the dashboard to trickle charge your car battery in cold weather, they increasingly appear as power sources for roadside signs and devices, and of course there are now huge arrays on some rooftops.

For charging leisure batteries they run from around 10W to 300W and can be connected in multiples up to almost any power level you require. In some desert areas they have been laid out to provide a low-maintenance alternative to conventional power stations, though climate change hasn't quite got us to the point where that is viable for the UK just yet.

Although they can be mounted almost anywhere that they will not be subjected to shade and are protected from accidental damage, and will work if the orientation from either side of south allows them to receive sunlight for a reasonable length of time in the day, the best option is for them to be set on turntables that track the sun as it moves, so keeping them aligned for maximum efficiency.

Those available and affordable for domestic use include monocrystalline silicon, polycrystalline silicon, and amorphous silicon types though new developments to improve efficiency, reduce cost and expand useability, are constantly being researched. The monocrystalline are more efficient in direct sunlight but more expensive and the polycrystalline or amorphous generally work better for the variable conditions prevalent in the UK.

More to the point, even in the UK the ones now available work, and though their output can be substantially below potential on overcast winter days they always put out something, and require no maintenance other than clearing off the leaves or snow and giving the glass an occasional wipe down to keep it clean. If the orientation allows the panels to be mounted at an angle, rather than flat or nearly so, rain will help to wash them and debris will not settle so easily.

As mentioned in the previous section, how many panels you need depends on the demands of your system. After you get above one thousand watts peak potential, your system is measured in kilowatts, or kilowatts peak (kWp). In general, if you are having an array fitted by a contractor, there might be a bulk saving so the more you fit the less per kilowatt it will cost.

If you want something that is less obvious than standard solar panels, you can fit solar tiles or slates over all or part of the roof in place of the standard coverings. These are unobtrusive but cost about twice as much as standard panels for the same level of output.

Something to beware of is the Feed-in tariff scheme that is subsidised by the government to promote green energy. Under these schemes the value of the energy generated is subtracted from your electricity bill. If you generate more than you use then you earn a rebate and could actually end up in profit. However, the system directs the energy produced directly into the national grid, and because of the contracts involved you are not allowed to have the output split or directed to a battery bank, so these systems do you no good whatsoever if there is a power cut. If the mains are off, you are in the dark the same as everyone else.

However, you do not have to go for large scale solar power systems. If you reduce your needs for mains equivalent electricity to a minimum you might be able to make do with a much smaller and cheaper kit.

You could operate with a single leisure battery or even a smaller sealed 12v lead acid battery and charge it with a 13watt briefcase solar panel. These come with a lead with crocodile type clips that will clip straight onto the battery terminals and with a female 12v socket that you can plug anything into that you would plug into the lighter socket in your car. Some also 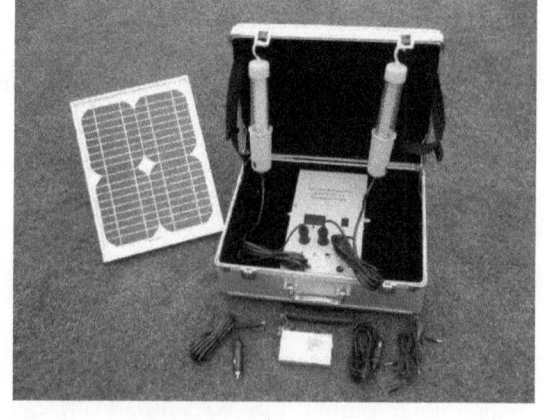 include a charge controller for use with the larger batteries and they are often available for around £50

Or you might choose a self-contained portable kit. Mine have an integral 10ah 12V sealed lead acid battery, a 12W solar panel, sockets for various output leads and voltages to recharge mobile phones, cameras, radios, and the like, and two 36 LED lamps. Leads for charging from a vehicle lighter socket or the mains are also provided. They are designed for disaster relief organisations and emergency services and come fitted in a sturdy aluminium case. Cost is very reasonable at around £100. Try eBay.

Wind Turbines

Whatever you think of the economics and visual or environmental impact of large-scale wind farms, you should consider the merits and drawbacks of a domestic-sized turbine as part of your off-grid power system.

Mechanical wind power has been around for centuries, in the form of windmills, water pumps, and other devices, and even using wind to produce electricity dates back to 1887. In the early 1900s many a farmer who recognised the benefits of electricity but was too far from the grid to be connected, built and erected their own wind turbine. Often they used components of a water pump connected to an automobile dynamo.

The results back then were variable but we now have the advantage of some modern, reliable, and relatively low cost machines from which, as with solar panels, you can choose a size and output to meet your needs.

Probably the first thing to consider is that, on average (the viability of sites differs), a wind turbine will only produce electricity for about 25% of the time and this might be at any time of day and any time of year.

People often think of adding a wind turbine to their system to supplement the power generated by their PV array, on the basis that they will get power from the sun in good weather or from the wind when it turns bad. There is some truth in that but unfortunately there are many times when we have clear skies and strong winds, wasting some of the available output, and others when it is overcast but still, so that neither system is productive. Even so a hybrid system does give some redundancy and alternatives, which is rarely a bad thing.

High quality wind turbines are not cheap. A reliable one will cost from around £500 to several thousands, depending on the type and power output. When looking at the cost of a turbine bear in mind that displayed price is often only for the turbine, the mast and cost of installation will be extra. Initial comparisons can make the price seem similar to, or cheaper per kW than, that of solar panels but do remember the extras and that unlike solar panels a wind turbine is a mechanical device with moving parts and will need regular servicing, with the associated costs.

In deciding whether a wind turbine is suitable for your use the main things to consider are site and wind speed, but in general you are looking for:

1. An open site with no obstacles nearby that might reduce the wind speed or create turbulence. Ideally the top of a gently sloped hill, with no buildings, trees, or higher hills nearby, or the top of a

strongly constructed building that is the highest structure in the vicinity. Doubling the height above ground squares the output.

2. An average wind speed of at least 5mps (18kph/11.25mph), although some authorities say 7mps (25kph/16mph)

3. Enough room for concrete mountings for the mast and associated guy lines, though some smaller turbines can be mounted on a mast that is secured against the side of the building.

4. Close enough to where the power is to be used to make the installation and cost of the cabling affordable.

5. Far enough away, or firmly enough mounted and buffered, that any noise or vibration does not cause disturbance and irritation for you, your neighbours, or any domestic stock.

6. A location that does not present a hazard to you or others in the event of a mechanical failure, or structural damage in a storm.

The big advantage of a wind turbine is that it does not need any fuel. The lifespan is usually put at 20 to 25 years. Nevertheless, from a self-sufficiency point of view you do have to consider the servicing aspect, particularly with turbines of over 3Kw and their associated masts. Can you do the job yourself, and will you be able to get the parts when you need them?

If you do decide that a turbine might be for you there are two main types and lots of variations on the themes. The most familiar type is the Horizontal Axis Wind Turbine (HAWT):

These are available in small models intended for use on boats, motorhomes or rural and suburban roof tops, rated from around 50Watts to over 1.5Kw and priced from £350 for the Rutland 504 on the left of these pictures to £950 for the Aleko WG1000 on the right, and upwards.

They are also available in the sort of models you will have seen on farms around the country, which produce several kilowatts of power and cost up to £20,000 when the mast, cabling, installation, etc. is calculated in.

Alternatively, and less familiar to most people, are the Vertical Axis Wind Turbines (VAWT) some of which are utilitarian, some of which are really rather beautiful, in my opinion.

  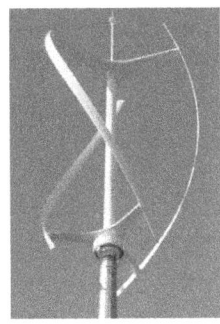

These are also produced in a wide range of models of varying output and at various prices, mostly comparable to or slightly more expensive than the HAWTs. They are not as height-sensitive as the vertical axis models but do take a bit more wind speed to get going.

For most readers of this book, the smaller turbines are probably the most suitable, as they are cheaper, quieter, safer, and require less servicing than the bigger ones. Even then you need to ensure your site will meet the criteria I listed above; otherwise it will simply be a waste of money.

Before setting up any wind turbine, check on the requirements for planning permission.

Hydro turbines

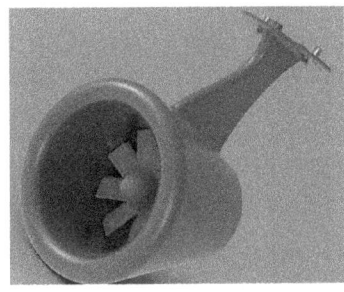

Unfortunately there are not many readers of this book with a Bug In location within the UK that is going to have a water source that is suitable for micro Hydro Power but, just in case you are one of the lucky ones, I thought it wise to cover this option.

To be viable for generating electricity using a hydro turbine your water source needs a high flow rate of water or a site that can provide a substantial

34

head of water i.e. a good sized drop between two levels of the waterway. For most systems you need a combination of both.

Many water courses only have one or the other.

The situation is changing as new technology develops and the inventors are constantly looking for ways to provide the power with only one of the two factors as shown by these propeller turbines but until these technologies mature they can be unreliable and expensive.

Another issue that affects many parts of the UK is the reliability of the water flow throughout the year. We have all seen or heard the news reports of floods in some parts while others have hosepipe bans in force because of a virtual drought.

When all the factors come together, Hydro can make a significant contribution to a household's energy needs or in some cases replace other supplies altogether.

The option might not be a cheap one. While small turbines can cost hundreds or in the low thousands of pounds, the Energy Saving Trust advises that a 5kW hydropower system that would provide sufficient electricity for the average off-grid home would cost around £25,000 including installation. However, a difficult site or the need for more costly equipment could substantially increase that.

Systems that produce between 500W and 3kW of power are referred to as Micro hydro plants and are generally less expensive than larger schemes. What they will power depends on the output but those at the upper level can be designed to provide AC power directly to the house electrical circuits to run standard devices such as an immersion heater for hot water, TV, vacuum cleaners, etc. though not all at the same time. Those producing lower levels usually provide 12v DC to a battery bank, from where it can run either DC equipment or be channelled through an inverter to run 240v items.

Where the output is fairly constant and at a high level (and this applies to wind turbines too) a resistive power user such as an immersion heater is essential to prevent excess power damaging the system. Unfortunately when the power produced is not so high this can gobble up all of the available energy. You could fit a switch to turn off the immersion so as to run other equipment but you would have to monitor the turbine's output to ensure it didn't start to overheat the system while you were doing so.

That said there are many smaller set ups, including DIY ones, that have been built on a tight budget and which work well to provide sufficient power for charging leisure type batteries.

Those systems that provide up to 500W are known as Pico hydro turbines and they can be created with small, easily installed equipment that has minimal environmental impact.

If possible, systems should be sited close to the place where the power will be used, to minimise the cable run, but where that isn't practical, batteries are charged near to the turbine and then transported to the battery bank.

This wheel is an example of an undershot water wheel, which is the most suitable style for a shallow stream with only a small head of water.

Where a higher fall is available or can be created, an overshot wheel can be used and these are more efficient. Where you have a fairly flat but high volume of water, such as in a major river, then a propeller driven turbine, such as those in the photographs at the start of this section, are required.

Whatever type of water driven power system you might think of using there are always some legal implications to be considered.

Firstly do you have the rights to use the water for this purpose? Waterways often form the boundaries between adjacent properties and even then might not be the property of either of the land owners between whose land it runs.

Next, do you need planning permission for the scheme? Unless the system is going to be very small then the answer is probably yes, which can involve delays, quite a lot of work, and extra expense.

Do you need to consider wildlife, including fish that use the water? In many cases water has to be abstracted from higher up the flow, diverted through the turbine and then back into the river or stream, so that the main water course is unaffected. Alternatively, suitable barriers are placed to prevent fish or other wildlife getting caught in the generation system and a separate channel must be provided for their movement up and down stream

When all the hassles of legislation and siting, construction and expense, are dealt with, however, what you should have is a fairly reliable source of power, which is cheap to run, requires relatively little maintenance, and is very environmentally friendly.

Voltage regulator

The voltage regulator looks a simple piece of kit, and they are cheap and easy to wire up but they are an essential component for the safety of your system. They are rated in Amps and depending on how much current you want to put through e.g., how many panels you have connected at the same time, they cost from around £10 to over £100.

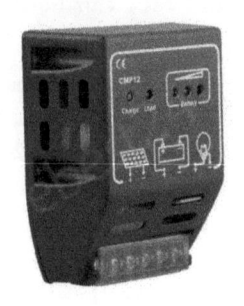

There are various types but they usually look something like this:

Batteries

The batteries most often used in 12v emergency systems are what are known as 'leisure batteries'. These are designed for use in caravans, motorhomes, and small boats. Technically they are referred to as deep-cycle batteries and although they may look similar to the shallow-cycle battery used to start your car the internal construction is very different.

A car battery is designed to give out a relatively high burst of energy for a short time, before being quickly recharged by the alternator once the engine is running. Only a small amount of the total capacity of the battery is usually drawn each time, normally a maximum of 20%. That is most noticeable if the car has been sitting out in cold weather for a long time and is difficult to start. The battery will quickly go flat while you try to turn over the engine, but if you get the car running it won't take long before it seems fine and, if the battery isn't getting old, after you next stop the car will probably restart without any problem.

37

A leisure/deep-cycle battery is intended to release a small but steady flow of charge over a longer time and will tolerate regularly being discharged by 50-60% of its capacity, and occasionally by 80%, if then gradually recharged, or to accept constant use while being trickle charged at the same time.

In a car that is run and stopped often throughout the day, the battery will often last only two to three years compared to seven to fifteen for a leisure battery.

Even more durable are 6 volt batteries connected in series to give 12volts (more about connections later). These often have twice the capacity of a comparable leisure battery e.g. 6volts 220 amp hours against 12volts 110 amp hours. Six volt batteries are often used in golf carts and milk floats, but are also available specifically for highly durable off-grid home electrical systems. The one on the right is 6v 450ah.

For very short term emergency use you could use car batteries to power 12v equipment or with suitable inverters to run mains items, and then recharge them by whatever means is available, and it would work, but you would not get long usage of the equipment before the battery went flat and if regularly used and recharged that way the battery would soon die.

Servicing and storage

Whichever type of battery you choose, you need to service it regularly. This simply consists of disconnecting the battery from the system, cleaning the terminals and wiping down the top, then checking and when necessary topping up each chamber in the battery. You will need distilled water and either a small funnel or a small bottle (0.5ltr is convenient) with a spout for topping up and suitable grease for the terminals. Vaseline will do or you can buy a tube of gel made for the purpose.

Servicing should be done about once per month. Make it a routine and keep a record. You should also check the status of the cells two or three times per year using a hydrometer and if necessary recondition the battery using a multiphase charger. Halfords stock all the necessary equipment.

If you have plenty of batteries you could change from one bank to another, service the one now off-line and then rest it for a month before moving back to it again. That would considerably extend the life of your battery banks

When they are under charge, lead acid batteries give off small amounts of hydrogen and oxygen and of course they are filled with water. Taking those things into account, the best place to store power system batteries is in a shed or box just outside the house. The box should be insulated to prevent the batteries getting too cold, and certainly never below freezing, but well ventilated to allow the expressed gasses to be dispersed.

*Safety point: Never use a naked flame or cause sparks around the batteries and do not allow liquids to spill across terminals or connections. If you do you might cause an explosion or damage your system.

The batteries should be sited low within the container but off the floor on a rack or pallet. You will appreciate the low placement when you have to move them; power cells are heavy! For your safety, the storage place must be arranged with enough light and room to allow you to use safe lifting technique and also so that you can easily access the cells for servicing.

The store also needs to be secure. Batteries are valuable, even for their scrap weight in normal times, but especially so when they are most needed. The structure must be strong, locked and preferably alarmed since any potential thief will probably come at night. You will also have to make arrangements for the security of your charging device(s), generators, fuel, and other essential equipment and supplies.

Connections

I will go into the complete system layout towards the end of this chapter on power, after we have looked at the various components available, but a few words on the basic connections is appropriate here.

Every battery has two terminals, one positive which is usually marked red and with a + symbol and one negative which is usually black and has a - symbol. When you are using more than one battery in a system, how you connect these can give you a higher voltage, the same voltage but with longer output duration, or destroy your batteries and pose a threat to your life!

There are two basic sequences of connections: Series and parallel.

Series

Batteries connected in series are linked positive to negative, like putting one battery after another into the tubular handle of a torch, and this multiplies the voltage

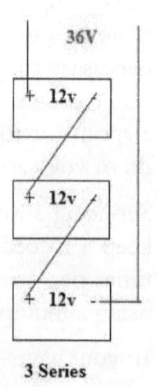

3 Series

by the number of batteries in the series e.g. if you have three 12v batteries connected in series the output is 36v. If you are using 12v batteries in a 12v system you should NEVER connect them in series.

Parallel

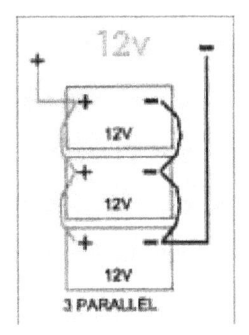

Batteries connected positive to positive and negative to negative are connected in parallel and this maintains an output of 12v but totals the time over which power can be delivered by adding the amp hour figure of each battery, so that a 12v 75ah + 12v 100ah + a 12v 110ah gives you a 12v 285amp hour system. Having batteries of the same voltage but different capacity in your system is not inherently dangerous, but it can make your calculations a bit more complex.

The one time you might connect batteries in series for a 12v system is if you are using pairs of 6v cells. In this case each pair must first be connected in series to create an out put of 12v from the pair. You then have to connect the pairs in parallel to increase the amperage.

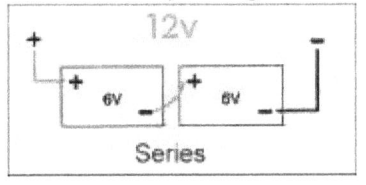

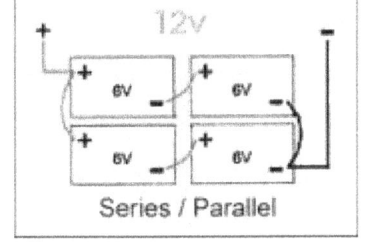

Importantly, when connecting batteries, and in fact any components in your off-grid system, you MUST use proper 12v rated cables. Although lower in voltage, the amperage of 12v systems might be higher than that of UK mains and appropriately thicker cabling must be used otherwise you will overheat the wiring and cause a serious risk of fire.

How many batteries?

How many batteries do you need? That depends on how much power it takes to run the various devices you want to use and the environmental conditions and equipment you have to recharge them.

In normal times, the average household wastes an awful lot of energy, every day. You might think that the power drawn by your electric bedside

40

clock, and the clock on your cooker, and the one on your microwave, and the stand-by lights on your TV, and cable box, and modem, PC, printer, phone charger, telephone, and the rest, is tiny and per item you might be right, but it all adds up! Factor in the old non-energy-efficient light bulbs, and low-rated refrigerator, freezer, etc. you are still using and they could be costing you dearly in electricity charges every month.

More to the point for our current calculations, most of them are totally unnecessary and should not be part of the system that you try to operate from an off-grid system.

If you look back at the list of electrical items in my home, or at your own list if you've already done one, how many of those devices do you consider essential i.e. for which you could find no appropriate replacement?

Now consider that less than one hundred years ago virtually nobody in the UK would have seen ANY of the electrical versions of those items, including the overhead lights, and less than fifty years ago most of them hadn't yet been invented!

Of course we get used to what we know, and it depends on what alternatives existed then and what you now have available, but it does put the term 'essential' into context, doesn't it?

That doesn't mean that you should necessarily give up all those things in an emergency, this book is about staying safe and comfortable not going back to the Victorian era, but there are alternatives, even convenient modern alternatives for many without mains power. We will look at those alternatives in the coming chapters but for this one, the point is that the more you can reduce your electricity demand, the cheaper, simpler, and more reliable your emergency system will be.

So, after you have worked through the various categories of use, and decided what your preferences for the off-grid alternatives will be, you can then work out the specifications of your electrical system.

Are you ready for some maths?

Each device you want to run will have a rating in either Watts or Amps; this is usually shown on a panel on the back or base. For example, my notebook computer is rated at a power input of 19volts, 2.1 amps. If, as a writer, I decided that I needed to use the computer for 8 hours per day that would be a drain of 2.1 x 8 = 16.8 amp hours per day. However, because the input is 19volts I couldn't run the computer directly from a 12v battery, I would have to use the power unit plugged into an inverter, both of which will steal some of the power. Looking at the specifications on those devices and figuring in their demand, the total is closer to 3amps or 24 amps per 8 hours.

To figure out how much battery power you need, you must do that calculation for each of the devices you want to use, including deciding how many hours per day you want to use them, and then work out the total.

Say, for example, I wanted to use the computer for 8 hours, my short wave radio for an hour, TV for an hour, the air pump/purifier for a couple of hours, and our little camping twin-tub washing machine for an hour some days or other devices on others, and the whole lot came to 120amp hours of demand, then without running a battery below 50% of its capacity I could power that with two 120ah batteries.

Of course, I could only do that for one day. If I had four 120ah batteries I could then switch over to the other two for the next day, while the two I had used were recharging.

All I would have to do then, is ensure I had sufficient power coming from my charging system to recharge the part-used batteries within one day, so that next day I could then switch them with the ones currently on and restart the rotation.

So, how much charging output would I need? (Just like being back doing exams again, isn't it!)

I want to replace 120ah of use. For convenience, let's assume I am using 12 volt solar panels. On average the UK gets 6 hours of useable charging sunlight per day, more in summer, less in winter. So 120/6 = 20amps of 12v output requirement per hour.

Remember WAV?

So how many W = 20A x 12V

Answer = 240

Theoretically, to recharge those batteries I would need 240 Watts worth of solar power. However we aren't done yet. The efficiency of a charging system, taking into account the panels, wiring, monitors, chargers, etc is only about 75% so you really need to up that to about 320 Watts. Then consider that although you would get far more than you need in summer, you might not get 6 hours worth of charging sunlight in winter, so you should allow for at least 400 Watts to be sure.

Just to put this in context: four 120 ah leisure batteries will cost about £400. 400 Watts of solar panel kits will add £600 - £1000. Add the inverters and other accessories and you are looking at £1500-2000 for this system. You could cut that by adding more batteries and less wattage of

42

panels, so that you spread the charging time, but generally, the more demand, the bigger the system, the higher the cost.

One final point on your main batteries: As I have mentioned previously, solar panels last for over twenty years, leisure batteries for a far shorter period. However, it is possible to buy the batteries dry, and sealed in that state they will keep without deterioration for many years. The only issue you have then is to be able to make or obtain the acid mix required to activate them, since the ready-made electrolyte will break down in storage. If this is of interest to you, research it in advance of need and find out how to obtain the necessary resources.

Inverters

The purpose of an inverter is to change the 12V DC current from your batteries to 240V AC on which you run devices that you would normally plug into a mains socket.

If you are only going to use 12V DC items, of which there is a wide variety, you don't need an inverter in your system, but they are useful to have for when you realise you really need to power up the TV for news or something for which you do not have a 12V or other equivalent.

Inverters come in many sizes, There are 75W models that plug direct into the cigarette lighter socket and will run small items; handy 150W versions that will allow you to run equipment such as a TV or computer; or bench or wall mounted equipment rated for several kilowatts of household appliances.

Inverters are available in many types for differing uses but the two of interest to us are Modified sine wave and pure sine wave.

Modified sine wave inverters are relatively low cost and are compatible with most electronic devices, but there are some exceptions. Fluorescent lights, audio equipment, and laser printers do not work well with modified sine wave and many flat screen TVs will work but with a reduced quality of picture and sound due to interference.

Pure sine wave inverters produce a power output that is comparable to mains grid power and are compatible with all electronic equipment but they are more expensive than the modified sine wave models. Basically you need to consider the devices you will use and decided whether your need for the devices that won't run on the cheaper models justifies the cost of the more expensive ones.

For large systems there are control boxes that feature various monitors as well as an inverter, and these can either have a socket or be wired straight into the circuit breaker panel. These will almost always have a pure sine wave output but it is worth checking.

After you have decided what type of inverter you need you then have to decide how much power it should be able to transfer. Remember that the inverter is only needed for items that have to run on 240volts so the more equipment you can power directly with 12V DC the lower the power of the inverter you will need.

To make this calculation you have to work out what items you need or want to be able to run at the same time, and add the power requirements of them all to get the total for the size of your inverter or inverters, if you want a mix of sizes and modified/pure sine wave output. Remember to figure in that about 10% of the power output from your batteries will be lost to heating the wiring and running the inverter. Also be aware that inverters will have two ratings, continuous and peak outputs. Some equipment such as freezers put out a short term high demand when they start up and then settle to a lower demand while running. Your system needs to be able to accommodate both levels of demand.

Each piece of equipment should have a label on it that shows its power requirements, although for some small items this might be in the instruction leaflet or on the box when you buy it. Items will vary but as examples:

Clock radio 5W

Food processor 400W

Microwave 600 – 900W

Vacuum cleaner 900W

Rechargeable hand vacuum cleaner 500W

Washing machine 900-1800W

Electric iron 1200W

Toaster 1200W

Dishwasher 1450W

Hairdryer 1500W

20" colour TV 110W

DVD player 30W

Fluorescent light 15W

Incandescent light 60 or 100W

Laptop computer 50-75W

Desktop computer and monitor 75-150W

Inkjet printer 35W

Electric drill 400-600W

Phone charger 25W

As you can see, it could soon add up.

Distribution box

Just as you have a distribution box or fuse box between where the mains supply comes into your house and where the cables go to various levels, sockets, lighting circuits, etc. so you need a similar box between your private power system and the wiring to your various sockets or devices. This is an essential feature to protect you and your equipment.

Distribution boxes with trip switches rather than fuses are the modern version and in addition to the safeguard feature of automatically cutting off a circuit if the supply or demand goes above the rated level, they give you the option to isolate some circuits if you are working on them or to prevent demand if a different circuit has higher priority and the system will not support both. If you have cabled in circuits for both 12V DC and 240V AC, you will need separate distribution boxes for each.

Devices

If you have a system that includes an inverter then you will be able to use any of your normal household items that your battery bank and associated equipment will support. Alternatively you can often reduce the draw on your system, and give yourself some additional versatility by using lower powered equipment intended for caravans or boats.

Some of these, such as the fridge, are designed to interchangeably use 240v, 12v or gas as available; some like heaters will use mains electric or gas; there are TVs with built in DVD that will use 240 or 12v; and the lights, water pumps, radio, and others are specifically 12v,.

There are also electric ovens, kettles, microwaves, washing machines, etc. that require 240v but which draw much less power than those intended for a house. They sometimes take longer to do the job, e.g. a kettle might take five minutes to boil instead of two, and have less features but they are viable alternatives.

One thing we have used a lot when I am working away from home and we are living in the caravan is a lightweight twin tub washing machine. The washing tub doesn't have a heater, so you have to put in hot water, and the only control is an on/off /time switch but it does a better job of washing clothes, and with much less effort, than doing them by hand and in winter the spin dryer is a real boon.

Another is a 6litre 800W oven/grill/toaster that Pat has used to cook an amazing variety of recipes (I do the washing but she is a much better cook!) It is compact, has only a timer and three pre-set heating levels rather than precise temperature control, but it makes a good job of things that the simple microwave in the caravan won't do and draws little power.

The main oven in the caravan runs on Propane but if that is not practical for you e.g. if you live in a flat, but you have an alternative power system, items like these can make life much easier than reverting to lower tech methods.

Have a look around the shop of a large caravan or boat dealer and you will find many mains and 12v items that you can adopt for off-grid or power cut living.

46

Putting it all together

So, you have many choices and the variations between systems are almost endless but hopefully this chapter will have given you the basic information with which to work and make some initial decisions. Take your time; setting up an alternative power system as part of your preps is an important step and often not a cheap one.

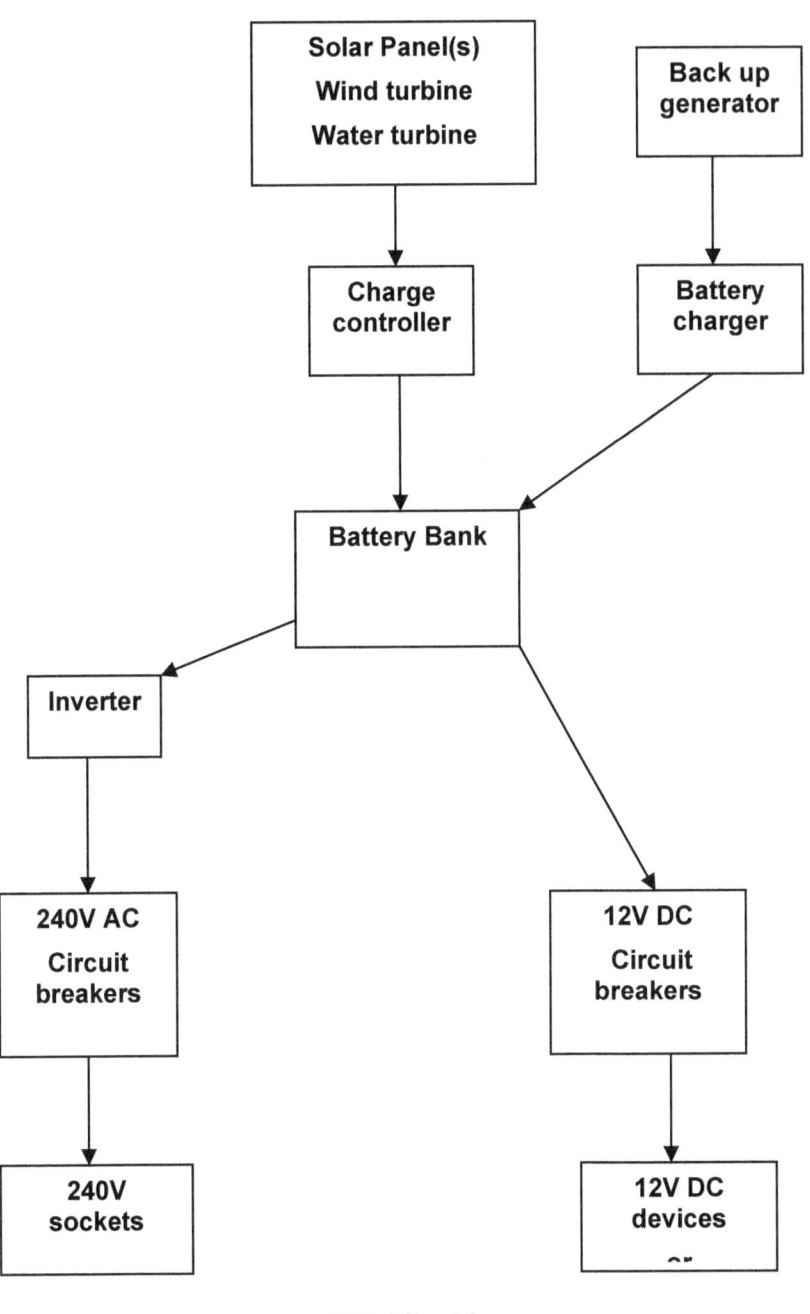

```
┌─────────────────┐              ┌─────────────┐
│  Solar Panel(s) │              │   Back up   │
│  Wind turbine   │              │  generator  │
│  Water turbine  │              └──────┬──────┘
└────────┬────────┘                     │
         │                              │
         ▼                              ▼
┌─────────────────┐              ┌─────────────┐
│     Charge      │              │   Battery   │
│   controller    │              │   charger   │
└────────┬────────┘              └──────┬──────┘
         │                              │
         └──────────┐      ┌────────────┘
                   ▼      ▼
            ┌─────────────────┐
            │   Battery Bank  │
            └───┬─────────┬───┘
                │         │
    ┌───────────┘         └──────────┐
    ▼                                ▼
┌──────────┐                   ┌──────────┐
│ Inverter │                   │  12V DC  │
└────┬─────┘                   │ Circuit  │
     │                         │ breakers │
     ▼                         └─────┬────┘
┌──────────┐                         │
│ 240V AC  │                         ▼
│ Circuit  │                   ┌──────────┐
│ breakers │                   │  12V DC  │
└────┬─────┘                   │ devices  │
     │                         └──────────┘
     ▼
┌──────────┐
│   240V   │
│ sockets  │
└──────────┘
```

12V Off-grid system

Alternatives

In addition to your main electrical system you might also want a portable backup for various purposes. For this the power units primarily designed as jump starters for cars can be useful.

These have 12v sealed lead acid batteries ranging from 10 to 40ah and, in addition to the jump leads, compressor and lamp many feature, they also provide power sockets in various voltages. The unit on the left has two 12v sockets plus a 300ma USB socket. The unit on the right has those plus a 300w 240v inverter and standard three pin socket. Prices range from around £25 for basic models to around £200 for the more powerful units. They can be recharged from either another 12v source, e.g. a car lighter socket or a solar/wind output, or from a 240v mains source with a suitable charging lead, which is usually provided when you buy the unit.

*Safety point: take care with some of these units, especially the cheaper ones, because the jump leads are not always switch activated and if not they are permanently live. An accidental shock from one of these is not fun and can be fatal!

Or you can go part way, with a standard 12v leisure battery within a box that has 12v connection points for crocodile clamps, rings, or plugs.

These cost around £35 and feature an on off switch for the terminals and a power meter so that you can easily check the state of charge of the battery.

People-powered dynamos

Home made and commercial hand-turned and pedal-powered devices have been around for a long time. Where smaller amounts of power are needed, for either short term use directly to devices or for charging batteries, they provide a relatively cheap and portable answer to the need.

Because of the strength of leg muscles compared to those in the arms, pedal power is often preferred but when the demand is limited, hand-cranked generators work too and are usually smaller and lighter. Dynamo devices such as radios, lamps, and torches really became mainstream when Trevor Baylis became involved and BayGen Power Industries (later to become Freeplay Energy) was formed. The products became so popular that other companies then got into the act and they are now ubiquitous. We will look at many of these appliances in future chapters on light and communications.

Bicycles often feature miniature generators to power their own lights and it doesn't take a great leap of imagination to extend this to using them to generate more power. And then not a lot more thought to take away the bicycle frame and just keep the pedals.

Link these to an integral battery pack and you come up with portable power devices such as the Gazelle from Power Plus.

The Gazelle has a 7ah 12v battery and can be charged from its own pedals or from either mains or 12v sources using the charging leads supplied. There is a charging indicator so that you know when input is sufficient but a pedal rate of 45 – 90 cycles per minute works efficiently.

It has an integral 100W inverter and output sockets for 240v, 12v, and USB. It also features a bright 9 LED lamp.

Total weight is only 4.8Kg but for even greater convenience the power pack is detachable from the pedal system.

Despite its light weight the Gazelle is sturdy and I have used both the power pack and the pedal generator quite extensively. Two of the problems with Bugging In can be boredom and lack of activity and apart from generating power the Gazelle can provide a useful means of exercise. Cost is usually around £100.

The same firm now produces a hand-crank device called the Elephant. It features some of the same facilities i.e. lamp, 12v output, 240v 100W inverter and socket, various input options but is mainly designed as a device for the car and is more expensive at around £150.

50

Or you could stick with Freeplay and go for the Weza. This is an exceptionally sturdy, and quite heavy, treadle charged power unit. Unfortunately Freeplay have discontinued the device but they are still available from various outlets. Cost is around £130.

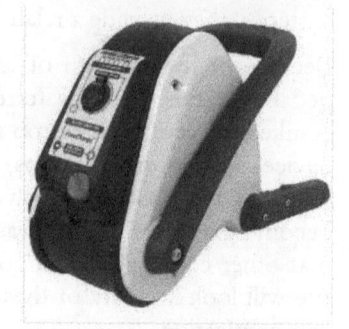

Like the Gazelle, the Weza has a 7ah 12v battery and various charging options including mains, 12v or its integral treadle but output is limited to 12v from either a lighter type socket or terminals. It also comes with heavy duty jump cables and a good quality bag that contains the Weza and all the associated equipment.

I haven't used mine for jump starting the car, but I have regularly used it at the caravan, including: with a 12v shower for bathing our dog, a couple of 12v multi-LED lights for illuminating the awning, and with a 75W inverter, to power a radio using its mains lead while sitting out in the sun, and then later with a notebook computer.

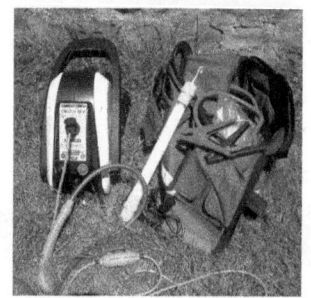

In the event of a power cut at home we could do the same and more, including using the shower for ourselves, which would have been a great relief for our Border Collie, Blue, who loved to swim but hated a bath!

And then there are the small hand chargers intended for things such as mobile phones and other hand-held devices. These are often quite cheap and very portable. Some sell from £4 to a pound or two more. The Datexx superbattery retails at around £15 in the UK and the Freecharge 12v hand crank charger cost from £20 upwards via Amazon.

These little devices are never going to power anything huge, but they can take some of the strain off your main power sources and are light and easy enough to use that even the younger members of the family can make a contribution and have a distraction while recharging smaller accessories.

Small batteries

Many of your portable devices will use standard small batteries such as AAA, AA, C, or D cell. All of these produce around 1.5 volts; the difference is that the bigger ones have a longer amp hour capacity. Depending on the demands of the device, they might be inserted in either series or parallel, or a combination of those, though you don't really have to think about that, just put them in the way the diagram shows you.

Many Preppers try to standardise the items they use, to run on just one or two sizes of battery, often AAA and AA. They then have adapters that will enable the small cells to be used, although for less hours per battery, in equipment designed to take the larger sizes, such as C or D cells.

Some of these fit a single AAA battery into an AA adapter, which will then go into an AA-C adapter, which will then fit into a C-D adapter as required.

Some connect several small cells in parallel and then banks of these in series to simulate the way the larger cells would be used. This system provides both higher voltage and longer working time.

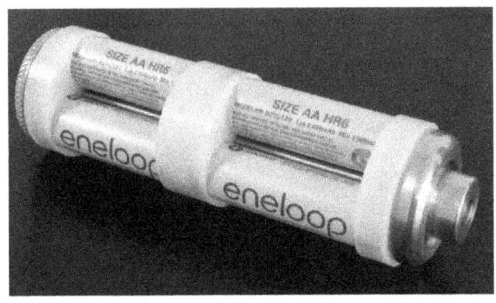

Rechargeable small cells usually produce around 1.2v rather than a disposable battery's 1.5v. Most equipment, but not all, will use the two types interchangeably. Check whether that is the case for your own items.

There are many types of charger for reusable cells, running from mains power or a car lighter socket, a PV charger or a hand crank. Prices and features vary, with some of them giving an indication of whether the battery is in good condition or starting to fail, and more expensive models showing how much charge and output life each cell is holding.

Some allow individual batteries to be charged, while others require them to be fitted in pairs. Fast chargers tend to quickly kill cells, while the solar charger shown on the right (sold by Maplin) is advertised as being able to charge four 2000mah batteries, of the same size and type, in six hours on a good sunny day. Unfortunately in the winter, when the batteries are likely to be needed most, it can take considerably longer. Batteries of differing capacity should have appropriately different charging times.

52

Especially in the winter, it can be more efficient to recharge small batteries by use of a mains charger running from an inverter connected to leisure batteries recharged by large solar panels than to use a dedicated small battery charger.

All batteries lose their charge over time but low quality rechargeable batteries often have correspondingly short retention life, with some needing to be topped up monthly. Good quality batteries can retain most of their charge for much longer.

You should maintain a routine for recharging your batteries and a record of when you last did so. Some keen Preppers organise their stock by condition, so that they know which to use first or for routine applications and which to reserve for more demanding roles.

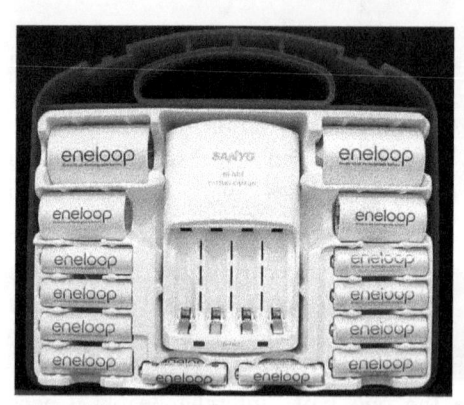

Front runner for quality products currently seems to be Eneloop, from Sanyo. These retain 85% of their charge after one year and can be recharged up to 1000 times. As you would expect, they are a bit more expensive than the competition but the retention rate and number of times they can be recharged is worth it if you are going to be using them routinely and repeatedly. The kit shown has a Sanyo charger, 8 AA and 4 AAA batteries plus 2 C and 2 D cell adapters for AA only. Cost is around £40 via Amazon.

Incidentally, there are still two main types of rechargeable battery that you might encounter: Nickel Cadmium (Ni-Cad) and Nickel Metal Hydride (Ni-Mh) but Ni-Mh seem to have largely taken over from the old Ni-Cads except in small solar-charged garden and shed lights. Most modern chargers will take either but some will only do one or the other.

Whichever type of battery you choose, four changes per item of equipment is a reasonable number to store, of either single use or rechargeable cells. Your usage of particular pieces of kit might demand more for that and less of others but standardisation can cut the total you need to keep in stock. That gives you enough for most temporary emergencies and provides time to recharge a reusable set even if daylight hours are short and dull.

Battery chargers are now available that will enable you to recondition and restore what are supposed to be disposable alkaline batteries. The process won't work on very old or completely dead cells, nor zinc or lithium ones, and number and depth of restorations varies according to the quality of the batteries, but these chargers can revitalise fairly new batteries that have been used until running low, between 2 and 10 times. You will notice the usable life getting shorter each time. Typical of these devices is the Battery Wizard which costs around £20 and is powered from mains supply. It will allow charging of different sizes of cell individually and indicates condition, sounding a warning if a battery is beyond renewal. Rechargeable batteries are better but if you have some disposable ones these chargers do work to extend their useful life.

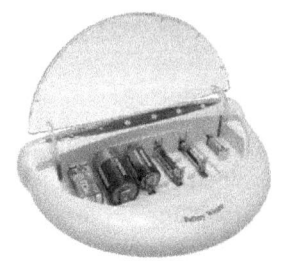

Shelter

Mains items: Door bell, Power drill, Clocks

The purpose of your shelter is to protect you from wind, rain, heat, cold, and harm. We will be dealing with keeping cool, keeping warm, and providing security in their own chapters so this one is mainly about maintaining the basic integrity of your dwelling place be that your home or somewhere else where you intend to Bug In.

The first thing you should do is study your surroundings to identify and then plan removal of anything that represents a threat to the structure. That might include trees, especially very large and old ones. I know that can be difficult; big trees can be old friends, but you cannot afford to risk a smashed roof or walls when it could be avoided. If you are lucky and the tree is on the outer edge of where it could fall onto the building, you could have it cut back and shaped so that it won't reach or is more likely to fall the other way, but whatever, it really should be dealt with. If the tree is not on your property, that is more difficult. Even good neighbours might be reluctant to cut back a beautiful beech or copper birch, but talk to them to see if you can reach an agreement.

Other things to consider removing are: any flammable items that could be a target for arsonists or provide fuel for an accidental fire, or scalable structures that could give thieves easier access to or from your house or garden. We will consider security and safety in more detail in a later chapter but while surveying your property, generally take note of the layout, compass orientation, distances, materials, and function of your buildings, features, plants and surfaces. Then review them in light of the potential threats you will by now have identified, whether that is flood, fire, attack, radioactive fallout or anything else. A diagram of the property showing the whole plan and a satellite image of the structure and surrounds are useful aids.

In addition to removing potential threats you could also consider ways to reinforce the vulnerable points on the buildings. Windows can be strengthened by fitting hardened glass, or if that is too expensive then by applying a transparent adhesive security film or by using smaller panes or lead strips in the style of older houses, or even by fitting external shutters. If necessary you can replace doors with ones that are stronger and don't feature any glass, or are made to be fireproof.

Flammable roof coverings can also be changed for less vulnerable ones, and you should look to the structure and condition of all outside features and coverings of the walls. Protective paints are available that will prevent water penetration, old wood can be replaced by modern laminates, pointing, brickwork, guttering and down pipes should all be inspected and renewed if they are deteriorating. Properly earthed lightning conductors should be installed.

Flooring your attic and applying a waterproof treatment to wood, then covering that with a cheap absorbent covering can help to prevent rain bringing down your internal ceilings if you lose some tiles, and the absorbent covering makes clearing up much easier and prevents water running into the wall spaces. The flooring over good layers of insulation will also increase the warmth retained in rooms below and give you extra storage space. Since less heat will be escaping into the roof space though, do ensure any water pipes up there are fully lagged.

These things will not only strengthen your home while lessening the chances of damage you might have to try to repair yourself, but also maintain and possibly improve its value.

The mains powered items for this chapter are easily taken care of: If the door bell doesn't ring, people can knock, though in a Bug In situation you might not want to answer. Time might be of less importance but for those tasks where it is, you can have a clock for a couple of pounds that will run on a rechargeable AA battery or even a hand-wound one for a few pounds more.

Availability of power for tools is the only real consideration in relation to maintaining your shelter if the mains are off-line. Yes, they can be replaced by hand tools, all the jobs for which they are now used were previously done with hand tools, but for the length of time you will likely use them and the comparative time and effort involved you might decide to start up the generator or run them from your 12v system and inverter. And before you sneer, have you ever tried punching holes in brick, concrete block or - God help us – stone, using a hammer and hand punch? Under the guidance of my dad I did as a youngster, to put up a set of shelves in an old cottage; never again if I can run a power drill by any means. I still remember the blisters!

However, for many jobs hand tools are perfectly acceptable and a good hand drill plus a brace and an assortment of bits of various sizes and types, plus hammers, saws, screwdrivers, pliers and cutters are basics that everyone should have. Add planes and shaves, chisels and gouges, mallets and markers and you are really starting to get there, though for working wood, metal and masonry there are so many more that could be useful, if you also develop the skills to use them.

Remember that an Event that prompts a Bug In could take many forms, but whatever the cause one of the main effects is that you will have to be self-sufficient in many things for which you might normally call on help. Whether it is fixing a broken window or damaged roof, a leaking pipe or a fallen fence, you and yours are now the workforce who will have to do the job.

Other than an extensive selection of tools, a major benefit would be a workshop with a sturdy bench, but even a folding bench like a black and Decker Workmate will be invaluable. You might be sawing planks or boards, Perspex or glass, drilling and shaping, attaching fixings, and so much more as you maintain and repair, build new hutches for your rabbits or traps for catching squirrels, raised beds for plants, or reinforcements for your windows. A firm surface on which to work is an essential every Prepper may need.

In addition to tools you will also need stocks of screws and nails, staples, wire, heavy-duty sheet polythene, tarpaulins, hoses, rope, string and cable ties, plywood, glass or Perspex, sand and glass paper, rubble sacks, a ladder, and potentially many other items for use around the house and garden. There are more suggestions in the Bug In Kit and Supplies list at the end of this book.

These are not the first things that many Preppers will think about when talking about preps for Bugging In, but any of them might be essential. Fortunately they are also all highly useful for non-emergency use

Nuclear

SEOUL | Last updated: 1 hour ago, Tue Feb 12, 2013 2:02pm GMT
(Reuters) - North Korea conducted its third nuclear test on Tuesday in defiance of existing U.N. resolutions

I had planned that I would include sections on radiation in the Safety and Security, and Health chapters but considering that this book is about Bugging In and the possibility of radioactive contamination is a damn good reason for doing so, I decided it would be appropriate to include some information here.

After the end of the Cold War, interest in preparations for surviving nuclear explosions dropped rapidly; understandably so. Effectively that was late 1991, although the date will always be debated and I write this section assuming that at least some of the readers will remember little of what life was like before then, or have much knowledge of nuclear protection. Concerns have been revived to some extent by news reports of nations hostile to the western world developing nuclear bombs, and of the possibility of nuclear materials or weapons being acquired by terrorists, and by accidents at nuclear power plants.

Probably the first thing to do is examine the differences between the potential threats.

Nuclear Power Industry Incidents

Despite wide-spread public perception, the nuclear power industry generally has a very good safety record. In the past 60 years there have been just over one hundred incidents world-wide that were sufficiently serious to be reported, but very few have resulted in deaths and only three – Three Mile Island 1979, Chernobyl 1986 and Fukushima 2011 – have cause wide scale evacuations or identified danger to anyone other than workers at the plant affected.

Incidents have occurred due to technical failures, particularly during refuelling, human error, and natural disasters. Where radioactivity has escaped beyond the boundaries of the facility, it is most often in the form of contaminated water getting into local waterways or the sea, or release of radioactive steam.

After the Three Mile Island incident, around 140,000 pregnant women and pre-school age children were evacuated from the area but there was no general evacuation, though inevitably some frightened citizens did decide to flee. There was no long term exclusion zone beyond the plant itself.

Chernobyl still rates as the worst ever nuclear disaster based on the amount of radiation released and its effects locally and internationally. The incident was initially caused by human error during unsafe testing procedures but this then led to a series of technical failures and eventual meltdown of the core.

Within two days, the 49,000 inhabitants of the city of Pripyat, which had been built to house workers at the plant and their families, was evacuated as part of the establishment of a 30 Km (19 mile) wide exclusion zone. Altogether, from 1986 to 2000, 350,400 people have been evacuated and resettled from the most severely contaminated areas of Belarus, Russia, and Ukraine. Although radiation levels in Pripyat have now dropped sufficiently for tourists to be allowed to visit the city, they are still too high for anyone to stay there for long periods and the city is a decaying and much-vandalised ghost town.

The figures are disputed but somewhere between 30 and 50 workers involved in the original incident and afterwards fighting to bring it under control died immediately or soon after and upwards of 4000 are believed to have died since as a result of radiation sickness or associated cancer.

The radioactive plume affected wide areas and within the weeks to follow, sheep in upland areas of UK were found to be unfit for human consumption due to having eaten grass contaminated with fallout from the event.

The next level 7 event (highest level on the International Nuclear Event Scale (INES) was the disaster at Fukushima, Japan, in 2011. This was caused by an earthquake but made vastly worse by the subsequent tsunami. The Fukushima plant had 6 reactors but 2 were shut down for maintenance and another had been de-fueled. Reactors one to three shutdown automatically when the earthquake hit but the tsunami caused flooding of the generator room which powered the coolant pumps and the result was a meltdown of the fuel rods.

A 'temporary' exclusion zone of 20Km was imposed, with a voluntary evacuation zone extending that to 30Km, due to the threat of explosions and the release of radioactive materials. At one time the event was considered to be so potentially serious that the prevailing wind direction caused the possibility of the need to evacuate Tokyo, (population over 13,261,000) over 200Km away to be discussed, but that was quickly discounted. Large amounts of nuclear material have been washed into the surrounding land, surface water and sea but the reactors and fuel rods were declared stable in December 2011. However, it is estimated that it will take decades to fully decommission the plant and decontaminate the affected area and until that is done many of the evacuees will be unable to return for any length of time.

In addition to these incidents, there have been some accidents to military and civilian transport while nuclear materials and weapons were being moved. Road and rail vehicles used for this purpose are massively over-designed for safety and none have resulted in release of any radioactivity. A US military aircraft carrying nuclear bombs did crash in the Mediterranean but the bombs were eventually recovered and again there was no leak of radioactive materials.

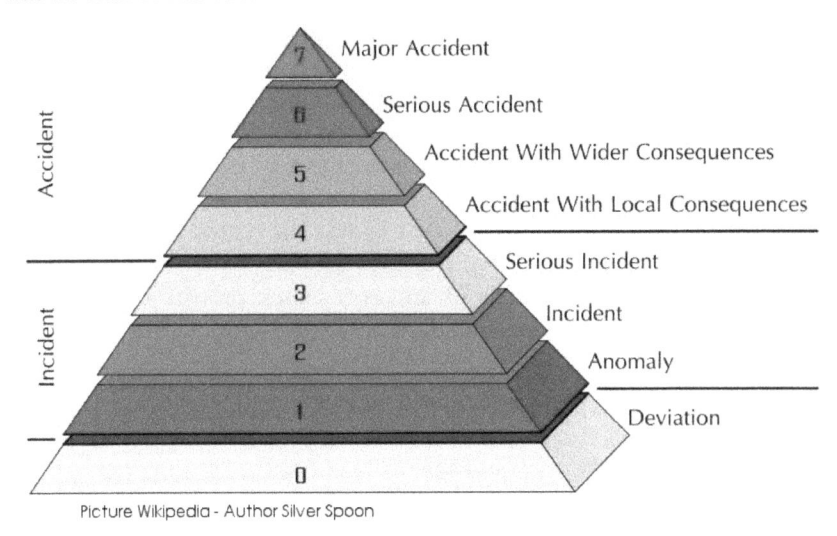

Picture Wikipedia - Author Silver Spoon

The UK has, so far, suffered three notable incidents:
1. Windscale 1957 – Level 5
2. Chapelcross 1967 – Level 3
3. Sellafield 2005 – Level 4

None of these have resulted in an evacuation of the public, though there has been contamination of local areas and effects on farmers, particularly those with dairy herds.

With all that in mind, there are a couple of conclusions to be drawn:

Firstly, when a Level 6 or 7 event occurs, the levels of radiation released are likely to be so high that, if you are within about 20 Km, Bugging In will probably not be an option and you may face compulsory evacuation. In that event you might want to apply the principles set out in my book, Bugging Out, bearing in mind that you might not be able to return for months or years, if ever.

Secondly, consider that even if you are beyond the immediate evacuation/exclusion zone but are down-wind and therefore initially follow Bug In procedures for a nuclear event, as you should, reactor fallout might still mean that you have to leave at a later date. That has been the case for hundreds of thousands of people after Chernobyl. Odd as it might seem, and although you don't face the immediate effects of a nuclear explosion, the elements in fallout from a reactor have far longer half life than those in fallout from an exploding bomb and the Seven and Ten rule I explain later does not apply.

So, be ready to apply safe Bug In procedures including safe movement and decontamination if you have to go outside but also be ready for a Bug Out at short notice.

Rogue states and others

Possession of nuclear weapons by 'rogue' states is, most likely, a political bargaining tool on their part. Just as the Soviet Union and NATO were ideologically opposed but an all out war was prevented by the threat of Mutually Assured Destruction, so any smaller state would have to recognise the inevitable result of an open attack on one of the major nuclear powers, which makes it unlikely to say the least.

There are some neighbouring states in the Middle East and Asia that are in perpetual if fairly low level conflict but that could resort to a nuclear exchange if things escalated. Even so, although increased levels of radioactivity would be measurable in the UK it should not pose a substantial danger to health.

Dirty bombs

The main threat related to radiation released by terrorists is the 'dirty bomb'. What you have to understand about this is that its use does not involve a nuclear explosion, with all the resulting effects that can have. A dirty bomb in this context is a conventional explosive device surrounded by non-fissionable radioactive material. This can be anything from the discarded coveralls of workers in nuclear facilities, to small radiation emitters from medical equipment, to fragments of nuclear material from reactors, possibly stolen when power stations, submarines, etc. were decommissioned.

When a bomb surrounded by these materials is detonated, the radioactive materials are shredded and dispersed around the local area. Some might be vaporised and distributed downwind. The radiation levels are low, especially after the materials are spread about by the explosion, and are unlikely to pose a major hazard to anyone except those caught in the immediate vicinity of the explosion.

The purpose of this type of bomb is to cause fear in the population, economic and social disruption in the affected area, and financial loss due to the cost of the clean up involved in restoring the area and reassuring the public. They are most likely to be used against financial, commercial and social centres. Government agencies are now well prepared to deal with these events. The initial explosion and radiation injuries to those close to it are likely to cause deaths, some immediate, some after long term illness, but the area badly affected will be relatively small, though travel around it might be severely disrupted for days or weeks.

If you live close to the site of the explosion but not directly affected by it, you will almost certainly be advised to go inside, close all doors and windows and remain where you are until further notice. You might find that telephone lines are blocked and mobile phone networks are unavailable; these are security measures often imposed after such an event. Depending where it occurs, the damage caused by the explosion might also cause loss of electricity, gas, and/or water supplies to the local area or they might be shut off due to danger of further explosions or the spread of contamination.

If you are within in the zone affected at the time of the explosion, or are evacuated from a building close by, you will be put through decontamination, not allowed to take out any personal possessions, and might be detained for medical and security checks until you are cleared for release.

If you are close enough to be told to Bug In but not close enough to be evacuated, then you are unlikely to need much in the way of extra precautions against the radiation. Ensuring all doors, windows, and other entry points e.g. letter box, cat flap, etc. have a good seal would be wise, and immediately moving all pets or livestock indoors, perhaps to the garage, would give them protection too. After that, monitor the news and local radio and get into a Bug In routine using your preps as required.

If you are downwind of the site of the explosion, you might have people in white suits wandering around waving survey meters. If they find sufficiently raised levels, your buildings and surrounds could be washed down and any edible plants removed for disposal. It wouldn't be foremost in your mind but in such cases you should be offered appropriate compensation, which would at least allow you to restore your preps.

Nuclear explosions

Whether caused by a device acquired or made by a terrorist group, or a suicidal rogue state, a nuclear explosion is in a completely different league to a dirty bomb.

There are 4 types of nuclear explosion, categorised according to the height of the detonation:

1) Subsurface burst – where the fireball generated does not break the surface of the land or sea below which it is generated. Subsurface based explosions on land are mainly confined to nuclear testing. Underwater bursts may be used for testing or could be a result of submarine warfare. A subsurface burst would cause local damage but little other effect

2) Surface burst – where the fireball touches the ground. This might be a ground level explosion or one above ground but low enough for contact between the fireball and the earth. A burst above ground will cause a wider area of destruction but both will produce all of the effects noted below, including radioactive fallout.

3) Air burst – where the explosion is above ground at sufficient height that the fireball does not touch the ground. The main characteristics of an airburst are the extended range of heat and blast effects, a wider area of immediate radiation, but little or no fallout.

4) Exo-atmospheric burst – where the explosion is outside of the Earth's atmosphere. These explosions can cause destruction of or disruption to satellites, a light flash observed over a wide area, and potentially long range Electro Magnetic Pulse (EMP) effects but no direct effect on the ground and no nuclear radiation effects.

The characteristics of a nuclear explosion are:

1) Immediate effects including: an intense flash of light lasting up to several seconds and of heat lasting up to a minute; immediate radiation including gamma rays, x-rays, neutrons and various other emissions; a blast wave of sound, compressed air and vibration; EMP

2) Residual effects including: neutron induced radiation and fallout. Neutron induced radiation only occurs at dangerous levels within

an area close to ground zero – the point at or immediately below the site of the explosion and only with a surface burst or low airburst. Fallout, however, consists of dust drawn up by the rising fireball and will emit a variety of forms of radiation but most noticeably Gamma rays, Alpha particles, and Beta particles. Fallout can be distributed over a long distance in whatever direction it is blown by the wind. Since wind direction and speed can vary at different heights the area covered can be large.

The range and intensity of damage will vary depending on the yield of the weapon. The yield, or 'size', of a bomb is calculated in terms of the blast damage caused by an equivalent amount of TNT explosive. During the Cold War some nations had bombs of up to 20 Megatons (equal to 20 million tons of TNT exploding at the same time) in size.

As an example, the range of effects of a 10 Megaton ground burst from ground zero would include:

A crater 1.25 miles across

A fireball 2 miles wide

Houses destroyed or seriously damaged out to 12 miles

Exposed skin charred out to 18 miles

Houses damaged by blast and fire out to 20 miles

A mushroom cloud nearly 30 miles wide

Where and at what intensity the fallout would land depends on wind strength and direction, rainfall and many other atmospheric factors.

Fortunately the chances of a terrorist or rogue nation getting their hands on a bomb of that size are extraordinarily slim. It is far more likely to be in the 'tactical' range of several kilotons rather than Megatons. However, that is still far from negligible. The atomic bomb dropped on Hiroshima was of less than 20 kiloton yield. It exploded at less than two thousand feet above the city. It instantly destroyed everything within a mile of ground zero and destroyed most other buildings out to around four and a half miles. It killed nearly one hundred thousand people and seriously injured almost as many more.

The only practical defence against the immediate effects of a nuclear explosion is not to be within range of them, either by being a long way away on the surface or very deep under ground.

During the Cold War there was some chance that if you realised things were getting hotter you could Bug Out to somewhere well away from probable targets, though that was difficult to predict because of the possible number of them. For a terrorist bomb there is unlikely to be any build up or warning but the variety of likely targets is smaller, mostly confined to the centres of major cities. If this is a concern for you, the only realistic option is to move out to a more rural area.

Beyond the immediate effects, Bugging In gives you much better odds.

Nuclear fallout mainly generates three types of radiation:

a) Alpha particles – which have a range of a few centimetres in air and very poor penetration, i.e. they will not penetrate your skin even if the speck of fallout dust is sitting on it. The threat from Alpha particles is if they get inside the body, where they can do great damage to the soft tissue.

b) Beta particles – which have a range of a few metres in air and penetrate more deeply. They cause burn-like damage to the skin and are particularly damaging if they get in the eyes or mouth and from there to the internal organs

c) Gamma rays – which have a range of hundreds of metres and can penetrate even solid objects. They cause damage to the flesh, brain and other internal organs and are the main residual radiation cause of what is usually recognised as radiation sickness.

There are three things that will reduce the amount of radiation reaching you: Time, Distance, and Shielding.

Time

You might have heard the term 'half-life'. This is the time that it takes the level of radioactivity generated by an element to reduce by half. Some elements have a half life of seconds, others of thousands of years. But remember that it isn't the case that if something has a half life of 20 days it will be harmless within 40 days. At 20 days it is half as active as it was at the start, after another 20 days it is a quarter as active, after another 20 days it is an eighth as active, and so on.

Luckily for us, the average content of fallout of the differing elements and the average of their half life, gives us a rule of thumb equation for predicting the decay of the intensity of fallout. This gets complicated if you receive fallout from more than one bomb detonated at different times, but in our scenario now that probably isn't something we have to worry about.

The decay rule is called the 7 and 10 rule and it states that for every seven fold increase in time the level of radiation will reduce to one tenth of what it was when it peaked at your location. So if at the time the radiation peaked it was measured at 100 roentgens per hour, after 7 hours it will measure 10, after 49 hours 1, and after two weeks and seven hours 0.1.

The problem for most people would be in measuring what level radiation peaks at, so that they can calculate when it is safe to come out of shelter. To solve that problem you can either buy a radiation monitor or meter, or you can rely on broadcasts and other information from official sources. At least after a single bomb, unlike in an all-out war, some government facilities and organisations should still be running, so you have some chance of that information. Whether you want to trust to that or make your own arrangements is up to you.

For comparison, although it varies according to where we live, we will each absorb about 0.1 roentgens per year from background radiation from our environment and that is negligible.

Damage occurs according to how much radiation your body absorbs, over what percentage of the body and how quickly. It also varies with age and general health of the recipient, but for short-time whole-body exposure of healthy adults:

- 80r accumulated will have no short term effects
- 120r will make around one in ten people feel nauseous
- 250r will make about half suffer from radiation sickness
- 400r will kill one in four within six weeks
- 800r will kill 3 in four within a week
- 1000r will kill everyone eventually
- 1200r will kill everybody within a week
- 5000r will cause almost immediate collapse and death within days

Distance

If you can keep fallout at a distance from you the effect will also be reduced. As I wrote in the list detailing the different types of radiation, some have a longer range than others. If you can keep Alpha and Beta emitters outside the house then they won't initially do you any harm. So, as we saw earlier, sealing all gaps in so far as possible, to prevent the radioactive dust getting into the house is the way to go. Use polythene sheeting, cling film, duct tape or masking tape, whatever you have, but do it!

If anyone has to go outside for any reason, then they must exit on a side where the wind is not blowing towards the building and be fully dressed in washable material. This will keep dust off their skin and make decontamination easier. Before returning to the shelter, they must wash down where the water can either be collected or will drain away from the building, then enter an outer area, strip off the outer layer carefully and enclose it in polythene bags. If the outer clothing is disposable, so much the better and for various uses a supply of cheap rain ponchos, decorators' shoe covers, rubber or surgical gloves, dust masks and goggles and duct tape will be useful, though you can improvise with bin liners and paper towels if you must. After getting rid of the outer layer, stripping off inner layers and then thoroughly washing or showering the hands, face and body should get rid of any contamination accidentally transferred from the outer layer.

Later, when it is safe to spend more time outside, you will also have to thoroughly clean any vegetables or other items before they are brought in, both to maintain that distance and also to keep the radioactive particles out of your body.

Keeping the Gamma emitters away is more of a problem, but if you can minimise the surfaces on which they can become embedded then there is more chance that they will be blown or washed away from the house. For this purpose: slate on the roof is better than tile, and make sure your gutters and drain pipes are kept clean and clear; smooth walls rather than pebble dash will hold less dust, concrete surrounds with the gaps rendered will blow or wash clear more easily than decking, flower beds, or grass. I'm sure you get the idea.

These things also work with the idea of keeping your near surrounds clear of flammable materials, but they do clash with some of the ideas for security that we will cover later. In the end it comes down to your priorities and choices.

Shielding

With shielding, it is actually the density of the material that decides how good it is, rather than its thickness but for a given material the thicker the layer the better it will be. For example half an inch thickness of lead is much better shielding than half an inch of wood, but you can get up to the same protection factor using wood if you have a thick enough layer of it. It's just that for the same amount of protection instead of a half inch of lead you would need eleven and a half inches thickness of wood.

Protection factor (pf) is generally calculated by the thickness of a material that it takes to reduce the amount of radiation penetrating it by a half. Some examples are:

Lead = 0.4 inches (1.0 cm)

Steel = 1 inch (2.5 cm)

Concrete = 2.4 inches (6 cm)

Packed soil = 3.6 inches (9 cm)

Brick = 5 inches (12.5 cm)

Timber = 7.2 inches (18 cm)

Air = 6000 inches (15000 cm)

A reasonable level of protection is normally considered as that given by 36 inches of packed soil, which gives a pf of 1024 (half to the power of ten). You can use that as a reasonable start for gauging the thicknesses of other materials that would be needed. If you have several different materials used in shielding you can also work that in. For example if you have a house with a double brick wall and each brick is 4 inches thick then for that 8 inches you could take about 6 inches off the thickness of packed soil you need in addition to achieve the same protection factor.

In a Bug In, if you don't have a purpose built shelter then a cellar is usually the best option. If you don't have a cellar then an internal room or hallway, that puts most walls between you and the outside of the house and gives you most distance from the ground and roof – which might both hold fallout – is your best choice. Then pack whatever dense materials you can against the walls. You could use books; heavy wooden furniture; containers of water; whatever you have will help. If you have some warning and can prop paving slabs or bags of soil or the like against outside walls then do so.

If you have to Bug In against fallout then your aim is to keep it as far away from you as you can, with as much stuff between it and you as you can, for as long as you can or until you know it is safe to come out.

I have only been able to include the basics in this section but I hope that will help as a starter if you are new to this subject. I'll include references and links to more detailed sources in the bibliography.

Although Chemical and Biological incidents share some of the features of a nuclear attack, the procedures needed for them are more in line with those for other general Bug In events and I will cover them in later chapters.

Light

Mains items: Overhead lights, table and standard lamps, bedside lamps, emergency lights, external security lights, battery chargers

OK, after that depressing little section, it's time to lighten up. (I know, I know, good intentions, bad pun!)

Gather any crowd of people into an underground train or an interior room, then unexpectedly turn off the lights and it is a good bet that at least one will scream. Many of us have an instinctive fear of the darkness based on genetic memories of the real or imaginary sharp-toothed predators that prowl in the concealment it offers them. The fact that most of us are rarely exposed to true darkness doesn't help when it happens.

We live in a world of artificial light indoors and out. House lights, street lights, vehicle lights, torches, advertising displays, computer screens and mobile phones illuminate our surroundings, and it is that way because we like it. Artificial light extends our days whether it is for work or play and it has been like that since our ancestors first discovered fire.

Watch any group of indigenous people in the remote African bush or the depths of the Amazonian rain forest and when night falls they will gather around a fire to talk and sing, eat and play. We communicate visually as well as with words and without artificial light a big part of our ability to do so is lost. If someone leaves the fire they might well take a burning branch to light their way, helping them to avoid snakes and thorns, rocks and branches, or anything else that might cause them harm, and to illuminate and repel those ravenous beasties.

Bringing a burning branch into a dwelling that is made of or full of flammable materials is a recipe for disaster, so smaller and more easily controlled lights were developed and so we have candles and oil lamps that are still viable light sources today. Even these though have their dangers and many a house has burnt down as a result. Fortunately devices that will lessen those dangers have also been developed.

Candles

Candles for illumination are available in almost every shape and size you could imagine, from 4 hour night lights to huge 'church' rectangular candles with several wicks that will keep on burning for days. They serve as a useful back up to other, more efficient, light sources and are an excellent potential trade item.

You can burn flat or wide ones on a saucer that will both catch any molten wax and give you an easy grip to carry the light, fit stylish ones into fancy candle sticks, or do as we used to with standard household candles and put them in a jam jar, that serves the same purposes as the saucer, shields the flame from draughts and gives it a higher level of safety. Or better still you can enclose your candles in purpose designed lamps that will give all the advantages of the jam jar and might also feature reflectors to enhance the light and make it more directional.

These lamps are cheap and easily available from many sources. The two on the right in this picture came from a factory outlet, while the ones in the centre and left are camping lanterns that telescope to protect the glass and minimise bulk when backpacking. They hold candles made from stearine that will provide light for up to 24 hours. None of these have a reflector but if you don't want all-round illumination you could quickly adapt them by fitting a piece of baking foil at the back of the candle.

Or you could make one yourself from a baked bean tin, like that between the two camping lanterns. Cut the top of the tin about seven-eighths of the way around and bend it upwards. Cut a section out of one side. Punch a hole in the base and thread a long screw through the hole. Warm the screw using a lighter then twist the candle down onto it. Bend the lid into a roof shape and push it down over the top of the tin. If you want to get fancy, punch a small hole at either side just below the top of the tin and fit a loop of wire to act as a handle. You now have a portable lantern that will keep your candle upright, protect it from draughts, reflect the light, catch the melted wax, and collect much of the soot from the smoke. Easy!

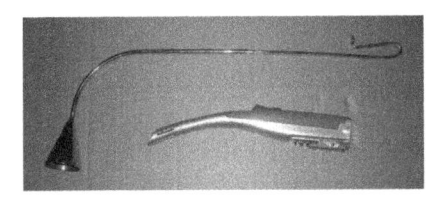

Whenever you are using candles and for some other lamps as well, you will find a long lighter and a snuffer help you to avoid burnt fingers.

Liquid fuel lamps

Early oil lamps were simply a bowl with a spout at one end to support a wick. A little later these developed into something more the shape of a gravy boat. Either type burns oil or melted tallow, such as sheep fat, and they are easily improvised from crockery you might have around the house. Instead of sheep fat or margarine you could burn cooking oil, which actually smells rather better.

Using the same basic format of a wick to conduct oil to a point where it is lit, but in a more modern format with the benefits of the candle lanterns, we have the oil lamps with a chimney or the Hurricane Lamp.

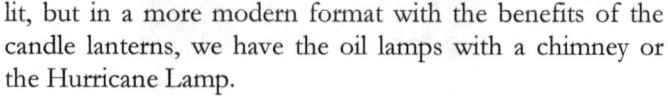

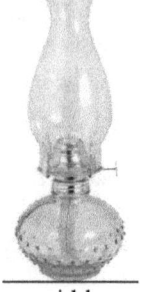

These are often used to burn paraffin rather than 'lamp oil' (which is much the same but more expensive!) but they will also burn diesel fuel, cooking oil, or other alternatives. The difference between fuels is mainly in the smell and smokiness, though the light quality varies to some extent too. 1mtr lengths of wick are available at £2-5 depending on width.

I have seen hurricane lamps for sale in pound shops but they are often made from cheap tinplate. They usually work but are intended more for decoration than serious light output and some are so poorly constructed that they leak. Considering that you can buy a good quality lamp made from steel for less than £5, the cheapo versions are hardly worth the saving.

Do be aware that although these little lamps usually give out enough light to allow you to move around a room without bumping into things, they are not sufficient for detailed work or reading.

Next up the hierarchy are pressure lamps. So ubiquitous was the product of one manufacturer, that in the UK pressure lamps are often simply called Tilley lamps. In fact there are several other quality makers in the market including Aladdin, Vapalux, Coleman, Thermos, and Petromax and, like the Hurricane lamps, lots of cheaper clones being produced overseas, especially in China.

Also like the Hurricane lamps, pressure lamps usually burn paraffin but not with the use of a wick. As the name implies, after fuel is poured into the tank at the base of the lamp, it is pressurised by pumping in air using an integral pump. When the valve is opened, the fuel squirts up through a tube and out of a jet into a chamber where it is ignited by a pre-heated mantle. When the fuel ignites the mantle is heated further and glows.

When pressure lamps burn, they do so with a gentle hiss which many people rather like. If the light starts to fade and the lamp splutters it can be pumped up to restore the pressure, but if it needs to be re-fueled then it should be taken outside and allowed to cool before you remove the cap of the fuel chamber to refill it.

Pressure lamps produce light that is more than adequate for reading or detailed work and can illuminate quite a large area outdoors. They do need to be serviced regularly and if you buy one for emergency use then you should also guy a variety of spares including: mantles, washers, globes, and various other parts.

Unlike the hurricane lamps, pressure lamps are not cheap. To be safe they have to be manufactured to high standards. Currently the cheapest I found was the Coleman dual fuel lantern, which will burn Coleman fuel or unleaded petrol, for £50 upwards. Many of the other lanterns will cost between £100 and £200.

I have to admit here to a prejudice. While I recognise that liquid fuel lamps, and particularly pressure lamps, can be cheap to run and efficient in their light production, and many users really like them, I cannot recommend them for use indoors, especially if you are Bugging In. My reservations come from my time in the forces when I was in my sleeping bag in a six man tent.

The lantern we were using started to fade and one of my colleagues went to pump it up. Perhaps it the pressure had fallen too low or perhaps it was caught by a gust of wind, but the lantern flared. The tent caught fire and our friend dropped the lamp which then set light to my sleeping bag. Luckily we all escaped from the tent unhurt and quickly extinguished the fire but we did

72

lose the tent and some of our gear. I dread to think what the result might have been if the incident had happened half an hour later when most of us were deeper asleep.

So I won't use them indoors. I admit I have heard of only a few other dangerous incidents so perhaps we were unlucky. Nevertheless, if you decide a pressure lamp is for you, then I urge you never to leave one lit unless someone is awake to watch it, and to have fire extinguishers standing by, just in case.

Gas lamps

Safer, simpler, lighter and cheaper than pressure lanterns, but still capable of producing a working level of brightness (about the same as an 80watt light bulb) are the camping gas lamps. There are several available from differing makes, but the most easily available in the UK are the models from CampinGaz.

As with the pressure lamps these little lanterns work with a mantle but burn Butane from disposable cartridges. You will often find older models of this type of lamp at car boot sales at very good prices. Old and new styles have a control knob to adjust the brightness and most have a sparker to light them rather than having to use a match or lighter. New lamps cost £20 or a bit more but are sometimes on special offer for half that. At car boot sales they are often £5 or less. Run time is 6-8 hours.

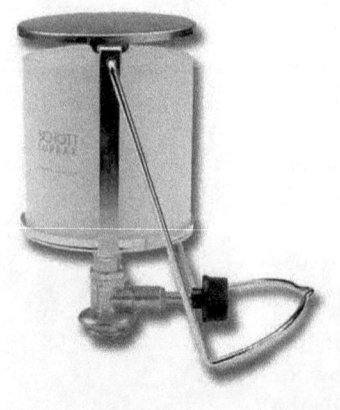

Similar but larger versions that fit the bigger Gaz cylinders are also available. These work in much the same way as the portable models but are even cheaper at around £18. The large gas cylinders are ever more expensive these days but give many hours of light at 100-120 watt equivalent. They are a bit too big for most houses but excellent for the garage or workshop.

Similar models are available from Bullfinch and Calor for the big red Propane cylinders that you often see at road works or on the back of works trucks. They will also work on any other Propane or Butane cylinder if you have the right regulator. They are very bright and run for hundreds of hours from a large cylinder.

Battery Lamps

The range of battery powered lamps and lanterns is vast, ranging from tiny things no bigger than your thumb to LED standard lamps and everything in between. You can get them in camping shops, supermarkets, garden centres, auto parts dealers, DIY shops, or online. Take your pick!

Battery lamps are relatively cheap, portable, and both safe and simple to use. They are an especially good option if you have pets or young children around. There are brighter lamps available than many of the battery ones but the larger models are more than adequate, even for detailed work.

At the upper end of sizes I can particularly recommend the Ring Endurance Essentials Storm Lantern. Ring has an excellent reputation for the quality of its power products, such as 'smart' battery chargers and this lantern does that reputation no harm at all. Reviews are consistently good.

It runs on 4 D cell batteries which power 12 high intensity LEDs and has a useful dimmer switch. On minimum setting one set of batteries will last up to 10 days continuous use and even on full you will get 40 hours. Remember, though, that rechargeable batteries will not give as long a burn time on one charge, so have a replacement set ready.

The lamp is sturdy enough for indoor or outdoor use, is waterproof and has a comfortable carrying handle. Recommended retail price is £21.99 but they are available from various sources including Amazon at anything from £13 to over £30.

Be aware that there is an older version of this lamp that has a fluorescent tube rather than LEDs. It is extremely bright but has no dimmer switch and the run time on one set of 4 D cells is only 4-6 hours.

Dynamo powered lamps

Dynamo/hand crank/wind-up lamps have all the safety advantages of battery lamps plus an integral recharge facility. What's not to like?

Many come with a charging cord for recharging from the mains or a car lighter socket and if it is the lighter socket type there are mains to 12v transformers available for charging in the house.

74

When fully charged you will get several hours of light from any of these lamps but even if you eventually have to top them up with the handle you usually get 30 to 45 minutes of light for a couple of minutes winding.

Freeplay sell two lanterns, the Indigo and the Indigo Plus. Both have LED main lights which can be controlled with a dimmer switch plus a button-activated directional beam that provides a more concentrated light for reading or other detail work. The Indigo can be recharged from 12v lighter socket whereas the Plus has sockets for input from AC (adaptor is an optional extra) solar (panel available optional extra) or USB (standard cable) and has an output socket for charging mobile phones. The Plus is brighter but more expensive at £35 as opposed to the Indigo's £25.

Burn time for the Indigo is 4 hours on maximum or up to 70 hours on minimum or 35 hours for the spotlight. The Plus gives 3 hours on full, 60 hours on minimum and 50 hours from the spotlight.

The Freeplay lights are high quality and the winding mechanisms and handles are strong but on the whole my preference is for a lamp sold by Ring as the Cyba-lite RT5114, though similar models are available with various labels and mine were bought from Blacks camping shop under the Eurohike name. This lamp is considerably brighter than the Indigo and price is from £20 upwards, averaging around £25.

The Eurohike lantern has the choice of 9 or 15 LED illumination and when fully charged using the 12v lighter socket cord supplied, the 9 LED setting, which is plenty bright enough for me to read by, will burn all night and beyond. The winding handle is not as strong as that on the Freeplay but none of the four I have has given any problems over several years of use. Should the pack of 4 AA Ni-Mh rechargeable batteries ever give out, it is easily accessible for replacement via a hatch in the base of the lamp.

As with lamps powered by disposable batteries, there is a large selection of this type of lamp available from various shops or online. Size, brightness, lighting time, price and other features will vary so shop around, but the ones mentioned above are the standards against which the competition should be compared, in my opinion.

Renewable energy lighting

There are two ways to go about RE lighting, one is to use solar rechargeable portable lamps and the other is to use fixed lights powered from your off-grid power system and 12v battery bank, charged by solar or other renewable sources.

If you decide on the latter then a trip to a caravan or boating shop is in order. Spot lamps, strip lights, dome lights, or table lights are available,

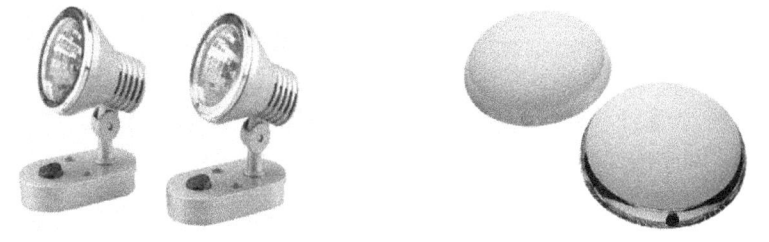

along with the necessary cabling. Most will have a switch on the light but it is something to check for because lights intended for exterior mounting are often wired to a switch inside the caravan or boat. Traditionally, either halogen or fluorescent bulbs have been used but LEDs are an increasingly popular option. The LED bulbs last much longer and the power drawn from the battery is less but you often need more for the same level of illumination.

These light fittings are designed to look good and if you have the 12v circuits permanently wired in, they can often be used in place of mains-powered wall or reading lamps without looking at all out of place.

Alternatively, fittings and kits are available which have bulb holders similar to the ones into which you would usually fit your mains ceiling lights but which take special 12v bulbs. Various types are available but they can provide lighting equivalent to a standard 60W bulb.

If you opt to use the portable lamps then you have many more from which to choose.

Some of these lamps are designed as security or courtesy lights and feature PIR sensors. Some of those have a control to adjust the level of time for which they stay on after being activated.

I find the 12 LED Solar sensor lights with a triangular side section ideal as emergency stair lighting. They come with a bracket you screw to the wall and the lamp then slides onto the bracket. Outside, this would put the blank side – which gives access to the batteries – against a wall, the built-in solar panel facing upwards and the light angled down. They have a key to lock the lamp to the bracket to prevent easy theft. Indoors the orientation is the same but the solar panel is inoperative.

The light comes on when anyone enters the area covered by the PIR and stays on for about a minute, plenty of time for someone to go up or down most staircases. It then switches off to preserve the battery charge, though these lights do have a switch to set them permanently on. I find the lights are bright enough for safe travel on stairs and will work for at least a week before I need to slip them off the bracket and put them in daylight to recharge. If you put them to charge each morning they will easily return to full charge during the day even if they have been used often during the previous evening. They usually cost just over £20.

There are other solar charged PIR lights available but most of them are designed as security lights and will be covered in the Safety and Security chapter.

Most other portable solar lamps are sold as garden or shed lights. Their output is often limited although the shed lights in particular are improving. Some cheap models still come with just 5 LEDs, which provides enough light to move around a small room without falling over things but is no good for any precise work, and they cost between £5 and £10. More recent products come with up to 48 'super bright' LEDs and higher capacity batteries, giving a much more useful level of brightness but costing 2 – 3 times as much.

Most of the garden lights are pretty but don't give out enough light to be useful indoors as anything other than nightlights. Perhaps the exception is the small spotlights. Because of their focussed beam, if you modify the support poles that have a spike for pushing into the ground, the lamps can be used as work or reading lights. With a couple of the brighter shed lights for area lighting and spot lamps for work, you can have a low-level but low cost, workable and flexible indoor system with no running costs that is much better than sitting in the dark. After a good day of sunshine, the spot lamps will run for 6-8 hours. The shed lights about half that depending on model.

The panels for the shed lights can be fitted to an outside wall or window ledge to make best use of the daylight, most come with 2-3 metres of cable to connect the panel to the lamp, but you will need to put the spot lamps out each day to recharge.

Mains recharged emergency lighting

Any building you enter, to which the public has access, will have emergency lighting, usually coupled with fire exit signs. Similar devices in your home can provide a useful, if temporary, emergency system that will give you time and aid safety while you bring your longer term preparations into play.

Emergency lights sometimes contain individual batteries and sometimes are connected to an emergency power system, be that battery or generator powered. If you have an off-grid power system for your home you could fit lights at strategic points that a sensor will activate when mains power fails.

However, as a temporary system you have a choice from quite a variety of mobile lights of differing types. For a long time now there has been hand lamps that you keep connected to the mains via a plug in cable. These lamps usually contain a 12v sealed battery and charging system with a battery status meter that disconnects the charger when the battery is at full capacity. They normally had fluorescent tubes, and some still do, but as with other lights the trend is for new devices to be

78

fitted with LEDs. These rechargeable emergency lamps are designed to give a bright light but they are heavy and bulky.

Latest entry to the market are much smaller devices that consist of a charging cradle that plugs into a standard three-pin socket and a separate light that can function as a night light while in place, an emergency light that comes on at full power if the mains supply fails, or a torch when plucked out of the cradle. Some have a permanently on night light, others are PIR activated.

There are now several competing models but at £10 - £15 they are a cheap, versatile, and less obtrusive, if less bright, alternative the big old lamps. They are now also being introduced in many care homes.

Torches

And now we're almost back to taking a burning branch from the fire to light our way and scare off the beasts of the night.

My wife says I have an addiction to collecting torches. That isn't true at all. I simply have a completely rational and justifiable technical interest in the study of an essential component of static or mobile preparedness activities for which reason I need to examine as wide a variety as possible in the interests of furthering my knowledge of the subject! Why are you laughing?

OK, so I like torches, have done ever since I got my first one for Christmas as a young lad. Odd really because I have no fear of the dark; in fact I love being out in the wilds after the sun goes down. But they are extremely useful and they have come a long way since the burning branch. In fact, after many decades when they hardly changed at all, they have suddenly gone through quite a renaissance in the past few years.

The range is huge: ones that takes batteries, ones that are hand cranked, and ones you shake to charge, small ones and big ones, simple ones and those with multiple functions. Until the current revitalization, top of the line were probably the Maglites. Prevailing opinion in professional and other high usage circles now seems to give the crown to Fenix but they are not a cheap choice. The tiny LD01 that runs on a single AAA battery and gives out a maximum of 72 lumens costs nearly £33. The LD41 with 520 lumens at £65 is highly recommended but top of the

79

line is the TK75 which uses special batteries has an output of 2600 lumens giving it a range of 600 metres, for only £160, not including 4 of those special rechargeable batteries for £13.95 each and don't forget the special charger they need at £21.95. That isn't the most expensive torch on the market but it should do for most people!

To be honest, for most purposes while Bugging In you probably won't need anything more than a cheap multi LED torch running on 2 AA batteries, though you should have one for each person old enough to operate it.

In some conflict situations, however, a brighter torch that will both illuminate and dazzle an intruder can give you an advantage and letting them know they have been seen could be the only defence you need to send them running.

Warmth

Mains items: Boiler, Central heating pump, Electric fire, Mains gas to boiler

Every year in the UK, some people, mainly elderly, die of hypothermia because they cannot afford to heat their homes. The cost is constantly rising and according to an electricity spokesman this week (Feb 2013) the loss of coal-fired power stations will mean importing even more gas, pushing prices higher again while lowering our potential generating capacity to minimally sustainable levels. If an emergency occurring in, or because of, a severe winter caused loss of power for a prolonged period, how many more – including people other than the elderly - would be added to the fatality figures?

Since the 1960s most new houses and flats have been built to be all electric or at best electric and gas. Older houses that were 'modernised' had the hearths removed and fireplaces blocked off, both to follow the trend and to comply with smokeless zone regulations.

The appeal of the open fire was recognised but it was provided for, in part, by electric or gas fires that simulated the effect of real flames. Only in more-expensive modern developments have open fires recently been restored as part of the design.

And this is despite the fact that the biggest part of the electricity usage of any house is usually consumed in heating and cooking, yet if the power goes off there is no provision for any alternative.

So, providing some sort of heating independent of the mains utility supplies is obviously essential. You might not be able to heat the entire house as you would in normal times but that isn't always necessary. What you do need to do is provide sufficient warmth to keep people safe and functional. Sufficient warmth at night to ensure proper sleep is particularly important, in order to maintain both physical and mental health and to preserve energy.

The two factors you need to consider while prepping in relation to warmth are how to create it and how to preserve it so that your resources aren't wasted. In this chapter we will look at both aspects.

Creating heat, for warmth, hot water, or cooking, places huge demands on any electrical system. These functions are, therefore, the least suitable to be replaced by most off-grid electrical generation even if you have gone for a fairly substantial system. It is more efficient and safer, in that it spreads your alternatives, to use other means for those purposes, and there are several available to you.

People and pets

People and other animals generate warmth. Cuddling together to share that warmth is one of our most instinctive, and often most comforting, methods of generating and preserving heat.

One of the standard immediate treatments for hypothermia victims in the outdoors is to strip them and a volunteer down to their underclothing and then put them together in a sleeping bag or other form of shared insulation, so that the body heat of the volunteer can provide warmth for the casualty.

The same principle has been applied by people and their pets and hill farmers and their working dogs. In the event of a Bug In situation, you and your family and pets can apply the same technique. Even if you aren't in physical contact, gathering close together in a confined space can considerably increase the temperature. Lowering the level at which warm air above you is trapped is especially effective.

One of the ways of doing this is to create a room-within-a-room. If you have a tent, then erecting that inside a room of your house can provide an extra layer of insulation to trap heat within a smaller area, keeping you warmer. This is even effective if you are on your own; though the more people there are the better it works.

If you don't have a tent then you can build a den for the same purpose. Rearrange your sofa, chairs, bookcases, standard lamps, and other items to create a frame and walls, and then spread sheets, blankets or duvets over it as a roof. Insulate the floor with mattresses, airbeds, backpackers' insulation mats, extra carpet, rugs, blankets, towels or cushions, then huddle in comfort and enjoy the warmth and closeness while reassuring the kids by playing at camping, or hibernating bears.

Clothes

After your body generates heat, your clothes become the first line of insulation in maintaining it. Again there are two sides to this. Wearing lots of clothes will keep the heat in your body but won't allow it to warm your close-range environment. So if you want other people to share the benefit of your warmth, you need to get them inside the same layer of insulation.

Generally people take off most layers of clothing when getting into bed, because it is more comfortable and the bedding is going to keep them warm, but in this situation that is especially useful if there is someone else with you under the covers; you then just need to cuddle up so that insulation doesn't sag down between you. The same is true inside your sanctuary. Outside wear plenty of clothing; inside remove some of it and share the warmth.

When you do have to operate in a colder environment, wear several layers of thinner clothing rather than thick items. This is more efficient and if you have to take on a physical task you can shed layers as required in order to stay warm but avoid sweating. In exceptionally cold conditions that is particularly important; wet clothes transfer heat much faster than dry ones and must be avoided. Strip off as you need to and pace your activity so as to avoid over-exertion.

Ideally, you want layers of clothing that will wick sweat away from your body while trapping the heat in. A polyester T-shirt next to the skin, with a couple of woolly jumpers outside that generally works OK, but silk against the skin is much better. Or you can use purpose designed thermal clothing, though it tends to be more expensive. If you go outside the house, a windproof layer, and then waterproofs if it is raining or snowing, completes the system.

Socks are useful all the time, indoors or out, but for outside in cold weather follow the layer principle and wear a thin inner pair and a thicker calf length pair over them.

Gloves too work well with the layer system, a pair of thermal inner gloves and a thick pair of mittens over them gives good protection but ensures you don't expose your hands if you have to remove the mittens for fine work. Fingerless gloves are often useful for inside where you are not exposed to the wind and don't have to handle frozen objects.

It shouldn't need saying but you do need a warm hat and it can be a real benefit indoors too. Choose a soft one that you can pull down over your ears to protect those sensitive lobes. A scarf or thermal snood will protect your neck, lower face and nose, and it will warm the air before you draw it into your lungs, so helping to preserve core temperature.

Blankets and sleeping bags

... and long woollen ponchos or quilted poncho liners, and snuggle blankets with sleeves and hoods, all have their place too.

Yes, I know the latter make you look either a bit naff or like you want to join a monastery, and no, I'm not admitting to having one, thank you for asking, but they are warm and don't fall off if you have to move around a bit. In private, where nobody but the family is going to see you, you shouldn't have to put up with too many giggles or clever comments either. Buckle a belt around your waist and you can pull up the hem so you don't trip over it as you walk.

In fact, if you don't have a suitable poncho, you can cut a slit just big enough to get your head through in the centre of a woollen blanket or fleece car blanket, then fold and stitch around the edges of the cut, to create a multipurpose cold weather garment and bedding. Adding a small tab of Velcro will let you close the gap so you don't have a cold spot when using the poncho as a blanket.

Sleeping bags are excellent for individuals, though double sleeping bags or singles that will zip together are also available. Some military issue poncho liners are designed to zip or button up to create a mild-weather sleeping bag or can be spread out like a thin duvet or quilt.

Thick woollen blankets are still hard to beat for warmth and flexibility, and they, duvets or eiderdowns are good for either couples or families. You can pile more or less layers of them on top or underneath you in really cold weather or more underneath for comfort but less on top when the temperature rises.

Food

Each of us has a genetically-controlled metabolic rate that determines how quickly we break down food to provide energy. For some people this means that after eating their temperature quickly rises. People who have a high Body Mass Index (BMI) i.e. a high fat to weight ratio, have inbuilt insulation and to them this effect might be particularly noticeable.

But whether you have a high or low BMI, in order to generate heat as a factor of breaking down food to provide energy you have to eat. Carbohydrates break down quickly and so provide a fast heat energy boost. Fats dissolve more slowly to provide a prolonged release of energy. Proteins aren't so important in this context.

Heating the food won't affect the amount of calories it provides but it will add some direct heat transfer from the warm food to the body for an immediate benefit even before digestion begins.

Conscious hypothermia victims are often given chocolate, which digests quickly, and/or hot sweet drinks to aid their recovery. Some studies have shown that strong coffee or tea with cream and sugar is even better for the purpose than the ever-popular hot chocolate. This is because of an effect caffeine has in helping the body to release stored energy, one of the reasons it also helps you to wake up. A hot drink will also transfer some of its warmth to the inner body.

However, anything that stimulates sweating, as some spices do, is a bad effect, since sweating is the body's way of promoting cooling. A spicy curry might make you feel hot at first but afterwards it could make you even colder.

Similarly, despite the fact that it might make you think it is warming, alcohol should be avoided in very cold conditions. It can dilate the blood vessels in the skin and increase heart rate, while lowering blood sugar levels. Blood is then pumped to the surface of the skin where it cools. When circulated back to the inner organs the cooled blood lowers core temperature, exactly the opposite of what you want in this situation. The reduced blood sugar can make you feel hungry and lead to a waste of food that could be avoided. Too much alcohol will also affect your judgement and lead to potentially dangerous mistakes.

So food has good and bad factors in keeping warm; eating is essential, eating chocolate is a good thing, but having a dram is not. You could put a tot in your coffee or hot chocolate to reduce the negative effect of the alcohol but it would also reduce the positive effects of the hot drink. I'll leave it to you to decide on the relative merits of the effects on morale of a small measure of alcohol versus a bar of your favourite confectionary.

Hot water bottles, warming pans, heat pads, hot rocks

Using off-grid power to run an electric blanket would be wasteful. The wattage might not be high but if left on for an extended period it adds up. Fortunately there are other methods that work just as well.

In times gone by, posh families might have had bed warming pans, usually made of copper or brass, into which embers were placed. The servants would push these into the beds to warm and dry the bedding in preparation for the family members retiring for the night, though the master of the house might have preferred the chamber maid to stay for the same purpose! If you fancy this idea – the warming pan not the chamber maid – originals are usually to be found in antique shops for £20 to £100 but reproductions are made and although some are intended purely for decoration there are functional models available for £20 upwards.

Alternatively you could go for the good old hot water bottle. These are regularly available for around £3 and work just as well as they always did. You might want to knit or sew a fancy cover for yours or just wrap it in an off-cut of blanket or a towel, both to prevent burns when you first introduce it and to extend the time that it stays warm.

If you don't have a hot water bottle you can use hot bricks or stones. Basalt is popular but any brick or stone will do. Ensure the stones are completely dry before heating them and even then take care because they can sometimes shatter and throw out hot, sharp fragments. As with hot water bottles, wrap the heated stones in a cover or bag and place them between the covers for a while before you get in. Move the bag around a few times to spread the heat. You can also use hot rocks in an open container to provide area heating; in this case stones first used to contain a cooking fire are an efficient use of resources.

For a more modern and portable version you could try heat pads. These are available from camping suppliers for warmth or from medical outlets for easing muscle aches and sprains.

There are several versions; some are simply bags of liquid or gel that you warm in a pan of hot water or microwave (see the instructions before buying, you might not have power for the microwave!), others contain an activator which, when flexed, causes a reaction that heats and hardens the pad. After use you restore the pad by heating it in water and then leaving it to cool.

This latter type is handy because you can keep them ready and initiate the heating reaction whenever required without the need for a fire or pan of hot water. There are also 'hand warmers' consisting of an insulated metal container into which you place a smouldering stick of charcoal, but I have never found them of much use. Prices vary from around £3 to £20.

House insulation

Improving the insulation of your home as an energy and cost saving measure has been pushed for years now but despite various schemes that provide the service free of any charge, a surprising number of people have done nothing about it. However, even if you do already have cavity wall and loft insulation that keep the place warm when the central heating is running, you might want to consider additional measures for when that isn't an option.

An additional layer of insulation in the loft is rarely wasted and double or triple glazing to replace old window sets throughout is equally worthwhile but unless you have a very efficient off-grid heating system, it is common in cold conditions to limit movement around the house as much as possible and to confine heating to one room. If you are prepping and recognise that as your potential situation, then it makes sense to choose a room now and to improve it as much as possible for the purpose.

If you are in a home that has more than one level, when possible choose an upstairs room as your citadel of warmth. Hot air rises and cold air sinks, so any activity that warms the naturally-colder lower floors will eventually pass some of the results to the upper levels. Normal building methods mean that often the ceiling of one room and the floor of the one above it consists of: a layer of plaster board, fixed to wooden joists - between which there will be no insulation other than air – topped with floorboards, over which there might be a laminate, carpet, or vinyl covering. None of these items provide for much effective heat retention, especially as there are often gaps between the floorboards.

An upper level room will have the same plasterboard and joists between it and the attic but the gaps between the joists should be stuffed with insulation and if there is boarding over that to provide extra storage space then so much the better as it will further trap any warm air to prevent it from escaping under the eves.

If the layout of the building allows you to choose a room with south facing windows then do so, because that will allow maximum warming by sunlight. A smaller room will be easier to heat than a big one, but if that isn't practical you can always apply the measures described in the People and Pets section. You can provide further insulation on or within the walls and floor of this room and pay special attention to draught proofing.

Unfortunately, other than in a home purpose designed and built for passive solar benefits and energy efficiency, there will always be some compromises to consider. Upper levels can provide the benefits described, but the flooring is rarely strong enough to support layers of heat absorbing material and thermal mass. Large windows let in lots of warming sunlight but are poorer at keeping it in than bricks and cavity insulation. Double or triple glazing retains warmth inside the room but can lower the amount that penetrates in the first place.

If you are in a single storey home, such as a cottage or bungalow, then you might have more options in this regard but some disadvantages too. Older cottages will be built from stone, with solid walls that do not provide an opportunity for cavity insulation, though you can install it on the inner surface of the wall or between the stone and an inner layer of plasterboard. Older buildings often have small windows, which have pros and cons and can be draughty. A modern bungalow is a better choice from this point of view but solid stone and small windows are good when it comes to security. You have to work with what you've got and your priorities according to your individual circumstances.

In addition to insulation you must also seek to reduce cold draughts, but while doing so remember that if you are going to use any active form of heating, be it wood, Propane, Butane, paraffin, or coal, then you must allow for sufficient ventilation, both to provide oxygen for efficient combustion and to prevent build up of carbon monoxide, which is a deadly and silent hazard whenever you burn something.

Open fires

When the South Yorkshire coal mining village council house in which I grew up was modernised, they took out the access to gas, removed the hearths, and blocked off the fireplaces. They also bricked up the access to the cellar, which was divided into two parts, one a 'clean' cellar for food and the other a coal cellar. The chimneys are still there though; one at one end of the house where the kitchen range stood and another at the other side in what was the living room.

If you have a house with chimneys but no open fires, you might have thought about being able to open up the fireplace for heating and cooking in the event of an emergency. If that is a practical option for you I urge you not to wait until a disaster happens, get it done now!

When the previous owners were having the fireplaces removed and covered over, there would have been no reason for them to spend additional money on having the chimney swept or preserving the flue. In addition, the hearth that would have contained the fire to prevent embers falling out onto the rugs or carpet, and the surrounds that made cleaning a little easier may have been removed too.

The chimney might, therefore, be thick with creosote and soot, possibly blocked by birds' nests, and the flue cracked, which poses serious risk of fire and of carbon monoxide fumes seeping into inhabited rooms. There might also have been a back boiler for providing hot water, which will have been replaced by either a hot water tank with an immersion heater or a combi boiler, but the old fittings must be checked to ensure that they pose no hazard.

Before the fireplace is restored, any cap on the chimney must be removed and the chimney swept and then inspected and approved or repaired as required by suitably qualified professionals. The lintel over the fireplace must be undamaged and fire bricks within the fireplace must be checked and if necessary replaced. A suitable hearth must be installed and a safe surround fitted. When that is done you will need to buy in a supply of fuel and build a stock of tinder or firelighters and kindling, plus suitable implements for lighting and tending the fire and cleaning the fireplace.

If you omit any part of that process you could be putting your house and the lives of all its occupants at serious risk!

Wood/multi-fuel burners

A safer, simpler, and more versatile, but more expensive option would be to install a wood or multi-fuel burner or cooker. There are many designs on the market, ranging from under two hundred to several thousands of pounds. There might still need to be a considerable amount of work done but the burner/stove will have its own flue pipe which might be run up through the old open fire chimney through a new liner.

You won't need to bother about firebricks or a surround but a burner must be set on a non-combustible plinth which extends at least 150mm (6") either side of the stove and 300mm (12") in front of it. The thickness of the plinth depends on whether the materials below it are combustible or not. At maximum it has to be 250mm but if the surface temperature of the plinth below the stove doesn't exceed $100°C$ then depth can be as little as 12mm. You can get a free download of the full regulations at: http://www.planningportal.gov.uk/buildingregulations/approveddocuments/partj/approved

Wood burning stoves are considerably more efficient than an open fire. With an open fire up to 80% of the heat from the fire goes up the chimney. With a wood burner up to 80% of the heat comes into the room. Some burners are intended primarily for heating and some come with a built-in oven. As an example, the Windy Smithy Louis Ranger burner with oven (picture above) costs £510 plus £75 delivery. Fitting is extra.

With a double skin flue, a burner like this can be installed almost anywhere, even if there is no existing chimney, as long as a suitable base can be fitted. Where there is a chimney, a full length flue isn't always necessary but does greatly aid combustion for efficient fuel usage and to avoid creosoting of the chimney when 'exhaust' gases cool too quickly. A full length double-skin flue with insulation is generally preferred to prevent that, and also means you can adjust how hot you have the fire box in order to run the oven at lower temperatures when appropriate for cooking. Be aware that a survey, cleaning, and installation could cost £1500 or upwards and must be HETAS approved. Sufficient ventilation is an important factor for approval.

As a cheaper, portable, alternative, I can highly recommend the Frontier Stove log burner from http://www.campingsolutions.co.uk/ I have one and consider it an excellent piece of kit. This £140 wood burner is designed for use in tents, classic caravans, sheds or workshops, outside or as a permanent room heater and cooker. It doesn't have an oven but it does have a hotplate area and a water heater that fits around the chimney is also available.

Camping Solutions offer a tough fireproof groundsheet for £28 and either more of these or fire blankets can be placed at the back and either side of the stove for greater protection. The stove comes with 5 flue pipes, extending up to a height of 2.41m including the height of the stove, but more sections can be bought for £9.99 per 410mm length as required. There are also other accessories available including a spark arrestor, silicone flashing kits to protect materials through which the flue passes, maintenance kits and, most importantly fire extinguishers and carbon monoxide alarms.

The latter two items are essential accessories whenever an open flame device is used indoors, whatever type of fuel it burns.

Before choosing a heater of any style you should think about the room where you will put it. Most wood burners will have a heat output equivalent to 5kW or above. A 5kW stove is adequate for a room of about 3.5m x 3.5m. For the size you need, talk to a dealer or do a search for an online calculator such as the one at: http://www.stovesonline.co.uk

You also need to calculate how much fuel you want to store. A 5kW stove will burn approximately six cubic metres of hardwood per year, but it could be considerably more if this is your only source for heating and cooking. That much seasoned wood (dried for a year) will cost £480-700 but you can buy unseasoned wood cheaper and store it until it is dry.

Depending on where you live and your relationship with neighbours, you might get it much cheaper or even free. You can burn almost any wood though the heat output varies. A hard wood like oak, for example, will give you about twice as much heat for the same volume of logs as pine.

If you have access to woodland and permission to cut timber you can provide your own, but you will need a chainsaw, appropriate safety clothing, fuel and transport, and most importantly proper training so that you can operate safely. After you get the logs home, you will need axes, a maul, splitting wedges and/or perhaps a log splitter, muscles and plenty of energy to turn them into fuel. Logs should be stored away from the house as a fire prevention measure, protected from rain but ventilated so that they can dry out and stay that way.

If your stove is a multi-fuel model then you should also consider other fuels, such as anthracite or smokeless fuel. Costs can work out cheaper than for wood and take less space for the same amount of heat output.

Gas heaters

Where properties are remote from mains supply, it is not unusual for the owners to use Propane gas for cooking and heating. The cylinders must be kept outside the building and properly mounted for safety reasons but that is a common arrangement for those places and is also the norm for static caravans. In these cases the gas is most often stored in exchangeable 19 or 47Kg cylinders but sometimes in a large tank.

The most efficient form of bottled gas heating is by the use of a wall mounted heater. These must be installed by a qualified gas fitter. There are two types of heater, vented and ventless. A vented heater transmits exhaust gases to the outside of the building via a pipe; ventless heaters emit the exhaust directly into the room in which they are mounted. Older models required the room itself to be vented by keeping a window or ventilator open but newer models do not officially need that, though it is still advisable.

The advantage of a ventless heater is that it is extremely efficient, emitting over 99% of its output into the room, which makes them economical to run, whereas some of the heat from a vented model is lost to the outside.

In general ventless heaters are considered very safe and do include monitoring features but the main disadvantage is that if one develops a fault, Propane or carbon monoxide can be released into the room, causing a deadly health risk. That danger is considered so severe in some places that ventless heaters have been banned. They also produce water vapour which can lead to condensation problems.

That said there are hundreds of thousands of these heaters in use and they rarely cause a problem. When they do it is often serious but you can mitigate that by following some basic precautions:

1. Have the device installed and certified by a professional
2. Have it serviced annually
3. Position and guard it safely
4. Do not use it for more than four hours per day
5. Ensure the room is ventilated to prevent build up of gas or humidity
6. Because of the risk of a Propane leak do not use any other open flame or heat source in the room (no candles or liquid fuel lamps).
7. Fit carbon monoxide and Propane detectors/alarms in the room

And remember that you always have the option of a vented heater. The heaters in most caravans offer the option of vented Propane or Butane gas, or mains electric operation. A caravan offers a small but very well ventilated living space, much the same as you will be trying to provide in your house if mains power is off. We have lived in our caravan over several winters while I was on contract in various parts of the UK and something we learnt quickly was how efficient the gas heating is compared to the electric. It isn't often on for more than a few minutes before the caravan is warm, even in the worst of winters, so these heaters are definitely an option to be considered if they are viable for your situation e.g. not a tower block flat because there would be nowhere safe for you to keep the Propane cylinders outside!

Portable gas heaters

More versatile and suited to any type of home are the portable gas heaters. Rather than Propane these use Butane, the cylinders for which are approved for use indoors. There is a variety of types, sizes and outputs using either refillable or disposable cylinders.

The models using refillable cylinders have higher output ratings and initially cost more but are also more economical to run. However, because of the size and weight of the gas containers they are less easy to move around.

Being portable they are inevitably all of the ventless type and therefore most of the precautions for wall mounted Propane heaters, other than those referring to installation and servicing, also apply to these models.

The large 'cabinet' heaters sell for £60 upwards and although they will take varying types of cylinder are really designed for the 15Kg size. A refill for one of those will cost approximately £30 though prices seem always to be rising.

The output of a cabinet heater is usually between 1 and 4kW and how long a cylinder will last depends on both the model and how high you have it set. On 2Kw setting, which is as high as you would normally expect to go in a house, especially if you have taken the measures outlined earlier, you should get at least 30 hours and possibly as much as 70 hours of heating from a 15Kg cylinder.

In my experience these heaters are reliable and the modern ones especially are simple to operate, often having only a single control for amount of heat and a button to activate the igniter. The gas can be turned off from the control or at the regulator if you are not going to use the heater for a while. The cabinets usually have castors for repositioning but a full cylinder is heavy enough that if you have to move the heater far it is better to remove the cylinder and move that and the cabinet separately.

LPG regulation BS: 4250 controls the storage of Butane and Propane cylinders. Basically Propane cylinders must be stored outside and there must be no cellars, pits, or openings to buildings within two metres. 15 – 400Kg of cylinders, other than those connected for use, must be no closer to a building than 1M (I doubt you'll want to store more than that but there are further regulations if you do!). The cylinders must be stored upright with all of the valves closed, even if you consider the cylinder to be empty, and a plastic plug fitted. For security the bottles should be in a wire mesh cage, which will also allow any leaking gas to dissipate.

If cylinders have to be stored or used indoors then the maximum is 70Kg total, with no cylinder of more than 15Kg in a domestic property or 20Kg in an office or workshop, and no more than 5 cylinders of any capacity.

93

For security, you will probably want to fix to the wall those cylinders that are in use. Casual theft can be discouraged by use of a padlock securing either a metal band or a chain shackled to the wall.

Parabolic reflector heaters that run from a 0.4, 1.8, or 2.7Kg Camping Gaz cylinder are available from around £20. The output is generally between 1 and 2kW. A 1kW model set on full will give approximately 12 hours of heat from a 1.8Kg cylinder or 18 hours from a 2.7Kg. A 1.8Kg refill will cost upwards of £17, a 2.7Kg refill £20 or so.

Much more easily available these days these days are small, easily portable radiant heaters. These are lightweight, run on disposable 227gm butane cartridges and have adjustable output up to 1.2kW. A gas cartridge will last for up to two and a half hours on a low setting but about half that on maximum. The heaters are usually priced at around £25 but are sometimes available from as little as £15. Cartridge prices also vary, with individual cartridges at around £2 but bulk packs reducing that by half.

My choice of these heaters for off-grid house heating is a cabinet heater for the main refuge room, with a store of at least four 15Kg cylinders, though if my home was suitable I would seriously consider a wall-mounted vented heater and 47Kg Propane cylinders. I also have a couple of the lightweight portables with 48 cartridges for short-term use in other rooms when required. The parabolic reflector heater is used in the workshop.

Paraffin heaters

Paraffin comprises 60% of aviation fuel and is very similar to diesel and domestic heating oil. In liquid form it is not easily ignited and is therefore relatively safe to store. It also resists deterioration better than many fuels and will remain fit for use in lamps or heaters for many years. Although paraffin does not ignite easily in liquid form, as it vaporises the fumes become combustible and with the use of pressure or a wick these can then be burned to produce heat or light.

If paraffin is not available, many heaters and lamps will work with the other fuels mentioned above; the main difference will be that they are smokier and perhaps give off unpleasant odours while burning.

For safety, any device that burns paraffin must be refuelled outdoors and for this purpose you should create a special refuelling point. This facility should:

1. be at least 10 metres from any building, store of fuel, or heat source

2. have a base that allows collection and disposal of any spilled fuel

3. Have dry powder or foam fire extinguishers close by
4. Be on ground that will present no hazard of contamination of water courses

When refuelling your devices they must be extinguished and cooled and no other flame or ember e.g. a lighted liquid fuel lamp or cigarette, or mechanical device that might generate a spark should be allowed within the vicinity.

Use a funnel or hand pump as appropriate and take care to avoid wasting fuel or creating a hazard by spillage. Also avoid breathing the fumes. After refuelling, clean and dry the exterior of the device and safely dispose of any spilled fuel or contaminated rags.

If you do use a paraffin heater indoors, be aware that the room should be well ventilated because a variety of gasses are given off during combustion. These gasses include: carbon monoxide, nitrogen dioxide, sulphur dioxide, and others. Normally, ventilation will ensure none of these gather in sufficient density to cause a problem but even so paraffin heaters should never be left unattended or burning while people are asleep and you should have the usual carbon monoxide alarms to warn of excessive concentrations. Water vapour is also produced and might cause problems with condensation or dampness and mould if the room isn't kept properly aired.

Like all heaters and especially those using live flame, paraffin heaters pose a fire risk, so ensure no loose flammable materials can come into contact, and keep children and pets away. Have a suitable fire extinguisher available nearby. All should have a cut off that extinguishes the heater if it is tipped over.

Most paraffin heaters work by use of a cotton or fibreglass wick, much in the same way as oil lamps, but usually in the form of a ring. This must be trimmed occasionally to remove burnt fibres from the tips of the woven material in order to assist clean burning. You can buy a special trimmer for the purpose or use sharp scissors.

There are some modern versions, though, that work in much the same way as a pressure lamp, using jets to direct the fuel onto a heated plate and a metal mantle that then burns the fuel vapours. There are also a couple of models that use a wick but then direct the heat into a second chamber where it is mixed with oxygen to burn at a higher temperature.

Most heaters are fairly simple to operate, with a battery-powered piezzo-electric igniter to light the wick and a control that raises or lowers the wick to adjust the height of the flame. If the electric spark fails you can use a match or lighter instead, though getting access to the wick is awkward on some models. Any odours from the paraffin usually only occur during lighting or extinguishing the heater.

Very modern heaters might have the electric ignition but also a thermostat that automatically adjusts flame height according to the temperature set, a timer that allows you to warm a room before you enter it, a booster start facility that produces higher output for a few minutes at start up and then adjusts when the proper temperature is reached, a battery operated fan to increase heating through convection, or even a motion detector that turns the heater down if there is no movement in the room for 10 minutes.

There are a variety of types but most of the domestic-sized models look similar to a cabinet-type gas heater. The output varies from 2kW to around 7kW depending on the model. Small versions intended mainly for greenhouses are quite simple, with a fuel tank topped by a wick chamber and a heat disperser. They have limited heat output and give off more smells but can be enough to keep a room above freezing.

There are also some models intended for heating very large areas or for drying out houses that have been affected by flooding. These will burn either paraffin or diesel and produce many tens of kilowatts of heat.

The fuel usage of a heater will depend on its design, method of operation, and kW setting but some greenhouse heaters will run for 14 days from a 2.25 litre tank and even a large modern domestic can last up to 59 hours on 5 litre tank. Prices run from £15 for a greenhouse heater to £250 for a new domestic model, and more for the very advanced designs.

Paraffin is used extensively for heat and light in the third-world because it is cheap, easily available, and stores well and you might want to consider it for the same reasons, particularly in a disaster situation because the heaters and lamps will also run on some other fuels. Nevertheless, in my opinion, under most circumstances the fire and fume risks put it low on the list for modern homes when there are so many other, safer, choices available.

Candles and stoves

Candles burn with an open flame and are automatically sources of heat as well as light. Although the amount of heat given off by each candle might be low, if you have several burning it can make a considerable difference compared to no heat, especially in a small space that is well insulated and where draughts and ventilation are controlled.

If you are making an indoor warmth-chamber in the form of a tent or den, then the fire risk has to be considered most carefully, but with proper precautions candles can help and if you are using them for light anyway then they will reduce your need to use additional fuel in other forms of heating. Enclosing the candle in an appropriate lantern will greatly aid safety and efficiency while doing little to reduce the amount of heat given off.

Using a cooking stove, however, is usually a very inefficient and wasteful form of heating. If you are also using candles, then blow out the candles and let the stove provide heat and light while you boil water or cook something. If you boil water then you should only heat the amount you need, to save on both fuel and water, but if you do have some left then transfer it to a thermos flask or hot water bottle to save fuel later. If you have nothing else available and the options are to use your stove or freeze then by all means go for it, but if you prep wisely you should never be in that situation.

Ground source heat pump

A ground source heat pump (GSHP) drives a mixture of water and antifreeze around pipes that are buried in your garden. As the water flows through the pipes it is warmed by the heat of the ground and then goes through a heat exchanger and back through the pump. Cold water flowing in a separate piping system is warmed as it passes through the heat exchanger and can then be fed to your radiators and hot water taps or into a boiler where it can be further heated as required but with a saving on energy because the water is already warm. Meanwhile, the water/antifreeze mix goes back around the pipe loops to be warmed again.

Below a certain level, which varies with the consistency of your soil but usually six to seven feet down, the temperature of the ground stays fairly constant throughout the year, so the system will still produce heat even in winter. The more piping you install the more heat it will be able to harvest but the more space and money will be needed.

For economy, piping is usually laid flat in a snake-like loop arrangement but if that is not practical due to a restricted amount of ground then at extra expense holes can be drilled and the pipes fitted vertically.

Ground source systems are not cheap to install – average is £10-20,000 - but after they are in place they require very little maintenance and don't always need any fuel to heat the water, so they can save you money. The temperature to which the water is raised is lower than would be the case with a conventional boiler and in winter the system might have to run constantly to keep the house warm. Because of that lower temperature, under floor or warm air heating systems are often preferable to radiators.

The down side of these systems is that they do need a continuous source of power to the pump, so for a Bug In event in which mains electricity was off you would need a substantial off-grid system to provide reliable power. Otherwise they are comparable with 'environmentally friendly' and energy-bill-savings schemes like grid-tied solar systems for normal times rather than useful for grid-down emergency situations.

Solar water heater

The absolutely simplest form of solar water heating is to put a black coloured bag or tank out in the sun and let it heat up naturally. This is the basis of how a portable solar shower works and in sunny weather it can perform well. However, for more complex systems you have several options.

A properly designed solar water heating (SWH) system has many of the advantages of a GSHP but without some of the disadvantages.

Generally, SWH systems are roof-mounted but can also be fixed to a south-facing wall. There are several heat collecting types including; Integral Collection System (ICS), Flat Plate, Formed, and Evacuated tube collectors. Then there are Direct or open loop systems and Indirect or closed loop systems, and passive or active pumping systems.

The simplest of the systems is an ICS, open loop, gravity fed system similar to some of the first ones produced. In these a network of black-painted thin metal pipes is enclosed in an insulated box with a glass plate on the front. Water is fed into the pipes at one end and as it flows through the network it is warmed by the heat of the sun. It then flows out of the pipes into an insulated water tank from where it is fed to the taps.

The 'open loop' part of the system refers to the fact that the water that flows through it is then used directly. It is used as domestic hot water for washing and showering then it is drained away after use and the water in the system is replaced by fresh water flowing in. If the water flows directly into a hot water tank, perhaps set in the attic below where the system is mounted on the roof, and from there down to the taps, no pump is required so it meets the criteria for a 'passive' system.

These systems were popular with DIY environmental enthusiasts and were often home made using aluminium cans or similar for the piping. The advantages are that they are very cheap to make, cost nothing to run, and in good weather can provide substantial amounts of hot water. The disadvantages are that they are subject to freezing in the winter and the small surface-to-volume ratio of the tubes makes them inefficient except in ideal conditions.

Flat Plate Collectors are similar except that they have heat absorbing fins between the tubes to increase the surface-to-volume ratio. Sometimes there is a pipe along the bottom of the box into which cold water flows and then a series of pipes between that and a top pipe. The cold water flows up the vertical pipes, gathering heat on the way, to the top pipe which is connected to the domestic part of they system. This can either be directly i.e. open loop, or more conventionally in modern systems, to a heat exchanger i.e. closed loop. The advantage of the closed loop system is that the fluid can be a water/antifreeze mix or other suitable fluid which avoids freezing in winter. Some new fluids are now being tried that it is expected will absorb and transfer heat more efficiently. The other major advantage of FPCs is that they usually feature a reinforced glass plate which can better withstand severe weather including hail.

Formed collectors are again similar but are not contained in the box or covered in glass. These are usually only used for swimming pool heating in sunny climates.

Evacuated tube collectors are again similar in basic design but the water tubes are surrounded by two glass tubes between which there is a vacuum. This allows the water tubes to be heated by the sun but reduces the heat lost by convection back to the environment.

Whenever a pump is required to drive water around a system, ether directly through radiators or through a heat exchanger then it is consider an 'active' system.

Depending on your requirements, commercial solar heating systems can cost between £1500 and £3000 but will provide up to 60% of your hot water requirements. They will provide less in the winter and perhaps more in the summer. Maintenance requirements are modest and expected serviceable life-span is considered to be 15 to 20 years.

If one of these systems is of interest then it is worth investigating further and talking to an installer who is fairly local to you. They do provide a much more efficient use of solar for heating than PV panels and might also qualify for various subsidies both for installation and against your electricity and gas bills.

For Bugging In use, just remember that you might have to power a pump, though not continuously or as powerful a pump as required for GSHP.

Passive solar

How about a form of house heating that once installed costs nothing to run, has no moving parts, requires no maintenance, uses no fuel, doesn't involve any work beyond normal household cleaning, and automatically adjusts to provide more in winter and less in mid-summer?

That is what you get with passive solar! It might not be as effective in the UK as it is in Nevada or Spain but even here passive solar can offer some great benefits.

To give maximum effect passive solar has to be incorporated into a house's design and incorporated into both the building methods and materials, but even if you aren't building from scratch there are often concepts you can add or take advantage of within the home you have now.

The most important factor in determining whether passive solar will work with your home is its orientation; principally orientation to the path of the sun and the direction of the prevailing winds. In the northern hemisphere, including the UK, the sun basically travels from east through the south to west; if you have one side of your house with big windows that face south then you are in with a good chance of being able to take advantage of passive solar. If that happens to be the side with most of your garden on it then you are onto a winner.

The basic principles of passive solar are to let the maximum amount of sunlight into the house during the daytime in winter, absorb it into the fabric of the house, and then let it slowly release during the evening and night to keep the house warm, while preventing too much entering in summer and taking advantage of natural cooling to prevent the rooms becoming uncomfortably warm.

The key techniques are: careful siting and/or landscaping for open aspects, shading and wind protection; an appropriate amount of glass facing south; use of materials with effective heat absorbent and retention properties; shielding where needed; insulation of the right type in the right places; and ventilation at the right heights and facing in the right directions.

Putting that together, the idea is that you consider not only the direction of the sun but its different heights in the sky at differing times of year. You fit windows so that when the sun is low in the sky during winter it shines through onto heat absorbing material that sits on a layer that provides thermal mass (TM) which will retain that heat. In addition, you have an overhang or awning that will shade the windows from most of the sun when it is at its height during midday in the summer. You then adjust which windows you open and at what heights to allow entry to cooling breezes low down while giving an escape route for hot air that has flowed upwards in the house in summer, or prevent cold draughts in winter while preserving warmth that has been generated.

If your present house layout doesn't allow for all of these things you might be able to adapt it by building a sun lounge with open glass on the south side and with a floor of dark coloured concrete with a textured surface. Solid concrete has a high thermal mass rating (2060 $KJ.m^3.k$). If this stands on sandstone or compressed earth foundations then that property will be enhanced. Ensure the walls are built of either reinforced concrete or brick rather than concrete block, as either of the former have better a TM rating than block (because the block has a hollow centre and therefore less mass).

Do not cover the concrete flooring with any cover such as carpet or mats and keep as much of it as possible clear of furniture or shading by pot plants, sun blinds, and the like. You can fit blinds if you cannot include an overhang outside, but keep them pulled up during the daytime so as to let in winter sunlight but slightly lowered to shade out the mid-day summer sun.

There is much more to passive solar design and adaptation than I can include here, in fact whole books have been written on the subject, but it is an important and potentially useful measure of which you should be aware in relation to warming your home and if you see it as practical for you then I hope you will investigate it further.

Cooling

Mains items: Fans, refrigerator, freezer,

As I sit here at my desk in April 2013, looking out of the window at two inches of snow covering the garden and far more on the hills in the distance, it seems odd to have to think about keeping ourselves and our food cold. Then again, there are many years in the UK when I might feel the same way if I was typing this in July, though probably without snow outside.

However, we have grown used to our refrigerators and freezers and in some cases air conditioning, and wherever you are in the world people face the same problems while trying to preserve the harvest and their own sanity in hot conditions. Over the centuries some of them have created remarkably effective and ingenious solutions that don't rely on electricity.

But let's leave those ideas for a few minutes and first look at methods that you can use to either avoid the problem or ease yourself into new ways without losing precious stores of food.

Keeping food cool

One of the main reasons many Preppers buy a generator is to keep their freezer running until the food in it has been used or preserved by other methods. Generators work most efficiently when they are running at near maximum load, so if your freezer does not take most of that load and your battery bank is fully charged, you can use the spare capacity for other cooling purposes, such as running the fridge or, in hot weather, fans to help cool the house.

Freezers work best and retain their cold for longest if they are full, so as you gradually use up your food, fill up the space with containers of water, freezer packs and the like, or visit friends and good neighbours to offer them the chance to keep food in your freezer until all the food is used.

While the freezer is not being powered, cover it with insulating materials, such as bedding, to help keep in the cold, and open the door or lid as rarely and for as short a time as possible. Efficient loading of the freezer will help in that. Pack the shelves or baskets so that the items you expect to need first come most easily to hand and keep food where the freezer is coldest. Pack the rest with your water containers but if you have a chest freezer then place heavy water containers on the bottom, then your food and finally some easily moved water packs on top.

Alternative power

As an alternative to using a generator, fridges and freezers are available that run on Propane, Butane or from 12 volt power systems. The fridges most often fitted in caravans and boats will operate on mains power, 12v, or gas but are usually much smaller than a domestic fridge and have an ice compartment that won't take much more than a couple of ice cube trays.

There are exceptions to that rule, such as the Thetford 140L fridge freezer and various models from other suppliers such as Dometic but be prepared for a shock when you see the price. A household fridge freezer of similar size might cost £200 to £300 whereas the Thetford will set you back nearer £1000. The smaller models are much cheaper of course but are still expensive compared to a domestic fridge of similar size. Unfortunately that is the price you pay for the versatility. Second hand models are sometimes available.

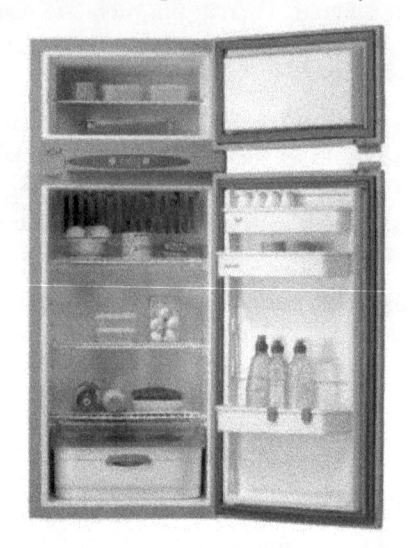

There are also portable fridge/freezers that run from various power sources. They are available in differing sizes and models but the better ones are chest types. These can cost from £150 to £1000 depending on make, size and features. The temperature is adjusted either by a dial or a digital control, so you can use the same device as a fridge or a freezer, but not both at the same time.

Ours is a Waeco CoolFreeze CF40 12/240Volt Portable Compressor Fridge or Freezer and cost just under £500 but it has been extremely useful and cost effective during long stays in the caravan and at home when defrosting the freezer. It also saved the most vulnerable and expensive items – meat and fish – from our chest freezer when that broke down. You might consider something similar to be a useful backup.

Ice boxes

Taking one step back in time from modern refrigerators we come to ice boxes. These are basically a cabinet, most often made from wood, with shelves for food items and a shelf or drawer at the top for a block of ice, though there were larger versions in which ice was stacked all around the walls of the cabinet.

The modern version of this concept is the cool box often used for picnics and camping, which will be filled with ice cubes and food, or beer and wine. They are also sometimes used for shopping trips in summer, with frozen ice packs to keep frozen or fresh foods in good condition until the shoppers get home.

If you don't have an ice box but you do have access to ice, of your own making or obtained elsewhere, you can use your fridge as an ice box by stacking ice blocks on the top shelves. The fridge is insulated and will serve this purpose even better than many of the old models. Keep the ice in a bowl or tray to contain the water as the ice melts.

If you don't have access to ice you can pack snow in a box and compress it as hard as you can to expel the air and make it last longer as a coolant. It won't stay frozen as long as proper ice but much longer than as soft snow. Take care that the snow you use doesn't include any contaminants or other unpleasantness.

Ice houses

A much larger version of the ice box was the ice house. These were often either underground inside or outside the main house, or were built on the surface and then covered with earth. Many differing designs can still be seen around the UK. Most have a domed roof and are reminiscent of a wartime air raid shelter.

The outdoors buildings were built from bricks or stone in a sheltered place, often among trees, and then insulated on the outside with earth and turf and on the inside with straw. Blocks of ice were stacked all around inside and then food placed on shelves or in containers that would protect them from predation by vermin. Although much of the ice would gradually melt, some of these structures would keep some of it frozen until the following winter when new supplies became available.

Evaporative cooling

Going back even further in time, but still in use in places that do not have mains electricity or supplies of ice, the main form of cooling was by the use of evaporation. It is also still in use in higher tech forms for air conditioning and various industrial processes.

Evaporative cooling occurs when air passes over a wet surface; the faster the rate of evaporation the greater the degree of cooling. Our bodies use this method by generating sweat, which evaporates to cool us. We increase the effect by standing in the blow of a fan, but for centuries the concept has been transferred to keeping other things cool.

The basic methodology is to put goods you want to keep cool into a vessel made from an absorbent material, then place it where it will be shaded from the sun but exposed to a breeze, and then wet the outside of the container. As the water soaking the vessel turns to vapour it draws heat from the material, so cooling it and its contents.

Taking this to the next level, the container is placed in a larger vessel and the gap between them filled with water. If a piece of cloth is then draped over both containers and allowed to contact the water it will soak up the liquid which will evaporate from it, enhancing the cooling effect.

There are many variations on this basic theme including using wetted sand between the containers. Much research has been done by relief agencies and government bodies in poorer parts of the world to identify ways of making this system more effective and to educate people in their use.

And the system is effective. Research in Sudan by Practical Action found that the storage life of various fruits and vegetables was extended by four to ten times what it would be without a cooling vessel. For tomatoes that was 20 days instead of 2.

I saw a much larger example of this in use in a village in Jordan in 1986. There a brick base had been laid, around the edge of which two brick walls were built to about waist high and with a gap of approximately four inches between them. A wooden box with a lid was fitted inside the inner wall. The space between the walls had been filled with sand, which was regularly rewetted with water brought from a nearby well. The whole structure was shaded by a pergola covered by vines. The wooden box contained several types of vegetable and other wrapped items plus bottles of cold tea, of which I was offered a drink. The liquid was wonderfully cool in that desert heat.

So with the use of a generator or alternative energy you can extend your current ways of doing things even when you are off-grid and by using old or even ancient methods, employing ice in winter and evaporation in summer, you could have ways to keep food cool and extend its life even without electricity or other non-renewable resources.

Keeping people cool.

I already mentioned that our body's natural temperature control mechanism employs evaporative cooling, and there are various ways we can enhance that. A wetted cotton bandana draped over the head or around the neck works wonders on a hot day. Or a hand fan, wide brimmed hat or a palm frond can be gently waved by a willing volunteer to increase the air flow across your face and body, generating a serene sense of calm as you lounge in the shade. Oi, that's my fantasy you're looking at; you go get your own!

For more technical cooling you could use a battery operated fan, either in the form of one of the hand held models, or a larger solar recharged type of which there are now many available in differing sizes and formats. Considering that if you need a cooling fan in UK the weather is likely to be sunny then solar recharging technology is particularly appropriate for this purpose.

For maintaining lower temperatures throughout the house you could make use of solar powered ventilators or air conditioning but for a low cost, non-technical solution it is simpler to use Mediterranean ventilation methods. In the UK, what most people tend to do when it becomes hot indoors is to throw open all the windows, but that is exactly the wrong thing to do, and people who live in countries used to high temperatures know that.

To cool the house you need first to think about ventilation. Consider two things: a) Hot air rises and as it does so cooler air is drawn in below it. b) Whatever the design of your house, the air on the side facing the sun will be warmer than that in the shade. (I know that seems obvious but they are important principles on which your actions will depend yet which most people seem to ignore!)

So, to make best use of ventilation you want to provide an escape for hot air in the house by opening windows or vents that are high up but shielded from the sun and let in cool air by opening vents low down where the air is cool. Open all room doors too, to encourage air circulation.

Take into consideration the direction from which any wind is blowing, not according to the weather forecast on the television but around your house, because many local conditions such as tree lines, buildings, and other barriers of that sort can cause local eddies and wind channels that might make air movements around your walls very different from those at higher levels or elsewhere on the street.

When you get it right, and you might have to experiment a little, this should provide a cooling airflow right through the house.

To avoid giving that flow more work to do than it should you must also consider how to avoid activities that will raise the temperature within the house. For this you should try to avoid:

1. Solar absorption – If you are using passive solar heating in your home then one of the features will be a roof overhang or awning that shields large areas of glass from summer sun when it is at its highest. You can extend that by lowering blinds or by laying mats over the heat absorbing layer and its underlying thermal mass so that they don't take up the solar energy. There is a judgement call here though, which you will eventual resolve with experience. After the sun goes down you might need that thermal energy to slowly release in order to maintain a comfortable temperature during the evening without using other heat sources. Exactly how this works in your home will depend on your individual setup.

2. Cooking indoors – this is inevitably going to generate a lot of heat and probably humidity as well. In hot weather you might not want so many hot meals and may prefer lovely cool crisp salads, which will ease the situation, but if possible you might consider cooking and boiling water for drinks outside.

3. Heat emitting light sources – such as candles, oil lamps, incandescent bulbs etc. wherever possible use fluorescents or LEDs instead.

4. Heat generating activities – such as washing, washing up, vacuuming, exercising, or using power tools. In fact try to avoid

using any machinery or doing any jobs indoors that will cause you and the atmosphere to heat. If you need to do them, consider if you can do them outside.

With these factors applied and good insulation, that as well as keeping heat in when you want to will also help to keep it out when required, you will be best placed to be comfortable while others suffer, and preserve foods while other people see theirs go to waste.

Food

Mains items: Freezer, refrigerator

Food comes quite low down in the hierarchy of needs for extreme survival situations outdoors. The order there, based on how long you can survive without the item, suggests that you can live: 3 minutes without air; 3 hours without shelter; 3 days without water; 3 weeks without food.

That is a bit general but not too far out in the majority of cases. If you are Bugging In though, you might find that your family will object to going that long without anything to eat. Even if the experts say they won't die because of it, you might, and become the main course at dinner in the process!

So for various reasons, Prepping to provide food is a good idea. I mentioned earlier that food is an important factor in maintaining morale, but it is also needed for maintaining energy and, contrary to what you might think would be the case, a Bug In situation can be far from sedentary.

When mains power is down, many activities that used to be automated become manual. You might spend more time: chopping, sawing and carrying wood; gardening; cleaning and disinfecting the house; hauling containers of water; washing clothes by hand; pedalling and winding dynamo devices; and many other physically demanding tasks. To be sure, there will be time spent relaxing or on watch, but you might find that you become fitter rather than couch-bound.

However, everyone's situation will be different. If you are single and living in a 7th floor flat and your Bug In activities will be mainly confined to changing the batteries for your iPod with ones from your solar battery charger or harvesting bean sprouts from the jar on the windowsill, then you might want to cut back a bit in order to avoid putting on weight; unless you are also making regular covert trips outside and having to sneak up and down six flights of stairs carrying those containers of water.

It all depends on the situation and whether you can venture outside or are confined to the house or even a single shelter room. For this reason you cannot assume when planning your stores that just because you are Bugging In your calorie requirements will be substantially lower than they are during normal times. That might be the case and if so your stores will last that much longer but unless you are routinely very physically active it could equally be that you are burning more energy than before. If not you might want to include exercise in your routine in order to stay or get fit for what might face you when you do get outside.

Your plan must also include all of the nutritional elements of a healthy diet, including: Proteins, Carbohydrates, Fats, Vitamins, and Minerals in forms that provide sufficient Fibre and Calories for your needs. What quantities and mix of each of those components you store or otherwise provide will depend to some extent on the nature of your family i.e. all adults, adults and children, or adults, children and infants.

Other than special foods for the infants if the mother can't breast feed, if you plan all requirements for active adults then with a bit of ingenuity you should be able to cover most needs and might have a welcome surplus. There might be some additional special requirements, for people with diabetes or those with digestive problems or allergies, for example, but you will know about those for your family and will take them into account when choosing your stores.

Another special requirement for which you will want to cater is food for your pet(s). They can survive on scraps but you will be trying not to have an excess so there shouldn't be much in the way of bits to give them. If you are going to stock for animals then it should be cheaper to buy pet food than extra of what you will eat and there are also alternatives they will stomach better than you will.

It's easy enough to joke about Polly Pie, or Poached Pooch, and it has certainly happened in places where starvation loomed, but not so easy to do when it comes down to it if the animal is your own. In survival literature you will also see many accounts of cannibalism and people eating grass or insects and read many a 'sage' spouting that, 'people will eat anything if they are hungry enough', some will even recommend that you should steel yourself to do the same. Well the truth is, some people will and some won't and if they do it will not usually be until they have been starving for a long period or have grown up not knowing any other way.

There are also accounts of people cutting off their own body parts, chewing them to make the flesh digestible and then feeding it to their babies, and many of those who have tried to 'eat anything' have killed themselves in the process by chewing on poisonous plants or insects or simply because there are many plants that our bodies simply will not digest and from which we cannot extract any nutrition.

There are wild plants and other food sources that are safe to eat and we will look at those later but you do have to know what you are doing when going that route. However, the whole reason for Prepping is to avoid getting into dire situations and both stocking up and developing skills and knowledge are parts of the process.

So, where do you get this food? In a Bugging In situation your food might come from one or more of five sources:

1) Food you store

2) Food you grow or raise

3) Food you gather

4) Food you hunt

5) Food provided by other people

A practical and well-considered food strategy will include aspects of all of those while relying totally on no single source.

Food you store

Initially, food you store will mainly be bought in. Eventually, if you use sources 2 – 4, this might be supplemented or replaced with food you grow or forage and then preserve by any of the means we will review later.

I'm going to assume a worst case scenario here, with an instant requirement to move in and close down and a concurrent loss of mains power; if the situation develops any more slowly than that, consider it a bonus.

Fresh food

Depending on your lifestyle, shopping habits, and preps, when you Bug In which food 'stores' you consume could differ over several time periods. The first thing you should do is take action to preserve or extend the life of, or eat any fresh items that will otherwise go off. In normal times you might not worry too much about that but now every calorie counts and in a few months you might seriously grieve over that over-ripe banana or orange you once casually consigned to the bin.

For example, if you have fresh meat in the refrigerator you could cook it, or put it in your freezer, or dehydrate it, or otherwise preserve it. Milk and some other items could go into the freezer too. The freezer will not be running but if you take measures to keep it cold then these will last longer than in an un-powered fridge. If you can run the freezer for a couple of hours per day from alternative power then it won't become a problem for quite a while.

For fresh vegetables and fruit: inspect each item carefully and set for immediate use any that are showing signs of deterioration. To keep those that are in good condition, find space and a suitable container such as a tray or cardboard box and separate each item so that it is not touching its neighbour, then leave in the coolest room or outbuilding available.

Construct a clamp for potatoes and other root vegetables. Put down a layer of dry straw, sawdust, or sand in a box or bucket, then a layer of individually-separated veg, then another layer of material, another layer of veg, and so on. Cover it with a top layer of the material used for separation and then seal it with a lid. Keep it in a cool, dry and preferably dark place protected from vermin and insects.

Make your onions and garlic into strings or put them into a net bag or a nylon stocking and hang them in a cool, dry, airy place.

Wrap up your bread in a tea towel or use a special bread bag such as the ones from Lakeland or Betaware.

Stand herbs with stalks in a jar of water and put a plastic bag over the top.

Transfer milk from a plastic container to a clean glass bottle or jar with an air tight top.

Tightly wrap in cling film any cheese packet, whether it has been opened or not and similarly seal the tops of any opened packet or jar and also foods such as cucumbers or squashes.

Place salad vegetables in a sealable plastic bag, put in a drinking straw at one side, seal the bag up to the straw then suck out as much air as possible before quickly withdrawing the straw and sealing the gap.

There are now some new products coming onto the market that are advertised as extending the life of fresh foods. These include substances to wash the produce in order to kill spores and bacteria that cause spoilage, and wrapping films that claim to exclude air far better than normal cling film. I haven't yet tried any of these of these products but they might be worth further investigation and possibly adding to the survival stores.

Otherwise try one of the evaporative cooling methods, or if there is snow on the ground an ice box, as shown in the previous chapter.

Eat these fresh products before any others and with these preservation measures, unless you often buy far more than you need, you will probably use them up before much if any goes to waste. If you tend to keep the fridge fairly full this could feed you for several days, though the menus for some of your meals might be rather different from the norm. If on the other hand you are one of those urbanites who consider fresh food to consist of energy drinks and a couple of ready meals, then working through it won't take long enough to matter!

Frozen food

We have already looked at the ways of keeping an un-powered freezer and its contents cold for as long as possible, and at using alternative power, from a generator or other source to keep the freezer running, so it might be that having used up your fresh food you can then work your way through the freezer until those goods are also consumed.

If you are like us the freezer will contain quite a few items that don't actually need to be frozen but last a lot longer if they are. We have homemade jerky and smoked fish in there, plus various smoked sausages, some cheese, and wholemeal flour among other things. But like most people we also have fresh meat, fish and vegetables, some portions of stews, soups, pies, etc. cooked and frozen, (these make for quick, easily prepared, low fuel-usage meals) bread, milk, and others plus some treats such as ice cream and fruit pies.

If you can keep it in good condition then this food also counts as a part of your stores. To use it to best advantage you need to have an inventory of what is frozen or better still to have a menu plan that combines it with what you keep in long-life fresh goods like root vegetables and dried or tinned foods, making a calculated number of portions of full meals. It doesn't have to be exact but you should have some idea of how much you keep in, so that you can work out how much extra you need of long storage life goods to cover the total time for which you decide you need to provide.

If you decide that in order to save on fuel or avoid the noise of running a generator you will only try to keep some foods frozen temporarily but still want to use them, then they should be marked and a suitable alternative method of preservation chosen and provided for. Dehydration, smoking, salting, and canning, among others, would be suitable for many foods you usually keep frozen but some items you might have to eat soon after they thaw or be prepared to lose them. Just think, the family might have to work their way through several litres of ice cream before it can all melt; it's a burden, but someone has to do it!

The logical approach is to recognise all your forms of stored food and to include them in your plans according to the resources you have available to extend the life of fresh or frozen items. Only after you have devoured all of those will you need to start on long-life storage goods, and even that might be delayed if you are also growing, raising, gathering, and hunting some food. How much forage you can reliably expect depends on how much garden you have, what other targets grow or visit and the time of year, so their part in the plan is less easy to calculate; one of the reasons self-sufficiency enthusiasts also keep a good store.

Long life stored foods

The things in your fridge or freezer are mostly going to be things you enjoy and use regularly. The same might be true of some long-life items on your shelves, such as soups, beans, chopped tomatoes, sandwich fillers and the like. When mistakes are made in building a store it is usually with those items that are substitutes for foods normally eaten as fresh produce.

There is a temptation when you first start in Prepping to get a bit carried away. A BOGOF offer on Value Brand Chilli Con Carne seems too good to miss, so into the trolley goes a 12 pack. It is only when you eventually open one of the tins to give it a try that you realise why they were selling them off cheap; once tried, never to be forgotten, but for all the wrong reasons!

There is a maxim in Prepping circles, 'store what you eat, eat what you store.' It isn't entirely practical because nobody wants to constantly eat tinned food when they could have fresh but the intent is sound. You might not regularly eat some of the items you store as substitutes for fresh but before you buy in bulk what you should do is buy one tin of something, or one tin of each of various brands of a similar product, and try them to find one you would be happy to eat at any time, not just during an emergency, and then store that.

The other reason for the maxim is to encourage rotation of stocks, but for most long-life items that isn't really a major factor. To put it bluntly, you can ignore the 'best before' date on anything; it is nothing but a marketing ploy to get you to throw perfectly good things away and buy more!

'Use by' has some value as guidance but is most often found on short-life food such as cream cakes, and even then relying on what you see, smell and taste should be your main guide, just as it was before dates were first put on food.

It is 2013 now. I am currently eating some packs of backpacking foods that were bought in 1999. Most of them have best before dates of 2000 to 2002. I haven't found a packet yet that even tastes less good than a new one, and unlike some these are very palatable. I certainly haven't suffered any ill effects. Admittedly they are stored in sealed, dark coloured boxes in a cool room, so storage conditions are good but tins we use from the shelf are often as old and rarely do we throw one away.

You should definitely examine any old containers carefully before opening, and discard any that are leaking, swollen or badly rusted, and also examine the contents and inside of the container after it is opened, to look for any evidence of spoilage, but most will last for many years. Be careful especially of tinned goods that are acidic such as tomatoes, or stored in brine, such as tuna, because the liquids can eventually react with the metal of the tin. Fish, such as tuna or pilchards, is better if packed in oil rather than tomato sauce or brine for that reason.

This longevity is even truer of dried food such as pasta, rice, potato powder, peas, beans and many others. Sugar and high sugar items such as honey and jam will last almost indefinitely while unopened; salt does last indefinitely. White flour will often keep for ten years in the UK if kept in a sealed opaque box, though wholegrain flour contains too much natural oil and will rarely keep for more than a year without going rancid. If you are worried about weevils in white flour: buy only containers that show no sign of leakage; freeze them for a couple of weeks to destroy any bugs before they can hatch; and then quickly transfer the bags to a tightly sealed container. Adding a couple of Bay leaves to the container is said to deter the flour moth.

If you want to use the flour for bread then bear in mind that yeast will only keep for a year or so but you can extend that for at least another year if you freeze it. If you don't have good yeast you can always make flat breads or develop a sourdough starter and use that.

Unopened vegetable oil and margarine will also keep for a year or more, and so will powdered milk, and egg powder, but always try to get them in containers that are not transparent.

Dried fruits last well, and well-packed nuts can last for several years but will fail if the package is breached. Chocolate is good, though eventually the milk fats will surface and the taste deteriorate. Boiled sweets like barley sugar might become sticky but never go off. Good fruit cake seems to improve with age for at least several years.

For meat you can either have tinned or dried or you can use Textured Vegetable Protein (TVP) meat substitute. The latter makes me ill but many people use it so I might have an allergy.

There are so many types of food available that I can't possibly list them all together with their predicted life expectancy but the basic rules are:

- Try it before you buy in bulk
- Buy good quality
- Ensure it is well sealed – do not store containers that are dented, punctured or otherwise damaged.
- Store in cool, dry, dark conditions – garages, cellars, attics and sheds are generally bad places; they get too hot in summer and too cold in winter. An unheated ground floor room with small, curtained windows is usually best.

- Store foods that are in liquid or sauce, in containers that you can turn over on a regular basis. This will best maintain taste, texture and colour throughout the food.
- Examine the container before opening
- Examine the food (look, smell, taste) and inside of the container before using
- For times when fuel or water is in short supply, store some items that can be eaten straight from the pack without any further preparation.

Exactly what you store and how much is up to you, according to your tastes, finances, and room for storage. My recommendation is to start with dried, tinned and otherwise preserved foods from the supermarket and have enough for two weeks, which might not be much if anything beyond what is usually in your cupboards, fridge and freezer. Then extend that to a one month supply, then three months. Beyond that you can continue to add tinned foods if you have the space and weight isn't a problem or you can add more dried foods or go to special long-life storage foods or the Mormon 'basic six'.

Bear in mind the fact that although you might eventually be fairly sedentary, in other circumstances you could be extremely active. You should plan for a minimum of two meals per day and to provide sufficient Calories to maintain the workload you foresee might be required. Include in your plan plenty of dried herbs, spices and other flavourings to improve the nutritious but bland items and some luxuries for special occasions or when a boost is required.

In the UK there are now some firms that advertise a 1 month, 3 month, 6 month or 12 month survival food supply. The shorter term plans might include foods from various sources including UK or US military 24 hour ration packs, which can also be bought separately.

Military ration packs offer up to 4000 Calories and three meals per day plus snacks and drinks. They are designed to be eaten cold when necessary but with some items that can be heated when practical. There is a variety of menus and quality of the UK packs is generally regarded as good. They are, however, not cheap, at £10 to £20 per pack, depending on the retailer. Cut down or alternative versions are sometimes available with less content but at a lower price.

For longer periods the favourite option is a selection of items from a US firm called Mountain House. These are provided as freeze dried products in #10 size cans. MH offer many different products including full main meal dishes or individual meat or vegetable packs. Some of the items available include:

Diced chicken

Scrambled egg

Pasta lasagne

Chilli Con Carne

Oatmeal and Raspberry

Salmon and Potato

Scrambled egg, ham & potato

Tinned peas

Custard and mixed fruit

Macaroni cheese

Mediterranean vegetable pasta

And a whole lot more.

Depending on the product, a single tin might offer anything from 6 to 23 servings and cost anywhere between £20 and £40.

Selections of the seller's choosing are offered as time based packs, including a 'one year survival pack' for around £1500. However, if you look closely at the contents list that is for a total of 366 servings, i.e. one serving for one person per day. That works out at about £4 per serving of 700 Calories or less.

You can put together your own selection, and for a more realistic pack for 2 people for 2 meals per person per day and a pudding each once per week my pack would have cost just under £4000 or about £3 per meal, which is a huge outlay for most people but slightly more affordable.

The major selling points of these products and packs are: the 25 year plus shelf life unopened (1-2 weeks after opening); the high quality and good flavour of the reconstituted food; the relative compactness of such a large quantity; the convenience of a single source of supply; and that the food can be reconstituted with hot or cold water and eaten when ready i.e. within around 10 minutes.

The disadvantages are: the price; and the requirement for water to reconstitute each product. At a real push you can chew some of the products dry and some even taste OK but you wouldn't want to eat many that way and it does make you thirsty, which defeats the object somewhat.

For a much cheaper but VERY basic supply you could try the Mormon (LDS) basic six items for survival. For one adult this consists of:

400 lbs of Wheat

60 lbs of Legumes

16 lbs of Powdered Milk

20 pints of Vegetable Oil

60 lbs of Sugar or Honey

8 lbs of Salt

With carefully shopping you could buy this lot for about £350 per person. You would need to add a hand grinder for grinding the corn for about £40, or if you are really masochistic a mortar and pestle, but it does last much longer than milled flour. In fact the shortest life items on this list are the oil at 10 years plus and the milk powder at 20 years plus. The others are at least 30 years in dry, cool, properly sealed storage containers.

With these basic ingredients you could make sourdough bread, tortillas, sweetened porridge, pancakes, biscuits, bean stew, or you could sprout the grain for fresh sprouts. If you can find one at a reasonable price, buy a copy of Passport to Survival by Esther Dickey, she includes dozens of recipes for these six items and many from the four excluding oil and legumes.

To these it is recommended that you add 90lbs of dried fruit and vegetables and 20lbs of meat or meat substitute. With those the variety of the dishes that can be created is substantially increased. Baking powder, herbs, spices, stock cubes and other flavourings are not essential but do help considerably in keeping things interesting. A daily multivitamin pill doesn't hurt either when you are depending on mainly dried foods. The basic diet would provide 1000-1500 Calories per day and up to 2500 with the extras.

For long term storage of dried goods, vacuum pack them in impermeable bags made from Mylar or a suitable substitute. You can either use large size bags or break down the stash into smaller bags, which can be a lot of work but has the advantage of you only having to unseal a small quantity at a time. Drop a couple of desiccants into an air tight container, such as one of the ubiquitous blue barrels, insert the bags of food, then add oxygen absorber sachets, seal it up and hide it away in a suitable storage location.

These barrels are available in sizes from 30 – 220 litres and sometimes in different colours. If you don't plan to place them and fill where they stand, remember the weight bigger ones will get to when full. They are available used, having contained food products and sometimes then cleaned, from as little as £6 per barrel. Search online.

You could either use a barrel for a single product, such as grain, or as a supply cache of various products in quantities you expect to use up in a similar time frame, so that you don't waste the O_2 absorber by opening the barrel for one minor item.

The other essential for this diet, as with the Mountain House foods, is plenty of safe, potable water. Ways of providing for that are included in their own chapter later in this book.

The Basic Six or possibly the MH 12 month pack would keep you alive if you didn't have to do much physical work and the extended LDS would do if even if you did, but you might often be hungry and even so you probably wouldn't exactly look forward to meal times. However, with the LDS basics as your base and a good selection and quantity of tinned and other preserved foods plus coffee and/or tea you would be considerably happier and better fed than most people in a long-term emergency.

That might actually present you with a problem if you made face-to-face contact with anyone from outside your Bug In retreat. If you are so obviously not wasting away while they are, there are going to be questions about how you are staying so well fed.

Food you grow

This isn't a gardening book and I'm not going to try to do an Alan Titchmarsh on you but I do want to examine some of the principles of providing food both from your garden and indoors in a Bugging In situation.

Of course, not all of you are going to have a garden or not much of one and even fewer will have the half to five acres (depending on whose estimate you are reading at the time) that is needed to become truly self sufficient in food, but it is amazing what an improvement a few fresh green leaves from a window box or tub, or some succulent crunchy bean sprouts, can make to a meal mainly comprised of items from your store.

It isn't just vegetables you can produce for yourself either. Rabbits and other rodents, chickens for meat and eggs, pigeons, goats for milk and meat, fish, and invertebrates are all potential home-grown protein, yet most of them do not need a great amount of space.

A word of caution, though; in hard times like those that would cause you to Bug In, any visible source of food is going to become an object of envy and a target for theft by human or animal predators. Protecting crops and livestock is going to cost you resources and time, some of it overnight when thieves are most likely to strike.

Anything you can do to reduce that threat will be worthwhile and you should take it into consideration when planning your garden. Secure fences and other barriers can be a deterrent but the Forces have a principle of defence that states, 'Any obstacle not covered by fire is not an obstacle.' i.e. any barrier that isn't otherwise protected can be overcome in time, with stealth or with force.

There are some passive defence measures you can take that will help. If you grow plants or rear animals in mobile containers that can be moved indoors and locked away each night, then they will be out of sight and alarms can be set to warn you of any intruders trying to get at them. Position rows of beans or peas on poles, sticks or wigwams so that they do not obstruct your view of other parts of the garden or provide cover for intruders.

Raising plants usually cultivated as ornamental, and some other food sources that less well-informed people in UK are unlikely to recognise as edible, can deter theft. Using freeform and companion planting rather than straight lines can disguise crops as well as protecting them from insect pests.

Providing that you and all your family/group know their location and can definitely identify them, mixing some plants that are

120

poisonous to one degree or another in among the edible ones should (perhaps permanently!) deter thieves from coming back. If the effect is less permanent, knowing which locals have become ill will give you an idea of whom the thieves were. If the plants you use have some similar features e.g. deadly nightshade among edible plants with black berries, or hemlock with its fern-like leaves near carrots or parsley, the effect is enhanced.

If you are concerned about prosecution or being sued in more normal times, you can stick a discretely-placed-and-worded warning notice among the plants so that anyone invited into your garden will be alerted but anyone looking over the fence will not. If the situation turns bad, simply remove the sign. In your defence, although these plants are dangerous if eaten or handled in ignorance, when properly processed and used in the correct dosage they are also the basis of many powerful medicines, and in a Bugging In situation with no other source of supply they might be essential.

I will include more general protective measure in the chapter on safety and security.

When deciding what to grow, particularly if you do not have much space, consider:

a) Your main needs

b) The food value of the item – calories, vitamins, etc – compared to the space, time and effort it requires

c) What reliably grows well in your area and what gardeners consider 'difficult'.

d) What is easily available elsewhere in the area

e) What is easy and cheap to store rather than grow

f) What alternatives there are so that you can grow a variety of species so that one disease does not rob you of all of one type of food

g) What resources you have to grow, protect and harvest the crop

h) Is a suitable perennial alternative available rather than an annual, even if the latter produces a bigger crop?

For example, although you can easily grow potatoes in bags, stacks of tyres, etc. and except in very wet weather they are both a staple of our diet and a reliable crop, it takes quite a lot of soil and space to grow enough for many meals. As an alternative, a stock of rice, pasta, powdered or tinned potatoes, and/or flour for bread, is cheap, long lasting and provides an equally acceptable source of carbohydrate.

On the other hand, a fruit bush or tree takes little care except occasional pruning and perhaps spraying but will produce for several years and any excess of the fruit might be easily preserved by jamming or dehydration and will last for many years in that form, without electricity. In some areas you might need 2 bushes for propagation.

If you have the ground and a suitable climate, then raised beds, greenhouses, espaliered fruit trees, nut trees, bee hives and much else is possible and can provide a satisfying, long-term supply of delicious produce and preserves both before and after a societal collapse. It is labour and resource intensive but for really long-term emergencies a possibly essential part of a complete survival strategy and lifestyle.

However, even if you only have a small plot, either at ground level or on a roof or balcony, you can often extend that vertically by either growing climbing plants such as beans or peas, or constructing a rack that looks like a staircase so that you can grow plants in containers one above the other while allowing all of them access to light and rain.

Whether you are planting horizontally or vertically, buy heritage or heirloom seeds. The garden centre varieties are usually hybrids and although you can save seed from them for the next year they might not breed true and quality will decline. Contrary to some opinion, older varieties have not necessarily fallen out of favour because their taste does not match that of modern hybrids; in fact they often taste even better. Heirloom varieties are sometimes more susceptible to disease, insect pests or weather conditions, and some hybrids do produce larger crops, but it is a trade off between the disadvantages this year and a continuing supply over many years if you allow some heritage plants to go to seed, save those seeds, and then use them for planting in future years.

Or you can garden indoors. Even in a small space you can grow sprouts or microgreens ready for eating within days of sowing them. These are available to you all year round, the only equipment you require is a tray or large transparent jar e.g. a sweets jar, some absorbent paper and a few CCs of water. Instructions are given on the packets, which are available almost anywhere you can buy seeds for outdoor vegetables, including at the supermarket. In fact, many of the seeds sold for sprouting are the same as you would use to grow the plants to maturity for larger leaves or other crops. A few packets of seed, at £1.50 upwards per packet, could give you a regular supply of fresh greens or sprouts for months.

If you have a bit more room you could opt for a hydroponics system. This could fill a greenhouse or your garage or you could go small scale with something like the Aerogarden (£120 - £150) or the Garland Grow Light Garden (£65). These indoor systems require a modest amount of electricity for the lights and water pump but we have run ours successfully from a leisure battery with a 13W solar panel and an inverter.

Or you could grow mushrooms. Many kits are available in boxes or bags that contain both the growing medium and the spores and come with full instructions. There is a wide variety of edible fungi from which to choose and prices start at less than £5 for a kit. The conditions differing types favour make some suitable mainly for outdoors but others have been chosen so that you can grow them in the kitchen and yet others are best in the airing cupboard. Be adventurous; all are safe so try a few to see which flavours you like in various different recipes.

With imaginative use of space, indoors, outdoors or both, even a limited area for growing food can provide you with a variety of fresh produce to brighten up your diet.

Whichever system you choose, one of the key factors in success is to start now, not after an emergency arises. Any form of gardening or farming has a multitude of skills and knowledge that you will have to develop over years of experience, and no matter how many books you read there is no better way of learning than by experience. Many real sages have said, 'I forget what I hear (or read), I remember what I see, I understand what I DO.'

A failure in a crop when you can replace it from the shops, rather than depleting your stores, is disappointing and frustrating but you can put it down to experience; a similar failure when you have to raid your stocks is a concern but that is why they are there; a second failure, when you don't know the cause or how to deal with it, might see your family starve. Learn now and learn by doing!

Food you raise

The first thing to learn about raising anything for meat is to never let it become a pet. Do NOT give meat animals names or let the kids play with them. If you do, you are setting yourself up for grief! When you raise multiple broods, killing and preparing them soon ceases to be a problem.

Then you have to choose what you are going to raise. When Bugging In this depends on: how much space and fodder you have, what you like to eat, and if you have any allergies or religious objections. Probably the smallest thing worthwhile raising for food is the snail, then the rat or guinea pig. The Romans bred dormice for the table but as a delicacy rather than a staple. The largest, unless you have a farm, is a goat or pig, but in between you have rabbits, pigeons, chickens, ducks, geese, and fish.

You will find books or web sites dedicated to each of the meat sources I am going to cover here and far more detailed information than I can give you in this book but at least I will provide the basics so that you can investigate further those that interest you.

Rats and Guinea pigs

The main advantages of rats and guinea pigs for food are that they take up relatively little room, are easy to care for, will eat a variety of scraps, breed regularly and grow fast. They have been and still are eaten as a normal part of the diet in many parts of the world and provide both protein and essential amino acids. If you maintain good hygiene in the cages then there will be none of the potential disease hazards associated with wild animals and the only issue most people in the UK will have to deal with is the social taboo on eating what are normally considered as either a pet or pest species.

Rabbits

Rabbits share many of the advantages of other rodents as food sources and most Brits aren't nearly as reluctant to eat the meat. They can be bred every 90 days, have a gestation period of 30 – 32 days and the young are ready to eat at between 10 and 12 weeks, though some might reach table weight as early as 8 weeks. A doe can usually wean 7 young successfully, so 1 buck and 2 does could provide you with around 50 young per year, each carrying 2-3 pounds of meat. If you don't need that much meat, then breed less often and/or cull some of the young at birth, which you might have to do anyway with large litters.

You can grow on some of the young in year 2 or 3 and use them to replace the original breeding stock, which will still be fine in a stew. Inbreeding of this kind is natural in rabbits and does not appear to cause them any problems.

You need more space for rabbits than guinea pigs and because they will probably be kept outside most of the time they will have to be in strong hutches to protect them from predatory species like cats and foxes. If you feed them on commercial feed and pellets they will put on weight faster than if you provide grass, clover and small weed clippings but they will be just as happy on the latter and occasional extras such as carrot and other vegetable peelings and the outer leaves of cabbage or lettuce that you might otherwise put to compost. Clear out any food left uneaten next day and provide fresh.

Chinchilla and Angora are good meat breeds and also have fine pelts. The Flemish Giant can grow to over 20 pounds in weight but needs more space and will eat a lot compared to the more conventional breeds. Californians and New Zealand Whites grow fast and provide good meat. Despite the fact that inbreeding does not seem to cause rabbits any harm, many commercial farmers like to cross-breed different types and since neither buck nor doe seem to have any prejudice that works as well as using a single breed.

Goats

When you get to animals the size of goats, you start getting involved with officialdom. To keep a goat in the UK both the place where it is kept and the goat has to be registered, even if you only keep one. That done, goats are much less trouble to keep than many people will have heard, though they are both agile and curious so a strong fence at least four feet high for small breeds and six feet for taller ones, with no climbable objects nearby, is necessary to keep them where you leave them. The goat(s) will also need a warm but well-ventilated shelter. They are clean animals and will avoid soiling their bed but should still be swept out regularly and fresh bedding provided.

Goats do not eat quite the variety of objects that people say they do but while they willingly munch on most plants, including ones you don't want them to(!) they will instinctively shy away from either food or water that is in any way contaminated, so keep it clean.

Size depends on species but a female pygmy goat will grow to between 30 and 50 pounds or a buck to between 40 and 60, while a full sized Anglo-Nubian can be over 240 pounds for a doe and over 300 for a buck. Most breeds common to the UK provide both high yields of milk and substantial amounts of meat. A kid will reach 70 pounds within a year and at that point will be ready for culling.

Does come into season every 21 days and stay on heat for about 48 hours. If they are successfully mated they will give birth in around 150 days. The kid should then suckle for seven to eight weeks, after which you can start to milk the goat again for your own uses and feed the kid on solid food.

I like goats and consider them an asset to a larger survival retreat but buying an animal of this size or bigger should be considered very carefully if you are only thinking about Prepping. They can be productive but are a substantial commitment compared to any of the smaller meat sources.

Birds

When my wife was growing up, her Dad raised pigeons for show and racing. Those that did not come up to standard ended up in the pot. When I started shooting, wood pigeon were one of my primary targets, and still are as it happens. Pigeon meat is as dark as beef and sometimes darker, slightly stronger in flavour on its own but otherwise can be used as a substitute for beef in almost any recipe, just as rabbit can replace chicken.

If you are raising them for meat, rather than show or racing, pigeons are easy and cheap to keep but do not provide much weight of meat per bird. In most cases only the breast meat is used; time spent plucking or skinning the whole carcass and cleaning out the innards is hardly worth the effort for the extra meat found, though in desperate circumstances you wouldn't want to waste even those slim pickings.

Chickens are more commonly kept for meat, and of course for eggs. They can also provide high quality manure and serve well for insect control. They are, however, noisy and smelly. That isn't a problem if you can put them well down the garden but more so when you need to keep them close in order to protect your investment. You can minimise noise by only keeping hens, not a rooster, and can control the smell by regularly cleaning out the coop but you won't entirely eliminate either.

Rhode Island, Orpingtons, Leghorns and most others are suitable for meat and eggs, some are slightly better for one and others for the other but any will provide food. Bantams are not so much a breed as a class that is comprised of smaller birds. They are easier to keep but do not provide so much in weight of meat or eggs.

For Bugging In purposes you would want to provide a solid but mobile coop that you can position where it is protected. Feed is not expensive but do be aware of new regulations that restrict what you can feed to domestic stock, supposedly to limit the spread and development of diseases such as bird and swine flu.

If you have plenty of space, you might consider ducks and geese. They can offer many of the functions of chickens but require even more space and ducks in particular need an open expanse of water. On the plus side they will give more weight of meat per bird than some chickens and more fat. They are noisier and harder to catch, though, and really don't like confinement even when you are doing it for their own good.

People don't usually get attached to birds to the degree they do to animals and hence find it easier to despatch them. Nor is there any taboo about eating them. But, they do take time and effort to care for so be prepared for another learning curve and area of knowledge on which you will have to build.

Fish

Traditionally, fish farming required big ponds or even lakes, but it is now coming to a living room near you! Well, maybe not a living room, unless it is a very big living room, but certainly indoors if you have about 4ft by 4ft of floor space somewhere warm and well lit.

In those ponds and lakes you would have found carp, trout, some other British fresh water species, and maybe a few predators such as Pike, but the indoor tank is more likely to contain an African fish called Tilapia.

These have become popular because they are easy to breed and fast growing but unlike many of the other types bred for food they are primarily plant eaters rather than predators. Certainly they will eat minced up meat scraps and insects, and the young need high protein food, but also finely chopped plant material. This makes them cheaper to feed.

They are most often kept indoors in either a standard tank with a recirculation pump or a system connected to a hydroponics arrangement in a hybrid now called Aquaponics.

The basis of a sustainable system is a breeder colony of several females and 1 male Tilapia. This can be kept in a standard fish tank. To avoid over-crowding these are usually hybrids with, for example, a male Hornorum Tilapia and female Mozambique or Nile Tilapia. This tends to produce all male offspring. These can then be grown consistently without further breeding in the growing tank(s).

These growing tanks can be any size or shape but must be maintained at close to 80F (ideal is 86F). They need to filtered, aerated, supplied with a rubble base and various plants and lit during normal daylight hours. Rocks, pieces of pipe and other natural features should also be provided in the base of the tank. Children's paddling pools are a good option but deep barrels or tanks will also work. Tilapia will tolerate crowded conditions but too much competition for food will stunt their growth.

If the extracted water is passed through a filtration system to collect the manure it can be used in the hydroponics arrays and the nutrition in the filter water will feed your growing plants. You can also grow snails in the fish tanks and have a tank in which you grow both ground-rooted and floating plants, some of which can be edible for you as well as generating food for the fish.

Tilapia will reach full size within six to twelve months and grow to anywhere between 2 and 8 pounds (1-4Kg), depending on the cross-breed strain, of which 30-40% will be edible flesh after bone and skin is removed. The flesh is darker than that of some fish used for food but flavour is pleasant yet mild. Some scientists complain that Tilapia have lower levels of Omega fatty acids than other species, which takes away some of the advantages of fish as such a healthy food, but others argue that they still offer a rich source of low-fat protein. There have also been concerns over the use by large farms of hormones that control gender and promote growth but that won't be a problem for you.

My main concern with Tilapia for a Bug In scenario in the UK is the requirement for continual heating and water pumping. Being a tropical fish they do not tolerate the cold and will die if the water temperature falls too far. However, home fish farming is a very current topic of interest and, if you have the alternative power resources to maintain the system, one that might be of use to you.

Snails

In addition to raising snails as part of an aquaponics system, where they also help to keep the tanks and water clean, you might want to consider growing them in controlled conditions as a meat source in their own right. I know they aren't anywhere near as popular in the UK as France, for example, and personally I get enough in my garden trying to steal my greens without breeding them but they are high in protein and easy to raise or find so for the sake of completeness, I offer them for your consideration.

Snails are hermaphrodite so you don't need to worry over how to sex them. To breed them place large examples in a pot or box with a base layer of moist soil and leave them to it. Make sure the box has air and is reasonably warm but protected from birds and rodents. Putting the box in a shady spot in a greenhouse or cold frame and covering it with snail netting is ideal. Or they can be bred and grown indoors in an old fish tank. Just be sure the lid is properly fitted or, take it from one who learnt, you will NOT be popular with other members of the family who find them in unexpected places!

The eggs will hatch in about three weeks and will be mature and ready to eat after three months. Over 100 per hatch is not unusual so make sure they have plenty of space and a source of calcium to develop their shells.

Snails hibernate in winter and if collected then can be cooked immediately, otherwise place them in a container where there is no food for them for a few days in order to clear out their gut. Cook them thoroughly and never eat them unprepared or inadequately cooked; they can cause major gastro-intestinal problems if you do.

So, that is vegetables and protein you can grow or rear, from land and water and air and dark places. You have choices of various fresh foods to supplement your stores.

Food you gather or hunt

When I defined Bugging In, I included a remote farm as one of the scenarios but I think for this section that opens the options rather too far for the majority of people. If we take into account all that you could gather or hunt in that situation we could include deer and game birds and perhaps wildfowl, or even lake, river and sea fish, seaweeds and shellfish. That could easily take a volume of its own and is actually more applicable to outdoors survival, which is adequately covered in other books. So for our purposes I am going to limit this section to those edible species you might find in the average UK garden and around its buildings.

Plants

My advice to anyone starting to learn how to identify edible or medicinal plants is always the same: begin with those you can already identify confidently and find out how you can use them. If you walk around your garden I will bet there are many more that you know than you would have thought and research might surprise you as to their potential. That might be as food or it could be as medicine. Many of those that are deadly if taken in quantity are actually very valuable if properly processed and used in the correct dosage. The key to your safety is knowledge.

The variety of plants you will find will differ according to where you live. Some do well in the south of England but are absent from Scotland and vice versa, but there are some that are common wherever you go, no matter how hard you might previously have tried to eradicate them if your gardening features constant campaigns against weeds.

I have to be honest, most of the greens taste either like a bitter version of spinach or of not much at all, but there are exceptions and even those you might not be tempted to add to a salad improve with some cooking and a bit of salt and butter, plus they are often rich in various nutrients. Maybe after reading this you'll at least put away the Pathclear for a while and give these free foods a try.

If you are sampling a plant for the first time, be cautious. Although it might be edible and harmless to most people that does not mean that you won't have intolerance for it. Just as some people are allergic to peanuts or olives so you might be to any of the plants you try. It is therefore wise to apply the 'taste test' even to plants you are confident you have identified correctly. There are variations of this test but most follow a similar pattern i.e.

1. Take a small piece of the plant, crush it and rub it on a sensitive area of skin e.g. your inner wrist. If after 20 minutes you have suffered no pain, irritation, burning sensation, soreness, redness or blistering then proceed to the next stage.
2. Take a pea sized piece of the plant, chew it and spit out both the pulp and juice. Wait for 20 minutes to ensure there are no ill effects.
3. If the plant passed that stage: for plants that are normally used as a vegetable rather than a salad ingredient you might need to cook a portion before proceeding, then take a small section, say one small leaf or section of stalk, chew it and swallow. Wait for 3 hours. If you are still OK …
4. Eat about a tablespoon full and wait for 24 hours.
5. If there has still been no illness then you should be safe to eat without any further concern.

Some things to note: although the above test can also be used to test the safety of plants you don't know, it is far safer to identify them by whatever means you can and only test in that way for your own tolerance to them. Second and most importantly,

THIS TEST DOES NOT WORK FOR FUNGI!

Poisonous fungi can taste wonderful, give you no ill effects for 24 hours and then kill you within the next 24. Do not take any chances with fungi. If you are not 100% sure of your identification based on shape, size, features, smell, texture, colour, location and surroundings do NOT eat it!

That said, there are not many worthwhile edible fungi that pop up in the average UK garden anyway, though there might be plenty in more open places and woodland nearby. If you want to hunt for them, get a good reference guide with colour pictures, otherwise stick to the kits you can grow indoors.

So, what of the weeds you might want to eat? There are actually many, but if you know the most prolific then you have a good start, so to give you a small sample, here are some to look out for:

The Dandelion

If there is one wild plant most people will know it is this one. The yellow flower, which tops a smooth, slender, unbranched and leafless stalk and turns to the white seed heads beloved of children as dandelion clocks, is probably the most visible feature, but closely followed by the long toothed leaves that give the plant it's name (from Dent-de-lion – tooth of the lion). There are up to 235 micro-species of the plant with variations such as depth of colour and sharpness of the 'teeth' on the leaves, but most are easy to spot as dandelion. The dandelion is one of very few plants with a milky sap that is safe to eat.

The plants nearest in form and which could be mistaken for a dandelion are hawksbeards, hawkweeds and catsears which can be identified by the fact that they have hairy stems that branch and have leaves. None of those are dangerous but nor are they beneficial, as is the dandelion.

The young leaves of the dandelion can be eaten in salads but, as per my warning, are rather bitter. They are generally better steamed or boiled and served with salt and butter or a vinaigrette sauce. The stems and flowers are also edible and the flowers can be used to make dandelion wine. The elongated tap roots are too bitter to be used for food but can be cleaned, chopped and roasted to produce a nutty, pleasant, but caffeine-free coffee substitute. The leaves in particular contain valuable amounts of vitamins A, C and K plus calcium, potassium, iron and manganese. The plant is a gentle diuretic and laxative and is used in herbal medicine in many countries.

The dandelion and its uses are especially useful to know because it is so common, and widespread; if its features are observed it is difficult to mistake anything dangerous for a dandelion; and it is a perennial that will self set and spread with alacrity, much to the ire of many non-Prepper gardeners.

Nettles

Once encountered, never forgotten. The stinging nettle is another perennial weed familiar to most people.

Growing up to 3m tall and with a sting that gets fiercer as the plant gets older, you would understandably give this plant a wide berth unless suitably dressed and protected. Yet it is also one of the weeds better known for its edibility and many of you will probably have heard of nettle soup.

The substances which might be the primary cause of the sting (there is still debate over the main culprit) include formic acid, serotonin, histamine, oxalic acid and tartaric acid but all are deactivated in the cooking process. The beneficial ingredients include Vitamins A and C, iron, manganese and calcium and young nettle leaves contain up to 25% protein.

As with most edible plants, nettles are best for food if the leaves are picked while young and definitely before the plants start to flower because they then become gritty in texture. They can be chopped, dried and used as a 'tea', soaked well and then eaten raw, made into wine or beer, or cooked as an ingredient in various recipes. I have eaten nettles at home in soup, with various other wild greens including Sorrel but they are also good as a green in place of cabbage or spinach with many main dishes. Nettles have an earthy, rather than bitter, flavour and I think they go particularly well with lamb.

The plant is also used in many other ways, including medically. It has been promoted in various different treatments from being used as a poultice or whip to stimulate circulation, reduce inflammatory chemicals and interfere with pain transmission in arthritic joints, to reducing the symptoms of prostate problems and even relieving hay fever.

However, nettles can have negative effects on some people (apart from the sting) including mild stomach upset if eaten or taken as a drink, or a rash if applied to the skin. There is some evidence that they can affect the menstrual cycle or even cause miscarriage, so they should not be used by any woman who is pregnant and only with care by others.

Dock

Where you find nettles, you will usually find dock leaves. This isn't because of any symbiotic relationship but simply because they flourish in the same sort of ground and conditions.

Docks are related to Sorrel and are part of the Buckwheat family of perennial herbs. They can grow into large plants and the wide, tough leaves are usually easy to spot. However, although the leaves can be quite tough on the plant, they break down to a very delicate consistency when cooked.

The flavour is slightly acidic, as with Sorrel, due to ascorbic acid (vitamin C) content, which is so significant the leaves were used by the navy in Nelson's day to prevent or treat scurvy. It goes well with fish, especially the earthy flavoured fresh water fish you might catch in UK waters, but has also been recommended instead of other greens as a layer in Lasagne; something I haven't tried yet but which sounds good and is a project for the future.

One recipe I have made and enjoyed when in the wilds is dock mashed with nettles and ramsons; you could make a similar dish at home, perhaps with some onion or garlic, butter and seasoning. One of the great things about Dock is that it is edible all year round. Strip out the veins from large leaves and just use the fleshy parts.

The practice of rubbing a dock leaf on a nettle sting to relieve the burning and itching sensation does seem to work but scientists have been unable to identify any substance in the dock that should neutralise those in nettles. However there are substances in the root of Curled Dock which are known to act as a general tonic and for treating everything from a tickly cough to cancer.

Goosegrass

Goosegrass is another plant many of you will formerly have tried to eradicate. It is an annual but self-propagating weed that spreads quickly and which, like the dandelion, is difficult to mistake for anything else because of its special combination of features. The stems grow up to 3 feet in length and are square or angular in section with rings of six to eight leaves every few inches. But it is the tiny hooks on the stems and leaves that make this plant so easily identifiable, as it attaches itself to woollen or fibrous clothing as you walk past.

They especially appear along the edges and fence lines of gardens but on rough ground can spread anywhere.

The stems and leaves can be eaten if boiled or steamed, during which process the tiny hooks melt away. They can in fact be eaten raw but the stalks tend to be tough and the hooks are unpleasant in the mouth. The tiny globular fruits, which are often, but not always, clustered in twos or threes contain caffeine and can be dried and roasted as a coffee substitute. The caffeine isn't as strong as it is in coffee but after a while without any it helps! The roots are small and thin and do not offer anything of value.

This is another plant that is used as a diuretic and also as a tonic for the lymph nodes; in the past it was used to treat tonsillitis. The leaves and stems are also good pulped for treating light wounds, burns or insect bites and stings. If dried and made into an infusion which is drunk two or three times a day, the leaves can also work as a mild sedative.

Rosebay Willowherb

Rosebay Willowherb likes open spaces and plenty of light, so it often appears where ground has been turned over and then left or on old expanses of weed suppressant cover and gravel. Another perennial, it is often the first plant to appear on burnt-out ground, which in the USA has earned it the name of Fireweed.

Both the young stems and leaves and the roots are edible, with the upper parts being used as greens and the roots usually boiled to remove some of the bitterness and then roasted. They are a good source of Vitamins A and C.

This is another of the edible but slightly bitter spinach substitutes and one that, because of its wide distribution in wild and rough places, I have eaten on more than a few occasions, without any ill effects but without much pleasure either. The leaves can be dried and used as a reasonable tea substitute and in Alaska the flowers are often added to sweet dishes.

Medicinal uses are mainly confined to using the mashed up stems as a poultice to draw boils or infection from wounds. Other uses include employing the downy seeds as tinder.

These are just five of the common weeds that you might find in your garden or close around your buildings but they are perennial, fast growing and nutritious. If you had to rely only on what you could find in a small area they wouldn't last you for long but if you get to know them well and can eventually forage over a wider area then you will find them in abundance.

Even though they might be weeds and potentially prolific, maintain your stocks by only taking what you need and not taking everything from one plant or area. Leave the roots and seeds so that the plant may regenerate, unless the roots or seeds are what you are after, in which case it is even more important not to take everything from one place. If you are starving it is not possible to think of preserving for the future - either you eat now or you might not be alive to see next year's crop - but by proper Prepping you should be ensuring that your pick of weeds is a considered and logical part of your food provision strategy, not an act of desperation.

Get out and do a survey of the weeds in your own garden or local area. When you find ones you don't recognise either pick a sample if it is present in quantity or take photographs. Make notes of the type of ground where you found it, and the general topography of the area e.g. open, against a wall, derelict ground, over-grown flower bed, damp (or arid), and what other plants were present in the same area, plus details such as how tall and wide it was. Then do some research to identify the plant and when you know what it is delve into its features and uses; it might be great for basic nutrition or as flavouring or medicine.

Even non-weed species you have planted for decoration might have uses you never realised or hadn't thought of employing; the hips on your rose bushes for high vitamin C syrup for example, or the petals of the flowers for flavouring in foods. Did you know that the leaves of Campanula and Violas, the leaves and flowers of Primroses and Day Lilies and the bulbs of the Tiger Lily are all good to eat, as are the berries, petals and young leaves of hawthorn? There are many more your neighbours wouldn't think to try but that you can easily discover.

Wild plants and garden flowers are unlikely to be a major part of your diet when Bugging In but they can be extremely useful extras and until then a fascinating source of study.

Animals

When we talk about taking wild creatures to use as food we are talking about killing. Whatever type of animal you are taking, and I don't care whether it is a rat, a hedgehog, or a pigeon, or how desperate your circumstances, it deserves the respect of as quick and painless a death as possible.

If you are using a trap then that means using one of the correct type for the intended prey plus setting, and if appropriate baiting, it correctly. It also means checking the traps on a regular basis, which you will want to do anyway to ensure your food isn't stolen by other predators. The type of trap and how you place it will also help to safeguard your catch and must be taken into consideration. For example, a snare with a pull-up mechanism might lift the carcass out of reach of hunters on the ground but only if it is far enough away from anything on which they can climb and might also give it greater exposure to crows, magpies, or gulls. If people are hungry, the potential prey-thieves might also include your neighbours.

If things are that bad, then some neighbours will not be able to feed their pets and some will release them to forage for themselves, adding to the natural predators that are on the prowl. Your traps should, therefore, take the potential presence of dogs and cats into consideration; whether that is to avoid accidentally trapping them, or as competitors, or as additional prey is up to you.

If you intend to shoot the animal, be it with a rifle, shotgun, airgun, bow, catapult, or other device, then for maximum efficiency of effort versus energy expended, you will not 'hunt' it, you will ambush it. Humane killing takes accuracy and accuracy takes practise and is best done from a fixed position with a firm rest for your leading hand if possible.

The target area for a kill quick enough to ensure that the prey does not get away, causing it to die uselessly and in agony and you to waste ammunition and lose your dinner, varies according to the animal involved but is generally much smaller than inexperienced hunters think. For a sure, fast kill, that means a head shot only and then into the area between the eyes from the front or just behind the eye from the side. Body shots will cause many animals to be lost.

Whether you regularly hunt game or intend to only in an emergency, before doing so you need to be sure that both you and your weapon will consistently put the projectile where it needs to go, at the range at which you will be trying to kill. Practise on a target until you know the weapon is properly zeroed and you can both put all your shots into the required target zone. And I mean be SURE; most occasional shooters are totally self-delusional about their competence with their chosen weapon!

Please note: it is illegal in the UK to hunt animals with any type of archery device and many animals that might be useful as food in a survival situation are protected in normal times. There are also many other laws which control where, when, and what you are allowed to shoot. It is YOUR responsibility to ensure that you comply with all these laws.

Prey

The types of prey you might get in the garden or around your building in an emergency include: invertebrates, mice, bats, rats, squirrels, hedgehogs, rabbits, cats, dogs, foxes, songbirds, pigeon, crows, magpies, and gulls. Bats, hedgehogs, many songbirds and some other species are protected in normal times.

Although none are inherently poisonous and all have been eaten by people at one time or another, the taste does depend on what they have been taking as food. I find the meat of foxes, gulls, magpies and crows generally disgusting to the point of inedibility, although Branchers i.e. young rooks just out of the nest are OK. Most other small birds are so tough when cooked that it would be easier, and possibly more nutritious, to chew your boot leather.

The flavour of mice, rats, squirrels, hedgehogs, rabbits, cats, dogs, and pigeon varies from OK to delicious, depending on how they are prepared and cooked, but none of them taste like chicken!

Eating something will do you no good if it makes you vomit and thereby lose even more energy and hydration. If you are maintaining pets or raising fish or rats for the table, they might eat the gastronomically rejected items. Otherwise you can use the carcasses for bait in other traps.

I mentioned snails in the section on raising sources of protein. Snails gathered from the wild are equally edible, though you should be even more careful to take measures to cleanse their gut before cooking them. Other insects can also be eaten, including worms, woodlice, ants, and various others, though some grubs and caterpillars are poisonous, so look them up before including them on the menu. All should be cleansed and cooked before consuming them. Worms are best dried and ground into powder, which retains the protein content but removes the 'yuck' factor. Hopefully your preps will prevent you ever having to get to that stage.

Many wild creatures also carry disease and vermin on their skin or in their coat. Take care to deter ticks and fleas by wearing disposable gloves, applying insect repellent at the wrists, ankles, neck, and in your hair. Tightly fasten clothing at these points. When gutting larger prey, avoid piercing the intestines as that can spoil the meat and although some parts might be edible it is safer to reject all of the internal organs. Skin or pluck and clean the catch outside and dispose of the dross well away or by burning.

Follow good food hygiene precautions when handling the meat. Avoid contact between your skin and the prey's blood or other fluids and cook the meat thoroughly. Hedgehogs are traditionally cooked by coating in mud or clay, roasting them and then peeling away the skin and spines with the clay.

Shooting

Under most circumstances requiring you to Bug In, any hunting you do should be discrete. The best weapon to use for the prey species I listed, below fox or dog size, is undoubtedly an air rifle with a telescopic sight. It will be quiet, safe, powerful enough for the job, and more accurate than you are until you become very good.

The calibre really doesn't matter, either .177 or .22 will do just fine, and nor does the make of the rifle or brand of pellets, provided the combination is accurate and powerful enough to do the job. The simplest and easiest to maintain for long and reliable use is a spring-piston, cocked by either a break-barrel or underlever action. You can pay anything from £40 to many hundreds but if you are in the bracket from £200 to £300 for a new rifle and scope then you should get quality that will last a lifetime and beyond. Look for a rifle that comes with open sights as well as the scope, so that if the scope fails you still have a useable gun. The open sights won't cost you any extra. I have been using a BSA Supersport

in .177 for the past 20 years and can't fault it but I've also tried many others in the same class that will do the job equally well.

At the moment no licence is required anywhere in the UK to buy or use such a rifle but there is a proposal to introduce a licence in Scotland. There are some restrictions as to where you can use such a gun but you can currently use it for target practise and controlling pest species in your own garden provided that you ensure the fired pellet does not go beyond the boundaries of your property.

If you live in a detached house in the country, or within extensive grounds of your own with open country beyond, then you might step up from an air rifle to a .410 shotgun or .22 rimfire rifle with a silencer. The .410 requires slightly less accuracy but range is limited to 25 or 30 yards, whereas you can add about 10 yards to that with a good air rifle. A .22 Long Rifle (.22LR) rimfire has an accurate hunting range of up to 100 yards and will take any of the species listed including foxes or dogs. A shotgun requires a shotgun certificate and a .22LR requires a firearm certificate.

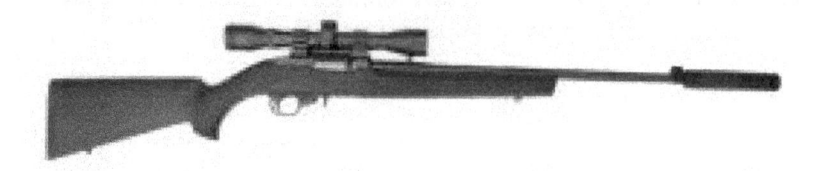

The shotgun certificate is somewhat easier to get but most police authorities will still require you to convince them that you have a valid reason for owning it and proper arrangements to keep it safe. A Firearms certificate has much stronger requirements. Don't expect to get either if you tell them you want it only for hunting in the event of an apocalypse! Full details can be obtained from your local police station or online at http://www.basc.org.uk/

A longbow or crossbow is capable of taking any of the potential prey species but developing the required level of accuracy takes longer than it does with a rifle. For the smaller prey a 'blunt' arrow or bolt delivered to the head will either kill the animal or stun it long enough for you to catch it. For the bigger animals you would want sharp broadheads.

A catapult will take the birds and smaller animals but needs even more practice to become proficient. A home-made frame cut from a forked branch, knicker elastic and small stones is traditional and might work but you won't have nearly as high a success rate as with a modern model and will lose many of the animals you do manage to hit. A modern catapult with a metal frame, wrist brace and high power bands makes accuracy slightly easier to achieve. Either steel or lead ball bearings are the most consistent and powerful ammunition. For practice I use aniseed balls most of the time; they shatter on impact with anything hard and are biodegradable.

Trapping

There are hundreds of designs for improvised traps and the triggers for them. With practise at making and setting them and the right type of bait they can be very effective.

One of the most common is the deadfall trap which features a simple trigger mechanism, usually made from sticks, that when displaced releases a heavy log or stone to fall on the hapless prey. These take some trial and error to get right because a weight sufficiently heavy for a clean kill requires strong support to keep it up until triggered. That places a lot of stress on the trigger mechanism which also needs to be delicate enough to be set off by a nibbling animal or bird. A cage trap with a similar trigger is somewhat easier because it does not rely on weight to catch the prey and generally works well for birds.

For rats and grey squirrels a tilting board trap sometimes works. This consists of a barrel part filled with water, on top of which there is a lid with one section separate. This section is designed to pivot approximately half way along its length. The concept is that you fix bait at the inner end of the pivoting board and as the rodent nears the bait it swings down, dropping the animal into the water below where it will eventually drown. An alternative is to use a material like cardboard for the lid and cut an X in the centre. The method is much the same. Chocolate spread or peanut butter works well as bait. The trap works better with rats than with wary and more agile squirrels but you can sometimes catch the latter.

Alternatively, you can go for commercial traps, of which there are many. For small mammals and sometimes birds the simple and familiar spring trap works well.

Differing sizes are available for mice and rats. Rat traps will also take hedgehogs, squirrels and the larger birds. Prey will initially be wary of any new object but if you place the trap where they either move or feed and bait but do not set it, the targets will eventually become familiar with the device and less cautious. After a few days, add new bait, set the spring, and then wait for a catch. It is sensible to secure the trap so that it cannot be dragged away by something that is caught but not killed.

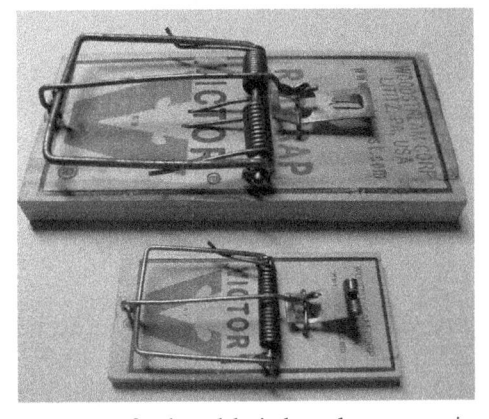

Larger animals can be caught by using snares. Wire is the most durable and effective material for a snare but leather, horsehair, and other materials will sometimes work.

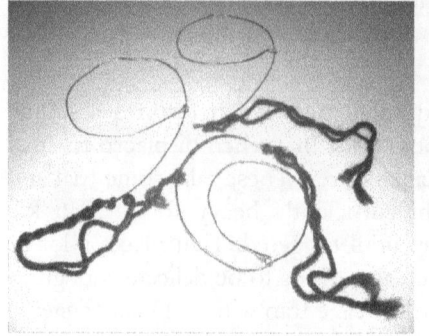

Snares should be set on a trail used regularly by the prey and preferably where it would normally have to push through an obstacle, such a fence or hedge. The snare loop is set slightly larger than the animal's head and at a height the cover causes it to adopt as it emerges. The free end can be attached either to the cover if that is robust enough or to a stake driven into the ground. Anything from a rat to a deer can be taken by a well set snare of suitable size and strength.

Snares can be set to catch and hold or to kill by strangulation. They can be made more effective by adding a pull-up mechanism triggered as the snare is dragged forwards by animal. This hoist can be raised by either a spring system such as a bent branch or sapling or a falling weight and serves to both tighten the snare and lift the catch out of reach of other ground based predators, but unless arrangements are made to hide the dangling prey it can be even more obvious to people or carrion-eating birds.

Now, a plea and word of caution is in order. By all means go out and practise setting traps and experiment with their trigger mechanisms, it is the only way to learn how to construct them effectively, but IMMEDIATELY after you finish your trials, disassemble and remove all parts of the mechanism. Never leave a trap in place where it could kill or injure an innocent animal. To do so would not only be cruel and a waste of the animal's life it would very probably be illegal. Killing should only ever be done by necessity, never by malice or thoughtlessness.

Food provided by other people

The whole purpose of Prepping is to be independent of help that might or might not ever come from official bodies. However, government agencies, NGOs or charities might eventually arrive to provide some assistance. That assistance might be offered to you in place or they might want to take you away to a communal shelter of some kind.

If that happens, do you accept what they offer or turn it down on the principle that you are doing OK by your own efforts and you shouldn't take resources that might be essential for others who are not as organised as you are?

If your situation is desperate, as it might be if your area is contaminated by fallout from a melted-down nuclear reactor for example, or you are surrounded by fast rising floodwaters or an advancing bush fire, but you have read and acted on the advice in this book's companion volume, Bugging Out, you should always have independent alternatives so that you don't fall into the trap of becoming a refugee.

If there is no urgent need to leave your home and the offer to take you away is purely on the basis that it is cheaper and easier for the authorities to provide communal care than it is to supply aid to small or scattered communities or individuals, then politely refuse on the basis that you prefer to stay where you are.

They will try to insist, perhaps by persuasion or sometimes by bullying and warnings of no future help if you don't go now. In return, remain polite but firm in your refusal. Don't reveal the level of your preps but insist that you are all right for the next few days and have friends or family outside the area that you can go to if you need to and don't want to be a burden to the authorities when there are others more in need of their help.

If the aid consists of food parcels and other supplies then you should accept these graciously. If you refuse, word will soon get around and both officials and locals will begin to wonder just how well stocked you are, and whether you have some to spare.

If the thought of accepting aid when you don't need it worries you, remember that you might not need it yet, but who knows how long the situation and food parcel deliveries will persist?

If it seems like you really won't need the extra then you can always pass it on anonymously, perhaps leaving it at night on the doorstep of someone who you know really is in need or offering it in trade for something you know someone has to spare that you could use. Perhaps explain that you or another family member can't eat a certain class of food item because of an allergy but you really do need ... whatever.

In all cases avoid appearing better off than others in your area. You might be of slender build anyway but if your diet is restricted then you could lose some additional weight, though maybe not as fast as your neighbours. If you have to be seen, wear clothes a size or two too big, to give the impression that you are getting thinner.

Food is one of your major preps. It will pay you well to give it due attention.

Cooking and Preserving

Mains items: Kettle, Ovens, Microwave, Bread maker, Mincer, Mixers, Blender, Deep fat fryer, Toaster, Sparker on gas hob, Dehydrator, Mains gas to hob

Does heating up a tin of beans qualify as cooking? According to a recent survey 1 in 4 parents think so. According to the dictionary, they're right!

Cook (Cuk)

v. cooked, cooking, cooks

v.tr

1) To prepare (food) for eating by applying heat

2) to prepare or treat by heating: *slowly cooked the medicinal mixture.*

3) Slang: To alter or falsify so as to make a more favourable impression: *disreputable accountants were paid to cook the firm's books.*

Hopefully your preps will be sufficient that you never have to cook this book, but whatever it is that you are cooking and whatever your own thoughts may be on the subject, while Bugging In the chances are that you will want to do so by heating the food.

Some forms of food preservation also rely on applying heat, so I decided to include preserving in this chapter, rather than in the previous one.

Your preps should definitely contain substantial amounts of foods that do not need to be cooked in order to be edible, because you never really know how long your fuel will last or if you will be confined indoors and unable to acquire more.

These foods might take the form of items normally served cold, such as sweet or savoury biscuits, cheese, jam, peanut butter, dried fruits, nuts, chocolate, tinned meats like corned beef, ham, or spam, cereal and milk, and others. It might also include foods that are usually served hot but that are pre-cooked and perfectly edible cold e.g. tinned custard, rice pudding, baked beans, stew, or meals from ration packs.

Whether manufactured to be eaten hot or cold, these items will give you the same nutritional value either way. Even so, your stores will probably also include considerable amounts of food that must be cooked in order to be digestible, or even safely edible, and for most of those you will need some sort of heat source.

Even if you are running a generator or have an extensive renewable energy electrical system, using the output to power an oven or some of the other high-drain heating devices, or low-drain but long-process machines such as a bread maker or dehydrator, is inefficient and wasteful. You might be able to operate a microwave or some of the other kitchen devices while the generator is powering your freezer, or from your battery bank on clear days if the cells are fully charged and you have no higher priority demands, but treat that as a bonus and enjoy it when it happens rather than relying on it.

If it is practicable for you then the most long-term-assured method of providing for cooking is undoubtedly a wood stove with oven, as long as you have a plentiful supply of wood within carrying distance. Remember that you might be relying on human-power – unless you have a horse - rather than an internal combustion engine.

There are several firms making these stoves, including the famous ones like Aga but also Esse and Windy Smithy. The one in the picture is an Esse Ironheart in my friend Hugh's home and the picture is from him too.

Prices vary widely, from £510 for the Windy Smithy Louis Ranger, through £3357 for the Esse Ironheart, to over ten thousand for a top-of-the-range Aga. The variety of features is just as wide, from one hotplate and a single oven compartment to five different oven compartments with varying heat levels.

Any cook who has worked with a wood or multi-fuel cooker will tell you that they take a while to get used to, so does any oven come to that but much more so with a live-flame burner. Not only the amount of fuel you burn but also the type of fuel affects the heat output and how long it will be maintained. Cooking on the hotplate is more easily controlled but using the oven successfully can involve quite a learning curve.

You do have the advantage of heating the room from the same fuel as cooking your food, and some models will also provide hot water from a back boiler, but while that is excellent when the temperature is low, and there is something undeniably wonderful about watching the flames in a wood burner, it can feel like hell in the summer if you have no alternative. Fortunately, while solid fuel gives you a sustainable heating and cooking source, you do have some simpler off-grid alternatives.

You could, for example, have a wood burning stove with cooker features set in your living room but mainly use it only for warmth and comfort, while having a Calor gas cooker in the kitchen. You can buy a Calor cooker in any format you would expect from a mains gas model up to and including professional multi-hob multi-oven layouts.

Calor cookers can be connected to either exchangeable cylinders, which will be mounted outside, or to a large tank. The gas pipes will be installed through the wall to where the cooker is placed. If you use bottled gas, it is usual to have two cylinders mounted side by side and you can either manually change cylinder as one empties, or have a switch-over regulator that makes the process quicker and easier - useful when chef is screaming that the gas is off and their soufflé is collapsing - or a monitoring device that will change over automatically when the pressure in the bottle that is in use falls below a preset level.

One thing you might note is that interchangeable cylinders are red. This indicates that they contain Propane. Butane is sold in blue cylinders. The reason that people use Propane for domestic purposes is that it will continue to vaporise down to -42C, whereas Butane stops vaporising at a nominal 0C, though because the remaining liquid cools as some of it turns to gas, this can happen at up to 5C air temperature. Either way, the last thing you want when it is cold outside is heating, cooking, or lighting that doesn't work because you are using Butane to save a few pence per cylinder on running costs compared to Propane.

Whether you choose Propane cylinders or a bulk tank, it pays to keep an eye on the levels in store and top up when required. In the chapter on Warmth there is a reference to the relevant storage regulations should you want to keep extra cylinders of gas.

Coming down from the domestic cookers we get to those intended for camping. Differing designs are made to run on Propane, Butane, Paraffin, Petrol, Methylated Spirits, solid fuel blocks, or found fuel. The 'found' models burn wood, pine cones, etc. either to provide heat direct from the flames or, more efficiently, by using the wood gas. Solid fuel block stoves are normally of the folding Hexamine cooker type used by the armed forces but there are now many variations on the theme. These stoves are small, light, quite cheap and burn long enough to heat a ration pack and make a brew in a light pan like a mess tin but the blocks do not generate enough heat for cooking larger amounts or with heavier pans and the burning fuel gives off poisonous fumes so it should not be used indoors.

Methylated spirits is best known in UK as fuel for the Trangia, which is, deservedly, highly respected in outdoors activities circles as a reliable and efficient little stove. Trangias are available with various sizes of cook sets and there are many rip-offs of the design on the market, most of which are serviceable but few of which match the quality of the original. Larger double burner Meths stoves, similar in layout to the well-known double burner gas stoves used by many family campers, are quite popular on small boats.

Paraffin cooking stoves are ubiquitous in remote areas of the world though both they and the fires and injuries caused by cheap, unsafe replicas of stoves from manufacturers of high quality products are often associated with poverty. The good quality versions can be both safe and efficient but do have to be treated with the caution associated with any liquid fuel device, including refilling them only outdoors and when cool.

Most easily available of all in the UK, and most popular with camping families and many other users, are cookers that run on gas. The gas is usually Butane but larger models can often also run on Propane if an appropriate regulator is fitted. Single burner types often work on disposable cartridges and are fine for one person out for the weekend or a little longer but they tend to be narrow based in order to fit easily into a backpack or travelling bag, although some have a folding stand to make them more stable and they will work if that is what you have and take care, they are not the best for domestic use when Bugging In.

Better are either the flat single burner types, like the one we recommended for Donald and Jane, or a double burner, perhaps with a grill. Many makers of camping equipment offer a model similar to this. Some are very basic and priced to suit, some feature stands, windshields, spark ignition, and many other extras and cost more, as you would expect.

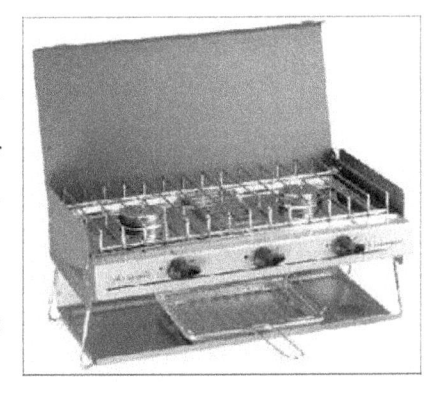

146

Butane cylinders are approved for use indoors and the 4.5 or 7Kg sizes are very portable. Most cookers will attach to the 15Kg cylinder and those are cheaper per Kg of gas but some users will find them heavy to move since they contain 15Kg of gas but the total weight including the cylinder is double that. In March 2013, a 4.5 Kg Butane cylinder refill costs £15.99, 7Kg £21.49, 15Kg £32.99. You can see the savings inherent on using the larger cylinders. If you don't have a cylinder to refill there will be a one-off 'hire' charge. Ensure you get a receipt so that if you ever decide to return the cylinder rather than refill it you can get that charge back. Otherwise, you can sometimes find cylinders much cheaper at car boot sales and since you are going to exchange them the condition doesn't really matter.

The similarity between all of these cookers is that the main feature is only a hob on which you can set a pan or two for frying, boiling, or similar. If you want to get more adventurous then you need an oven.

Coleman makes a double burner stove with oven but I haven't found one available in the UK. Camping Gaz is due to release a similar model in spring or summer 2013 that is reported to achieve temperatures of up to 250C and will cost around £250. Most of the others are intended for more professional use and are almost as big as domestic oven.

The alternative is something that has been around for quite a while and is still in demand and that is the Coleman oven.

The Coleman folds flat for easy transport or storage, and features a built-in temperature gauge but no heating system. It is basically a metal box designed to be used on a gas stove, wood stove or open camp fire. They are not currently available from a UK supplier but you can buy them, new, from the US for £60 including tax and shipping through Amazon.com.

It is easier to maintain an even temperature on a gas stove than it is on a wood burner or open fire (there are reports that the temp gauge on some isn't reliable, though ours is OK and checks out close to the readings on a separate oven thermometer) and if you need the higher temperatures then you might want to cover the oven with a fire blanket as fireproof insulation and/or line it with foil but ours works extremely well and among other things we have baked bread and even cooked Yorkshire Pudding – which needs a very hot oven - in it. Ours in now a little less pristine than the one in the pictures!

Without an oven like this you can, of course, use any heavy metal pan with a close fitting, preferably flat, lid as a Dutch oven. Some of the technique is different but many of the same results can be obtained. If the pot has a good wire handle, it can also be suspended from a tripod or other support. The original form has three short legs to help keep it stable and above the coals or embers of an open fire on which it is placed but they aren't essential and are often a hindrance if you want to use the pot on a stove. The flat lid is so that you can also pile embers on top of the pan for all around heating. You can make stews, bake bread, roast meat, and all manner of things in a good heavy pot

Pat, my wife, used this method with a cast iron pan in our caravan when she found that the oven would not get to a high enough temperature for baking bread to the standard she would like, and she got better results but eventually decided that the extended time needed and amount of gas used was not worthwhile. As an alternative she makes excellent tortillas or chapattis, which are much quicker and simpler to do.

The Dutch oven is primarily intended for use on an open fire, indoors or out, and if you do not have facilities for cooking indoors, or you want to preserve gas, or it is summer and you do not want to heat the house, then there are alternatives.

You might have a brick-built barbeque in your garden or have a portable one that burns either gas or charcoal, or you could have some of the disposable ones left over from a previous summer, like the ones I found in a box in our shed a little while ago, though I have no idea how long they have been there! Barbeques can be used for grilling, in the way they are normally intended, or when they are fired up and glowing they can be considered as a bed of hot coals and used like a raised campfire, either with a Dutch oven, or food wrapped in foil, or simply with a pan placed on the grill for boiling water, vegetables, etc.

If you don't have a barbeque or a supply of charcoal (something else to add to the preps list!) you could make a fire pit or an open fire surrounded by bricks or stones from the rockery and go for good old campfire cookery. For a more efficient use of fuel there is the rocket stove, such as the one in our back garden seen here being used last year by our Granddaughter Claire.

This one has a concrete patio slab as the base, raised on bricks for convenience, and then the rocket stove built on that using 14 loose whole bricks and one half brick and a piece of garden fencing for a grid. The opening is towards the wind. The arrangement of bricks causes a chimney effect, drawing air in at the base and containing the flames while directing the heat up to the pans. This is more efficient than an open fire and saves fuel. Does it work? Claire gives it the thumbs up!

If you don't have facilities to build your own rocket stove, you could even use a short-chimney garden Chimnea for the same purpose.

A simpler stove can be made using a large can, such as a catering size vegetable can, or a metal bucket or any similar container. This is usually referred to as a hobo stove.

Holes are punched around the side just above the base and just below the top. Fuel can be fed in from the top like a brazier and some wire mesh placed over it to hold a pan. Or a hole can be cut in the side and the container used upside down with the base as a hot plate and fuel and air let in through the hole.

These stoves save on fuel, protect the fire from wind and rain, and also limit the light and smoke emitted when that is a consideration.

Thee are commercial versions available that use various modifications to make the stove more efficient but the original purpose was to make something that works using a no-cost resource that can be left behind if necessary and replaced when needed.

If you want to get rather fancier you could build a pizza oven. These can be made of brick and clay or concrete and with a simple design or raised and with various extra chambers. In essence they are a variation on the traditional clay oven used worldwide. Some are a domed chamber with a chimney at the front and an arched doorway. A fire is built inside the chamber to heat the oven and the embers then raked out and food put in to cook. A door is usually placed over the entrance while cooking is taking place. Other forms have a lower compartment in which the fire is built, an oven compartment above, and a chimney at the back. The oven has a door but the firebox is often open to allow fuel to be fed in as required.

These outdoor fires and ovens will burn any fuel, and a mixture if that is all you can find. Hardwood will cause less smoke and blackening of your cookware and will burn hotter and longer for the same volume of fuel but softwood, charcoal, or home-made logs of rolled newspaper and old oil or anything else that will burn will suffice. The only thing you should watch out for is fuel that might contain noxious chemicals that could either contaminate the food or harm you if you inhale the smoke.

The other issue to bear in mind with outdoor cooking is that you might attract the attention of neighbours. Cooking shows that you have something to cook on, fuel to burn, food to cook, and the skills to put them together outdoors. The last of those might be a good thing, enabling you to offer advice and build good relationships without cost but if other people are not so well prepared in their stores then their interest in what you are doing and what you could spare might not be so welcome.

One of the important considerations is 'how' you cook. Even if your fuel stores are reassuringly substantial they will not last forever. It therefore makes sense to cook efficiently, especially when resupply is limited or uncertain. If you can cook in a room where you will also be living then you make double use of the warmth.

Single pan cooking of soups, stews, and the like is often the most economical method but you can expand on that and have separate items by boiling meat or boil-in-the-bag ingredients in the bottom pan and stacking steamer pans of vegetables one above the other. Items cooked in a single pan can also be separated by wrapping them in foil or cloth bags. Some flavour might transfer but that is often to the good.

If the water has been used through steamers and has some of the juices from them in it then add a stock cube and turn it into a nutritious drink, or use it with other things to make a sauce or gravy. If that isn't appropriate immediately then pour it into a thermos flask to use later or even into a hot water bottle if you have no culinary purpose for it.

Frying can be a one pan option too. It might not be the 'healthy' option but when you are eating under Bugging In situations it isn't probable that it will be a regular occurrence so it will do no harm and could make a welcome change.

In the forces we would heat a tin or ration pouch in a mess tin of water and then use the water to make a hot drink; or to wash and shave with; if you are cooking from your stores you could do something similar. That way you save on both fuel and water. When heating water for any purpose, only heat as much as you need and only as hot as you need it.

If you are cooking from stored foods when you are under pressure, the result can be adequately nutritious but not particularly appetising in either flavour or presentation. You can help yourself and your family to accept these meals by using the ingredients on a regular basis so that you get a chance to experiment in ways of using them and you all become accustomed to eating them but there is no reason for them to be boring.

Adding some imagination in the ingredients you use, flavourings such as herbs or spices, and texture in the form of fresh greens or croutons made from dried bread can make a huge difference. They give the cook an opportunity to concentrate on something they enjoy and the diners a boost to morale as well as energy. With a few extra ingredients included in your preps and a bit of research, you can ensure your post-apocalypse meals are cordon bleu not cordon bleh!

Preserving

In modern life we have lost our connection with the seasons in which differing foods are available. By importing from all around the world we can have almost any food apparently fresh on the shelf at any time of year. Fresh strawberries or 'spring' lamb are available at Christmas. But if a major crisis of any type hits, whether natural, financial, or technological, this system of international trade could easily grind to a halt.

The population of UK is growing and for generations now we have not had sufficient arable land to feed everyone, even if every inch that could be tilled was put into use. If we could not import, many people in the UK would starve as surely as they do every year in parts of Africa.

Even for those with some land on which to grow their own crops, in days gone by one of the regular features of each year for the poor in the UK were 'the hungry months'.

The actual months to which this referred differed according to the environment in any particular area. For England, Wales and large parts of Scotland it was the late winter and early spring, when almost all of the stored food from the previous year was gone and new growth and animals were still too small to pick. In Ireland it was June to August, when they were also known as 'the growing months', relating to the spring sown potato crop that was the mainstay of the diet and economy for rural folk.

In most of the western world our routine way of preservation is now freezing, or for shorter periods refrigeration, and as I covered on the section on Cooling that is not new. The difference is that these modern methods are not sustainable without electricity. We also still use canning, drying, jamming, pickling, and various other processes. Unfortunately when I say 'we' use these methods, for most of us that will mean that we buy foods in that state after they have been produced by other people, mainly large firms.

For the future, we are going to have to learn how to apply these processes ourselves if we are avoid using all our emergency stores during what will otherwise be our hungry months.

The method of preservation you use differs according to the crop to be saved, because some lose nutritional value or flavour or structure by some methods but can actually be enhanced by others. However, in most cases after the original processing, any preserved food needs to be kept in a cool, dark, dry place to maintain the preservation to best effect.

We will look at the individual methods by which various produce keeps well but in general the choices you can apply at home are:

Cooling, Dehydration, Smoking, Salting, Fermentation, Bottling (Canning), Jamming, or Pickling.

Cooling has already been covered to some extent and includes the use of clamps for root vegetables but also of a cellar for extending the life of food preserved by other means. Any cellar should be dark, dry, well aired and fitted with containers that will protect food from attack by insects or rodents. The light you fit in the cellar should be powered by a means that does not create heat and in winter you might well want to wrap up before going down there, even if you access the cellar from within your home. Cold air sinks so if properly sited and constructed the cellar will definitely be the coldest place in the building, as it is intended to be.

Because it will probably be below ground, however, you should always be aware of the danger of flooding. The cellar should have a drain but you will also want to use water-tight containers, have a pump available in case the drain becomes blocked or backs up, and to be ready to move your stores if it becomes necessary. For that purpose try not to pack so much to a container that it is too heavy to carry. Using smaller barrels, jars, etc. will also help to ensure that if some of the preserve goes bad you don't lose all your stock of that item.

Dehydration will be the method by which many of your long term storage foods will have been preserved, including goods such as pasta, rice, potatoes, beans, fruit, meats, and many others. Commercial firms will have used high-tech methods such as accelerated freeze drying but you can achieve successful results at home for many foods while using much simpler processes.

Dehydration is an excellent method for preservation because with most foods it substantially maintains both the flavour and nutritional value while making it more compact. In fact the flavour is often concentrated by the process

Even in the UK you can dry foods by solar dehydration, though usually only in summer. The design of a solar dehydrator is very similar to that of an electric model except that it needs a transparent - preferably glass - top sheet to let in the sun.

In this design the box is made of wood. It must have tray support bars on each side onto which you place or slide the drying trays and legs so that air can be drawn in through holes drilled in the base. The air then passes up through the mesh drying trays to carry away the moisture being evaporated from the food and is drawn out of the box by a solar-powered extractor fan. If you don't have a suitable fan you can simply drill some holes in the back, near the top, again protect them with mesh to prevent entry by pests, and rely on the natural convection of rising warm air to vent the box. You can make the glass top detachable or hinged and put the trays in from the top or, more conveniently, hinge the front or back at either the top or bottom, or make it detachable, so that you can slide the trays in and out from there.

I find it more convenient to have the hinges at the bottom so that the front rests on the ground while I am inserting or extracting the trays, rather than having a top hinged door clonking me on the head when the wind catches it and blows it down, as a previous model did. We all live and learn!

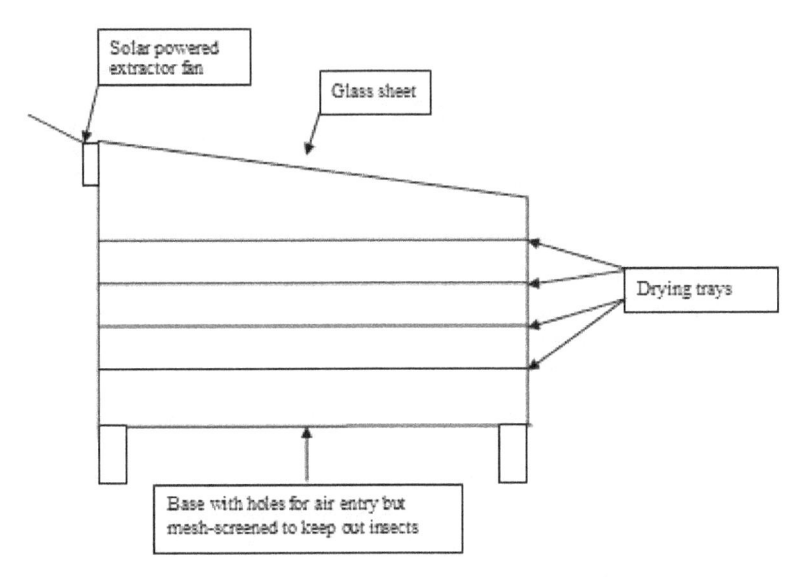

As with most solar devices this functions best if you rotate it as the sun moves but it will work pretty well if you just place it facing south somewhere that it will never be in shade.

You can put different foods on the trays or even different items on the same tray. Space them out so that there is good air circulation and leave until dry to the level you want. Meat should be dry to the point of becoming brittle but fruit is good when it becomes leathery.

Alternatively you can use oven drying. For this you put the food to be dried on a non-stick tray then into an oven set to minimum heat, leave the oven door open slightly, and if the oven is not fan assisted place a fan or similar to ventilate the oven. Leave the food until it reaches the required level of dryness; this will take several hours.

If you have electricity available you can use an electric dehydrator or make your own. Home-made models often feature one or more incandescent light bulbs as the heat source. Although neither commercial nor home-made versions have a very high wattage they can eventually consume a considerable amount of power due to the length of time for which they have to be running. There are several electric models available commercially but the top of the line is usually recognised as the Excalibur.

Four, five and nine tray models are available, generally retailing around £239, £259, and £279 respectively. This is our 5 tray model. It is very good but from experience, for the extra £20 we should have gone for the 9 tray. You can use it with a single tray if that is all you need and the difference in running cost is negligible.

The cheaper makes cost from as little as £40 upwards but take less food per load and do not have the quality or features of the Excalibur. Nevertheless, customer reviews of the mid-range models between one and two hundred pounds are generally favourable.

Some highly coloured foods you can dehydrate simply by slicing them fairly thin and putting them into the dehydrator. Apples will go brown if done that way but will maintain their colour and look much more appetising if first dipped in lemon juice. That also works well for bananas. Pineapple rings are wonderful without any conditioning and so are strawberries.

Meat is often better if marinated overnight and there are many different recipes for making jerky in this way. Select one according to your tastes. I dislike spices but many people make theirs quite hot; your choice. When making jerky from any meat, choose very lean meat and cut away any external fat, otherwise it will go rancid. Meat cut across the grain will be easier to chew but tends to break into pieces; cut with the grain it is more durable but if the meat was tough in the first place you need strong teeth and jaws to chew it. It is easier if you soak it in hot water first.

Take care when eating dried fruit, it is easy to over-indulge and the fruit is very high in sugar. Too much can also cause diarrhoea. Do not eat un-reconstituted dehydrated foods, and particularly meat, if water is in short supply as it will draw water from your body and may dehydrate you!

Most fruits, meat, fish, bread, green beans, peas, peppers, mushrooms, onion, tomatoes, herbs, and yeast are all good candidates for dehydrating.

Smoking is another of the methods still in common use commercially in the preservation and flavouring of meats e.g. smoked bacon, salmon, continental sausages.

There are actually 2 methods of smoking: cold smoking, which is done at a temperature of around 20 - 30C and requires the meat to be cured first but is a proper method of preservation, and hot smoking which is done at 50 – 80C and results in food that is fully cooked and ready to eat.

Home-made smokers have been created from just about any container you can think of, including: wooden boxes, beer barrels, oil drums, refrigerators and even old filing cabinets. Basically all you need is an enclosed container that will allow wood to smoulder and smoke rather than burn, with containers high enough above the coals that the meat is not directly cooked by their heat but is thoroughly enshrouded in the rising smoke, and a chimney or vent to let the smoke gradually escape. Various woods can be used but in the UK alder, oak or apple is often favoured. What you definitely need is a hard wood, because softwood like pine burns too fast and the smoke contains too much tar, which can give the meat a bitter taste.

For cold smoking the meat needs to be soaked in a 10 – 15% brine solution, or repeatedly rubbed with salt, for four to six weeks and kept very cool at 2-3C, which is why in the past cattle or pigs were killed in the winter if their meat was to be salted. Freezing reduces the penetration of the salt and so extends the soaking time. Temperatures above 3C reduce the effectiveness and safety of the process. The salt used should be curing salt or sea salt not table salt which contains iodine. Around 5% sugar is sometimes added to combat the strength of the salt flavouring while not reducing the preservation. The curing process darkens meat or turns it grey but if the salt is combined with sodium or potassium nitrate it will react with the meat to a produce a much redder colour that most people prefer. After the meat is salted then it is smoked, which seals the surface of the meat to extend the preservation by restricting bacteria from getting in.

The curing and smoking of meat is an old and proven method of preserving and I recommend that you research the subject further if it is of interest to you.

Salting of meat is related to the above process but can be used without the smoking if required. However there is an even simpler and older method that has been used for centuries. In this process fresh meat, usually beef or pork is rubbed with salt and the salt pounded into the surface by hand. A layer of salt is poured into an earthenware or wooden tub and alternate layers of salt coated meat and salt to fill the gaps and cover the meat are then laid in the tub until it is full, after which it is sealed with a lid. The meat is extracted as required and soaked in water for several hours before cooking.

Lactic fermentation also employs the use of salt and is probably best known as the process used in creating sauerkraut but it was the standard way of preserving vegetables in the middle ages and beyond and is suitable for cabbage, cucumbers, green beans, lettuce, radishes, and turnips.

The basic process is really simple: Remove outer leaves and core or strings, grate the vegetable, cover it with pickling salt on a basis of 1-2% salt to weight of vegetable and leave it to soak in its own juices. Place in a glass jar and pasteurise in a hot water bath at 80-85C for 30 minutes. Either seal or transfer to an earthenware pot and seal then store in a cool dark place. Alternatively, the vegetables can be cleaned and pierced, placed in a sterile glass Kilner jar and covered in brine. Use spring water for making the brine as chlorinated tap water can hinder the fermentation process. Various herbs and spices can be added to the jars according to taste.

Bottling, or Canning as our American friends would call it, is a long proven preservation method but it does require attention to detail in order to ensure a properly preserved product and prevent nasties like botulism getting in.

The main factors to ensure are that all components of the system are clean, or where required sterile, and that all required temperatures for both the produce and equipment are reached and maintained. Some acidic produce such as fruits are slightly safer than others as the acid content adds another layer of safety against bacteria but even then you should take that as a bonus and pay no less attention to detail than with non-acidic produce.

Within these guidelines there are two acceptable methods for safe bottling, according to what it is you are preserving: boiling-water bath for high-acid foods, and pressure canning for low-acid foods.

To apply these you are going to need several essential items of equipment:

    A large, deep pan for water bath bottling

A pressure canner for pressure canning

A large enamelled or stainless steel pan for processing the food

Mason or Kilner jars plus lids, seals and gaskets

An accurate food thermometer

References with cooking times and temperatures for various products

Muslin bags

Various other cooking utensils and equipment such as scales, trays, oven gloves, clean tea towels, etc. All of which must be thoroughly clean.

Detailed instructions on processes

What can you bottle? Fruits, vegetables, meat, meat products, sea foods, soups, sauces, ready made pie fillings, and others.

Get the most up-to-date information on bottling and ensure you understand it before you start. There are many old references on this subject, including instructions in classic books from famous cooks and old-time authorities. As much as that information might have been acceptable at the time it was written, modern techniques of food hygiene and biological testing have proven that some of those references are not reliably and consistently safe. 99 times out of 100 or even 999 out of 1000 the outcome might be fine but it only takes that one time to see you ill or dead!

When you have finished bottling, ensure the jars are properly sealed then carefully clean the outside. Label the jar including the date it was filled. Store the jars in a cool, dry, dark place.

Before opening a jar look for any signs of a leaking or bulging lid, any visible mould or bubbling, shrivelled or discoloured contents. If you do open the jar then be aware of: spurting contents, gassiness, sliminess, unpleasant appearance or odour, any mould on the surface of the food or underside of the lid. If you spot any of those signs before or after opening the container DO NOT EAT THE CONTENTS however hungry you might be!

And there I am going to leave it. You should now be aware of the potential and dangers of bottling. I don't want to over-emphasise the latter, this is a valuable technique and a safe one if it is done properly. Get yourself a good modern reference specifically on this process, all the right materials and equipment (beware charity shops and car-boot sales, the equipment might be serviceable for modern process and it might not) and then have a go.

Preserving in Sugar, including jellies and jam making, is a firm favourite of country housewives running stalls at village fetes and is closely associated with bottling in that you are putting a hot preserve into a sterile glass jar and sealing it, but allied with the ability of sugar to reduce the availability of water to any potential spoiling organism, and the acidity of the fruit, and the heat used in the process, and the lack of oxygen in the jar when sealed all add up to a potentially very safe form of preservation.

There are several output forms in this class including: jams, conserves, preserves, marmalades, jellies and butters but all are based on fruit and sugar and it is mainly the consistency and type of fruit used that decides into which category they fall. Because of the nature of this book I will concentrate on apples, crab apples, pears, plums, and berries that can generally be grown in the UK. Where possible, I'll also recommend the use of natural rather than added pectin. However, what you are going to need for these processes is a good stock of sugar.

Pectin

Pectin is a natural ingredient of fruit. It combines with sugar and the acid in fruit to make it gel. Too little pectin will result in thin, runny jam or jelly.

To test whether a fruit has sufficient pectin, mix a spoonful of cooked fruit juice with a spoonful of alcohol. If it forms into a lump that can be picked up with a fork it doesn't need any additional pectin; if it forms little clumps then it does.

Commercial pectin is available in powdered or liquid form but you can make your own from the juice of crab apples or under-ripe apples. This can be added to other fruits to raise the level of pectin.

To make crab apple pectin: add 1 pound of fruit to 1 – 1 1/2 cups of water, bring to the boil and then simmer for 30 – 40 minutes. Press through a colander and cheesecloth then heat the juice and pour through a muslin filter or bag. Collect the juice in a sterilised jar then seal it.

To make apple pectin use 1 pound of apples to 2 cups of water. Simmer for 3 minutes then sieve and press the pulp and collect the juice. Heat the juice until it is reduced to about half the quantity then filter and bottle.

Jam

A jam is primarily made of crushed fruit and sugar and has the consistency of thick syrup, often with some pieces of fruit in it. It holds together to some extent but will not keep shape as will a jelly.

The traditional recipes for Jam called for equal quantities of sugar to fruit but if you want to reduce the quantity of sugar for reasons of health or economy then you can do so, providing you remember that the sugar is one of the reasons jam preserves so well. To reduce the quantity of sugar you should use slightly under-ripe fruit with its skin so that it contains the maximum amount of natural pectin and acid, but add crab/apple pectin as required.

Generally, sour apples, crab apples, blackberries while still red, plums, cranberries and gooseberries will have enough natural pectin and acid but ripe apples or blackberries, cherries, pears, raspberries, strawberries and elderberries will need more added.

Cooking time will vary according to the fruit but if you are using only natural fruit plus sugar then you will need to bring it to a boil and maintain that for 15 – 45 minutes, constantly stirring to ensure it doesn't burn.

Berries don't normally require any additional water but, depending on the variety, apples and crab apples might do so, up to 1 cup of water per pound of fruit

You can tell when it is done by watching for the point where it will hold its shape when scooped up in a spoon.

While this is happening sterilise your jars in a pan of boiling water.

When the jam is ready remove it from the heat and stir gently to allow it to cool slightly.

Ladle the jam into the jars, leaving about a quarter of an inch of space in the top. Wipe the top edges of the jars carefully using a cloth dipped in boiling water. Cap the jars and put them into a pan of boiling water for five minutes, then remove, and set aside to cool. Swirl the jars around at regular intervals in the first 30 minutes or so to distribute any fruit pieces around in the jam.

Allow to cool and store in a cool, dark place.

Conserves

A conserve is basically a fancy jam which includes more than one type of fruit.

Preserves

A preserve contains whole or large pieces of fruit in thick syrup which is sometimes slightly jellied

Jellies

A jelly is made from fruit juice rather than fruit pulp or pieces. It is clear and holds its shape when set.

Butters

Fruit butters are made from fruit pulp and sugar cooked until they are thick but smooth.

Marmalades

Marmalade consists of a jelly which contains small pieces of citrus fruit. You might be lucky enough to be in an area of the UK where you can grow citrus but you will be in a very small minority. However, I've include marmalade in case you happen to have a large quantity of citrus available when you need to Bug In.

The alternative forms of cooked fruit preserves use a similar process but with modifications according to the consistency required. Cooking times, amounts of sugar, type of pectin and when it is added, and various other items may differ according to the recipe. The main features and need for sterile containers and process remains the same. There are lots and lots of recipes for different jams and it can be great fun trying them and devising your own. As with most things in developing Preparedness, becoming proficient when a failure isn't disastrous is definitely the way to go.

Pickles and Relishes rely on acid as the main preservative in much the same way as jams depend on sugar. Similar sterile containers and processes are also required. The main difference between pickles and relishes is that in the former vegetables are left whole or in large pieces whereas in the latter they are chopped, cooked and pickled with various other ingredients.

The major difference in process between making jam and pickles comes from the fact that for pickles you will be using vinegar and salt and therefore need to be selective in the material from which pans and utensils are made. Stainless steel, earthenware or glass is fine, galvanised pans, copper, brass, cast iron or aluminium should never be used.

Only use perfect very fresh vegetables for pickling. Only use proper pickling salt as other salts can contain chemicals that will either spoil the preservation process or cause the pickling solution to go cloudy and the pickles to darken. Only use high quality cider vinegar or, for less chance of discolouration, pure white vinegar of 5-6% acidity. If you find the pickles to be too tart, don't reduce the quantity or quality of vinegar, add 5-6 % of sugar by volume to the quantity of vinegar.

Squashes such as cucumbers or gherkins are prepared by washing and then soaking in 10-15% salt solution for 2-4 weeks before processing. Any scum must be removed from the top of the solution each night. They are then transferred to clean jars, covered in fresh brine and pasteurised for 30 minutes or subjected to a boiling water bath for as long as recommended in the recipe (varies according to vegetable to avoid softening them).

Other vegetables can just be left in solution overnight and then treated in the boiling water bath as per cucumbers.

Pickled eggs

If you have too many eggs to use before they go off then pickled eggs are even easier than cucumbers:

Prepare a sterile jar with a tight fitting lid.

Mix pure white vinegar sufficient to fill the jar, cloves, chilli, peppercorns and whatever other spices you prefer. Bring to the boil and then simmer for 10 minutes.

While the vinegar is boiling, hard boil as many eggs as will fit in the jar. Allow them to cool and then peel them and transfer to the sterilised jar then replace the lid.

Leave the vinegar to cool to room temperature then strain it and pour over the eggs until they are completely covered.

Seal tightly and keep in a cool dark place for at least 2 weeks.

Eat the eggs as required, topping up the vinegar if necessary to ensure the remaining eggs stay covered. Keep stored in a cool place after opening.

Pickled Onions

Prepare a sterile jar with a tight fitting lid

Pick small onions, top and tail them then remove the skin and outer layer. Place them in an earthenware dish and liberally sprinkle them with salt. Roll them around in the salt to ensure they are through coated. Leave overnight.

Mix malt vinegar sufficient to fill the jar, cloves, chilli, peppercorns and whatever other spices you prefer, with 170g sugar per litre of vinegar. Heat to bubbling and stir until the sugar is dissolved but do not boil..

Pack the onions into the jar and pour the liquid over them. Do not filter the liquid, let the spices go into the jar. Seal and leave to cool.

Store in a cool dark place for at least one month and preferably two. Keep stored in a cool place after opening. Enjoy!

There are other preserving processes using oil, chemicals or micro-organisms as in making cheese but I doubt they are really appropriate to the circumstances we are considering in this book. That isn't to say you shouldn't investigate them, all knowledge might be useful, but they, and further details on the methods included here are available elsewhere.

Water

If an emergency lasts for more than a few days and you do not have a sufficient supply of drinking water, all your other preparations will be wasted, because you and your family will be dead before you can see the benefit of them. It is as simple and as stark as that.

You can make do without washing yourself or your clothes, without cooking with water, flushing the toilet, watering your plants, or anything else, at least for a while but you must keep your body hydrated.

Water is so important, and the need so urgent, that even if you are Bugging In any shortage might force you out of your refuge to seek new supplies. In the relevant sections of this chapter we will therefore extend the potential sources to include those beyond your immediate residence but consider the dangers accessing and using them can present and how to deal with those threats.

Quantity of water to store

The medical advice is that you have to take in 4 litres of water per day to replace that lost through normal bodily activity, including breathing, perspiration, urination, etc. In fact in an environment like the UK about half of that is absorbed when you breathe in and from fresh food, particularly plants.

If you are surviving on stored foods you might need extra water to rehydrate some of them but if water is extremely short then you should be eating mainly carbohydrates not protein or fats, which draw water from the body for digestion. This is one of the reasons for the popularity of sweet high-carbohydrate foods among desert dwellers.

When planning your storage you should allow for a MINIMUM of 1 gallon or 5 litres of water per person per day. That will allow enough for drinking, preparing food and very basic hygiene such as essential hand washing. We will look at some of the ways you can make that last as long as possible in a later section but for now reflect on that storage quantity.

For a family of 2 adults and 2 children for the basic 72 hour emergency kit that would require 12 gallons/60 litres of water. Consider that is 30 of the standard big coke/lemonade bottles. If you had to take a 72 hour Bug Out bag and head off into the wilds, can you imagine carrying 30 of those 2 litre bottles with you, in addition to all your other kit? Fortunately if you are Bugging In it is a bit easier.

Nevertheless, if you are not already a Prepper it is probably much more than you are used to storing. Extend that from 72 hours to 14 days and you are looking at 56 gallons/280litres.

Small garden water butts usually hold about 120litres/26gallons and large ones 210 litres/46gallons, so if you have room for a couple of the smaller ones or even one of the large types, plus some containers indoors, you are getting nearer to the mark.

Remember, though, that we are still talking minimums; you and the family are staying hydrated and fed but have now gone 14 days without anything more than a wipe down with a damp flannel and using alternative toileting .

For something approaching acceptable standards of life rather than pure survival, if at all possible double or treble the amount you store. The extra will either make life more pleasant or extend the time for which you are prepared, according to the need. In a high level flat storing large amounts of water would be difficult to say the least but if you have even a small yard at the back of a terraced house a couple of water butts is not intrusive.

A 120litre tub will cost around £30, a 210 just £5 more. Add £16 per barrel for a proper stand or you can improvise with paving slabs or make one from wood. If making your own, remember that a full 210litre water butt will weigh over 460lbs/210Kgs. Either way, ensure the barrel is raised high enough to get a decent sized container under the tap.

Some indoor storage is essential. In winter your water butts might freeze solid. If you get warning of a contamination hazard that will confine you indoors then you should empty the barrels, bring them indoors and immediately refill them. If you don't get sufficient warning to do that then any containers you keep in the house will give you a buffer until you can arrange access to what you have outside. In the meantime, if there has not been a warning that mains water might already be unsafe, fill any other containers that you have in the house.

20, 10, 5, and 1 litre containers with 2 litre pop bottle for comparison

Smaller containers are more expensive, litre-for-litre. A good quality 20 litre container will cost around £15 and a 10 or 5 litre about £10. Less durable versions are available at lower prices. Or you could save 2litre pop or water bottles and refill them for nothing. It might be a bit less convenient but they are a lot more portable and if you would normally buy them for the contents and throw them away afterwards you save on recycling too.

A 5ltr container full of water will weigh around 5Kg/11lbs and is about the maximum for many people to lift to kitchen counter level without strain, so one or two of that size or smaller should be kept. They can be refilled from the larger containers as required. Containers with taps rather than just caps are much more convenient.

Alternatives that you can have ready in the house or even filled include water beds, and purpose made bags that will fit in a wheelbarrow or a bath.

If you have plenty of room outside then you could opt for one or more steel-framed, pallet-mounted 1000litre IBC containers. These are available new from about £130 or used from £30. If you are buying used, find out exactly what they previously contained, even if they are advertised as having been cleaned, to ensure that they have never held anything other than food-grade materials. Even larger storage tanks, up to 50,000 gallons, are available if you have room for them and they can be mounted externally or buried and provided with pumping systems.

What is the maximum it is reasonable to store? That depends entirely on how much room you have. If I could have an Olympic-size swimming pool in my back garden I would, and a lake, and a well, and a rainwater collection system. In any emergency, there is no such thing as too much water unless it is threatening to drown you!

Sources of water

Apart from the water you deliberately store you have several alternative sources. Firstly, there is the water in your domestic water system. How much is available depends on the type of system you have installed, with older configurations usually holding more than modern ones.

If you have a combi boiler then your water will be sourced direct from the mains to your cold taps and the boiler. In this case there will be little available except what is in your pipes. To access this water, immediately you hear either that the water supply is going to be interrupted or that it could become contaminated, turn off the stop cock on the main inlet pipe. You should know where this is but if not you must find out. It is often under the kitchen sink.

To drain the water from the pipes, first turn off the boiler and any electrical heating element and allow them a few minutes to cool. Then starting at the highest part of the home, open the hot and cold taps and collect the water in a suitable container. Leave the taps open and then work down through the house draining the water at each level. Do NOT drain water from your radiators; it contains poisonous chemicals that will not be removed by any of the filtration and purification methods likely to be available to you!

If you have an older system, with a cold water cistern in the attic or a cupboard in your flat and a hot water cylinder in an airing cupboard, then you have access to far greater supplies. The cold water cistern will hold 25 to 50 gallons, depending on the strength of the support system below it (a full 50 gallon cistern will weigh nearly a quarter of a ton!). A hot water cylinder will also usually hold from 25 to 50 gallons, though some are even bigger. For one person that would be 50 to 100 days supply from both, if you could access it all. That is unlikely but you might be able to get 75% or more of it in usable form.

You can draw off most of the water from your taps as specified above but you will notice that the outlet pipe on both the cistern and the cylinder is not attached to the bottom of the container but a little way up one side. This is done to allow any dust or other sediment to settle below the level of the water that is extracted and, in the case of the hot water cylinder, to ensure that it is always above the level of the heating element.

To obtain what you can from the level below the outlet pipe you would have to remove the top or the outlet pipe and then scoop or pump it out. This water will probably be murky and heavily loaded with sediment but you can make it usable by the methods explained in the next section of this chapter.

In blocks of flats, any cold water storage will be on the top level or roof and the boiler and hot water cylinders in the basement. Any taps in the basement are the places to get the last dregs out of the system but there is a chance of contamination from above. Stay alert for notices identifying any outlets as being connected to water not intended for drinking. This water might be from storage cisterns that are not regularly refreshed, or a recycling system, or other sources not considered potable. The water will still be usable but will have to be fully processed to ensure it is safe to drink.

Unfortunately, some modern buildings and complexes are fitted with systems that might contain water storage cisterns but then rely on electric pumps to distribute it. I was talking to a friend who is a plumber and who was working on such a system recently. That sheltered housing complex has two 100 gallon storage containers but no back up system for the electricity to the pumps if there is a power cut. Residents might have water in storage but none to the taps or toilets!

You, however, might still have water in the cistern of your toilet if you haven't flushed it after turning off the supply. Whether this is usable depends on whether it is as it came from the pipe or you have some sort of chemical in there to add disinfectant and/or colour to the water. It might contain bacteria through cross-contamination with the toilet bowl but they can be removed by appropriate filtration and purification methods. The cistern will hold 2 or 3 gallons.

If you have an air-conditioning system it might have a water tray or container to collect condensation. In Central America I was in one location where they had window-mounted systems on portacabins surrounded by earth berms. Each conditioner had a pipe leading to a plastic 5 gallon jerry can. These would be changed once per day and the water used for servicing batteries. It is unlikely that we would get such humid conditions in the UK, but that does depend on the nature of the emergency that is causing you to Bug In. Even so, large systems can produce substantial amounts and even my portable air conditioner has a condensation collection and drainage system, though it sometimes takes several days to fill the 0.5 litre container.

- Position a flat container or dish on the floor under the drain hole. Do not allow the water to drip continuously into the container as it might easily overflow.
- Remove the drain knob.
- Remove the rubber plug, the water will flow in the container. When this is nearly full, replace the plug to stop the water flow and empty it. Repeat this process until all water has been removed.
- Replace the rubber plug into the drain hole firmly, the ☼ warning light should not flash any longer.
- Replace the drain knob.

Rubber plug   Drain knob

The water produced is distilled water and shouldn't need any further treatment if you keep the container clean but purify it if you are at all unsure.

If the mains electricity fails and you do not have a suitable alternative then do not forget to collect any ice from your freezer and refrigerator as it defrosts and keep this in a suitable container until it thaws. You might have ice cubes or containers of water stored in the freezer to help preserve the low temperature for as long as possible and this will eventually become available to you for drinking.

Soft drinks, soda water, tonic water, and the like are, of course, alternatives but treat alcohol with caution. Wine, beer or cider will initially quench your thirst but lead to dehydration later. Spirits are even worse.

We are really getting to the dregs now, but if you have drained the rest of your pipes and are looking for anything else available, pull out your washing machine and dishwasher, put a container under the junction of the waste pipe and the house mains pipe and then disconnect them. You could use the drain water for flushing a toilet, or put it through a filter and then spread it around plants, but although there might be several litres of liquid to collect the only way to make it fit for most uses will be to distil it (see below).

However, if you have exhausted all other resources, and the situation gets really desperate, you might have to eat the fish from your aquarium and then put that water through a suitable filter and purification system! Sorry Goldie, but when needs must!

Before you get to that level, if you can go outside your building there are other potential sources.

Not intended as storage perhaps but ready and waiting to be used is any swimming pool, paddling pool, hot tub, or fish pond. Any open source of water should be treated as suspect in regards to its quality but all are potentially viable. Then there are rainwater butts earmarked for watering the plants but still useful for more immediate needs and any other container left open to the rain might also be full of water. If you have a garden parasol it might be supported by a base that is filled with sand or you might have been forward thinking enough to use water in that too.

To extend the use of rainwater beyond what you already have, any roof surface should have guttering below its edge and those gutters should be fitted with down pipes from which water is diverted to storage containers. If you are concerned that conventional water butts are rather obvious, there are more discrete models now available (like the one shown from 3P

Technik UK) that are designed to blend with the house, or be fitted under decking or to be buried.

The tops of the drainpipes should be fitted with filters to prevent leaves and moss from blocking them and the inlet to the butt should also be filtered.

If you do not have water collection systems fitted, or you need more water, you can set up tarpaulins stretched out for maximum collecting surface but drawn to a point at the bottom edge to direct the collected rain into a container. If you are really pushed you can let the grass grow and then drag clean tea towels through it after the rain and wring them out into a pan. In winter you could collect snow and icicles and take them indoors to melt in a pot, but you need a surprisingly large volume of snow for relatively limited amounts of water. Outdoor survival manuals will show various other emergency sources, such as the solar still, dew sources and plant respiration bags. The quantities of water that these yield, especially in the UK, are small but at worst they can slake your thirst while you are establishing more efficient methods. In short, be alert and ready to take advantage of any source of supply.

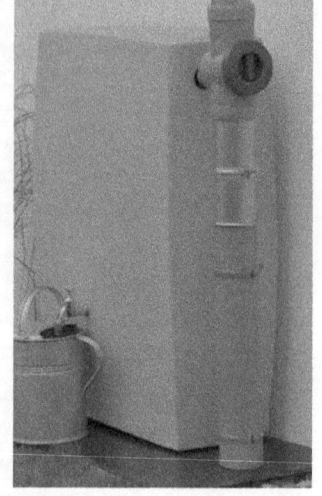

If you are truly Bugging In then any movement outside of your property might involve a serious breach of security but, as I said at the beginning of this chapter, a shortage of water is one of the very few circumstances under which that might be justified if there is no other reasonable option.

Beyond your boundaries you might have a river, stream, canal, lake, pond, reservoir, water tower, municipal swimming pool, drainage ditch or simply low ground where water collects every time you get heavy rain. Any water that collects after flowing over roads, paths, roofs, or other surfaces that will be fouled by multiple different contaminants must be treated unless you only intend it for watering plants, flushing toilets or other non-critical purposes, and if that is the case why are you breaching your boundaries for it?

When you make this sort of expedition under dangerous conditions you must take all possible precautions. If you are confined because of contamination or similar, dress appropriately in the best protective clothing you have and take great care with sealing all joins between different items of clothing. Because of the way you use your hands, gloves should go over the cuffs of sleeves but because of the open tops on boots trousers should be worn outside them. If you roll the end of sleeves or the legs of trousers because they are too long, turn them inwards not out, so contamination will not be caught in the folds.

When you get to water, try to choose a deep, slow-moving source if possible. Use a branch or whatever is available to gently sweep weed, dust, and any other surface film clear from the area where you are going to insert your container. Insert the container slowly until it is fully submerged and press it down as far as you can without disturbing the sediment at the bottom of the source. When the container is submerged, remove the cap and allow the container to fill. Refit the cap and then lift it clear. When you return, decontaminate yourself and the outside of the water container thoroughly and then filter and otherwise treat the water as required by the type of contamination.

Be under no illusions; obtaining water in a contaminated zone is dangerous. Depending on the effectiveness of your gathering technique, filtering and other treatment, the water *might* eventually kill you. If the alternative is certain death from dehydration within a few days ... the choice is yours to make.

During a disaster, some of the people who don't have water and are afraid to expose themselves to get it, or those who are simply lazy and predatory, will try to steal yours, so follow meticulous security protocols. Go only when there is least chance of being observed, even if that is at 3a.m. Choose a route which provides the best cover from view and protection from attack, with the fewest and shortest periods of being in the open; better to take longer than not get there or back at all! Move carefully and quietly, stopping frequently to observe and listen. When you get to your destination, scan for any threat before moving into the open, and then do what you came for quickly before moving away as soon as you can. Take a different route back from the one you took to the watering hole, so that there is less chance of you being ambushed on your return journey.

Water is heavy to carry so the journey back could take you two or three times as long as the outward trip. You can ease that by choosing your type of container or transport. You could use a wheelbarrow or shopping trolley or you could use a container with its own handle, such as the Aquaroll or Water

170

Buggy that are barrels with a central axle, rubber tyres and a forked handle. Differing models are available with capacities of from 29 to 50 litres.

We use 40 litre Aquarolls all the time at the caravan but also keep a couple in the garage for emergency use at home. They are durable and do exactly what they are supposed to, in the way they are supposed to. You can also buy a tap to replace the standard cap and a stand to raise them when back at your base. They are available in all caravan shops and Halfords or online, including from the makers at http://www.aquaroll.com/. RRP for the 40ltr model with handle and filler pipe is £75 but you can often find them on offer from various stores or second hand for even less. The very similar alternatives now available might be as good and slightly cheaper but I have never tried them so I cannot comment as to their quality.

If the authorities are still operating during the emergency they might provide an alternative such as a water bowser. The water in this will initially be safe but if you are going to use it you should get in quickly. If you want to wait until others have been and gone all the water might have been taken before you get there. If you wait for long after the crowd has dispersed you might find the bandits move in, either demanding payment for water direct from the bowser or emptying as much as they can into other containers and then contaminating the rest before advertising their stolen goods as for sale, as has happened in various places in UK when bowsers have been provided due to drought, floods, or broken pipes. There have also been cases of yobs contaminating or damaging bowsers, not for gain, simply as vandalism.

Filtering and sterilisation

Depending on the source and conditions, your water might be contaminated with any or all of a variety of harmful substances. There could be biological contaminants such as viruses, bacteria, protozoa, cysts, funguses or their spores, or chemicals from industrial, agricultural or domestic sources. The chemicals might include harmful heavy metals like lead or mercury, nitrates and nitrites from farm land run-off, arsenic or petroleum products, detergents, and many more.

Not all water will require full treatment before use, and how you treat it depends on whether you are going to take it into your body through drinking, cooking or cleaning your teeth, use it externally for washing or decontamination, or for cleaning other surfaces or watering food plants. Some of the contaminants might be harmful for one purpose but acceptable for another. If in doubt, deal with it as if it is poison and give it the maximum treatment available to you.

If you buy bottled water or fill containers with water straight from the tap in the UK it will usually require no further treatment, though if your containers have been standing empty for a while you should give them a soak in a sterilising solution such as Milton before filling them. Milton is available in liquid or tablet form and various sizes of container. Follow instructions on the bottle or packet for the concentrations to use.

If you use a hose or other pipe to fill larger containers, ensure it is made of food-grade material and give it a thorough internal soak and flushing with the same sort of solution as your containers; garden hoses can develop all sorts of nastiness when left for long periods.

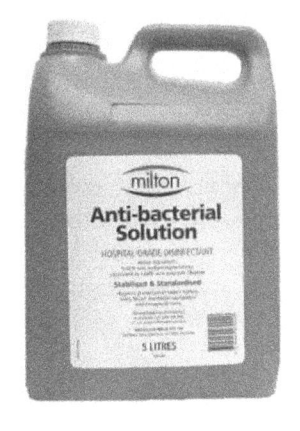

You can also use a bleach solution for sterilising your equipment but, unlike Milton, it could leave an after-taste or damage rubber seals.

If you cannot treat the containers or pipes before use, then when you fill the container add sterilising tablets or bleach as specified below. When you take water from the containers for use, treat it as you would for any apparently clean water from a biologically unsure source. Use your water and replace it with fresh supplies as often as practical but at least every 6 months – more often in summer if the water is stored outdoors. If water has been standing longer than that, treat it as suspect and purify before use for drinking.

Water containers should preferably be opaque but many of the smaller ones are at least translucent and many are transparent. That is OK if the contents are to be used and replaced within a few days but not ideal for the long term. If the container itself isn't opaque you can always store it in a bag or box that is or in a dark cupboard. As with most stored goods, water keeps best in a cool dark place.

Even if water looks clear it might still contain various chemicals in solution or suspension and organisms that are invisible to the eye, so a combination of filtering and sterilisation is the best policy.

Filtration

Filtration can remove many of the forms of contamination, depending on the fineness of the filter and the form of its media. The best filters, whether commercial or home-made, contain various media that will remove solids, organisms, and chemicals. This might consist of a fine filter material and substances such as charcoal, resin, and silver that will each react with and/or remove differing contaminants.

If the filtration system is sufficiently complex it might be all that is needed to make water safely potable. Course filtration will remove particles, while finer filters will remove protozoa, cysts and some bacteria, and very fine will even remove viruses. Differing materials will remove various metals and chemicals. For anything but the finest of filters the water must be sterilised after being filtered.

There are many models of commercial filter/purifier available, including large domestic filters and portable ones designed for backpackers and adventurers travelling in remote places.

Among the smaller filters there are ones shaped like a thin tube. These are designed so that you put the filter end into any puddle or other small amount of water and suck it through the tube and directly into your mouth. Depending on manufacturer and model the straws will filter up to 1000 litres of water and are advertised as removing particulates, organics and chemicals.

Jug type filters will give similar filtration using membranes, charcoal and in some cases silver filtration to reduce various contaminants and will generally treat 3-7000 litres.

Then there are pump activated filters like the Katadyn, which features a pre-filter and a silver-impregnated ceramic main filter plus intake and output tubes. There are various models with capacities from 7000 to 50000 litres and prices from £60 to nearly £300.

If you want a higher capacity filter for the home then the best are products from British Berkefeld.

These have filter 'candles' that consist of a ceramic shell integrated with silver and activated charcoal interiors. Some also have ion exchange resin filters.

The system has a top container, into which you fit from 1 to 4 filter candles, and a lid. Fitting more filters doesn't increase the purity but the more you fit the faster the output. This sits on top of another container into which the filtered water flows. This lower container has a tap for drawing off the water. Capacity is around 9 litres and according to model and number of candles you can get between 40 and 90 litres of water per day. Price is from £106 - £136 and new candles are available from BB or Freshwater Filters for £15 upwards.

Or you could make your own filter at any size from a 1 litre pop bottle to a 55 gallon drum! For this you take a container and if it is a pop bottle cut off the bottom, if it is a big drum cut out the top. On a drum you then need to fit an outlet in either the base or low on one side. At its most basic you simply punch holes in the base. If you are using a pop bottle just take off the screw cap.

Lay a piece of fine weave cloth in the base of the container. On top of this put a layer of fine gravel or very coarse sand and over that another layer of cloth. Then a layer of fine sand, a layer of cloth, a layer of charcoal, and so on up the container until about ¾ of the way to the top. Make each layer of sand or charcoal 2-4" thick. On the top put a piece of coarse cloth, straw or grass. To use, gently pour in raw water at the top and wait for it to filter through and out at the base.

This type of filter will remove many of the same organisms and chemicals as the commercial filters. The deeper the container and layers of sand and charcoal the more effective it will be. The top layer is disposable and can be replaced as it becomes clogged or smelly. Fine, clean, builders sand and crushed lump wood charcoal is best for the filters.

I have made these in a 1 lire bottle with pocket lining for the cloth, sand from under patio slabs and charcoal scraped from fire wood and had rain puddle water come out substantially clear. However, it is always best to then boil or otherwise treat the water to ensure all microscopic organisms are destroyed.

Sterilisation

Heat

Microbiological sterilisation is defined as a process that removes or kills all forms of microbial life present on a surface or contained in a liquid. Filtration is one method or stage but the others include appropriate application of dry or wet heat, chemicals or radiation.

Most of the harmful organisms likely to be present in water are killed at or below the boiling point of water at sea level. Lower pressure at higher altitudes lowers the temperature at which water boils but you don't need to worry about that anywhere in the UK that you might be Bugging In. If you are travelling in other countries it might be a factor. Perfectly clear water will be treated by this process but cloudy water might contain a suspension of matter that provides protection for the organisms. The resolution for either lower boiling point or murky water is to boil it for longer. One minute will normally kill any of the organisms but if you are not sure then 10 minutes will do the job anywhere.

A combination of filtration and sterilisation can be achieved by distillation. Boiling will kill micro-organisms but it will not remove or render harmless all chemicals. Boiling the water and then collecting and condensing the steam will do both in most cases although harmful chemicals, such as methyl alcohol, with a boiling point lower than water will pass off before the water boils and could contaminate your water unless you take steps to remove them.

In the distillation of spirits for drinking this difference is used in the opposite way to what we require. Alcohol evaporates at 80C while water does so at 100C. Distillers therefore collect the spirit by maintaining the temperature in the still at a lower temperature than that where water will boil. If you can measure the temperature of the water you are heating, you can reverse that process by maintaining it at 90C for several minutes (time depending on the quantity of water and therefore amount of contaminant that might be present). Let the unwanted chemical vapours vent away and you will remove most if not all of the alcohol. If you then allow the water to come to boiling point, let the steam vent for another couple of minutes to clear out the pipes, throw away any distillate and then start to collect and condense it from that point, you should have removed any harmful chemicals it might have otherwise contained. As a double-safety measure you could pass the water through a charcoal filter either before or after distilling it.

Water stills are available from some home-brew shops, though their unlicensed use is intended strictly for producing distilled water, of course. But you can make a simple version yourself using a kettle or pressure cooker, some tubing and a collecting vessel. If you have the resources you can get a bit more inventive and create a system to cool and condense the steam more quickly which could give you less loss of steam and therefore usable water.

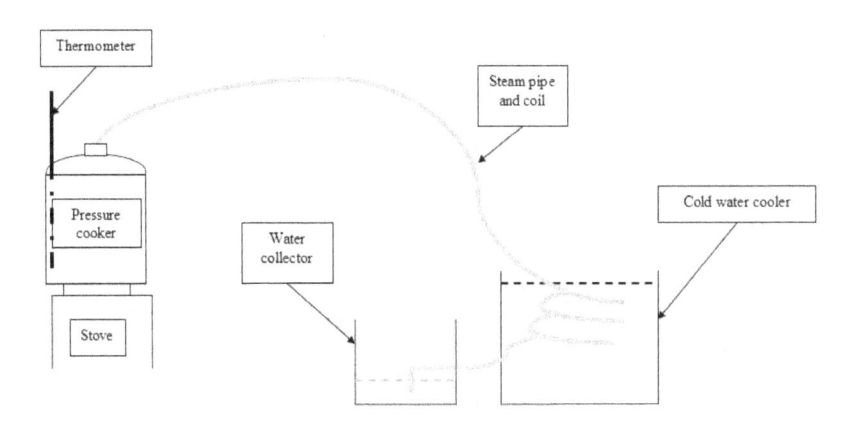

Home made water distiller

Chemicals

The chemical used for sterilising water is usually either Iodine or Chlorine. Iodine is slightly more effective but some people don't like the colour taint or the taste, though the latter can be neutralised with vitamin C.

Either is available in liquid or tablet form from chemists and many outdoor activity suppliers.

The brand of iodine you will most often find in the UK is Potable Aqua as either a tincture or as tablets and with their own brand of neutraliser as well but if you buy from a chemist then it is much cheaper. Instructions for use are on the bottle or packet but you will want 5 drops per litre of water and leave it to stand for an hour before use (minimum is given as 30 minutes but an hour is safer) and for very heavily clouded or contaminated water double the dose and allow it to stand for 24 hours. Note that women who are pregnant and people with thyroid problems and some other health issues or on certain medications should not take iodine; check the leaflets with your medication for any contraindications.

Liquid and tablet forms of chlorine are available from the same sources as iodine and the main commercial forms in the UK are Oasis and Aquaclear. Much cheaper is thin, unscented bleach that is 5% chlorine. To treat clear water add 2 drops per litre (9 drops per gallon) and leave to stand for at least 30 minutes. For cloudy water double the dose of bleach and the standing time.

A third option more recently on the market is silver ion/chlorine dioxide, with Micropur being the most visible provider here. This method is more effective than iodine or chlorine alone and leaves virtually no disagreeable taste but costs are several times that of the others and waiting time can be longer i.e. up to 4 hours per litre in badly contaminated water.

Irradiation

Ultra Violet radiation will also kill any of the organisms that infect water. Devices are available to fit onto the piping of normal household or caravan systems or for portable use.

SteriPen is the main supplier in the UK and offers a variety of battery operated, rechargeable, hand-wound, and mains equipment.

These will sterilise 1 litre of water in around 90 seconds and total treatment life will differ according to the individual device.

Prices also differ but range from £33 - £75. Check them out at http://www.steripen.com/

Saving water

By now you will see that although a safe supply of water is absolutely essential, obtaining, purifying and storing it for, or in, an emergency will not be easy or without cost. It is therefore obviously sensible to make the most of what you have, and as with so much in Prepping, the time to start learning and gathering things you will need is not after the event but now!

The repeated droughts in some parts of the country and rising costs often monitored by the installation of water meters, will make these steps sensible for many readers even before any emergency might arise.

The average use of water in a household in the UK is apparently 120 – 150 GALLONS per day per person for all uses. For comparison, when living in the caravan, my wife and I and our Border Collie live quite happily on 40 litres per day in total, which is just under 9 gallons. However, just to show what is possible, in winter when both the supply and drain pipes froze we managed without any issues on a total of 10 litres per day for all 3 of us for over two weeks at a time, and without our going thirsty or anyone backing away wrinkling their nose in disgust!

I will make some suggestions of ways that you can save on your use of water when it is in short supply, but to put that into a personal perspective, I suggest you begin simply by thinking about your use of water throughout the day and considering at each stage how much you are using and if you could reduce that amount.

We are so used to an unlimited and cheap supply of water that we tend to take it for granted, but having read this chapter hopefully you will understand that you shouldn't do so. For example, when you go into the bathroom first thing in the morning do you:

Flush the toilet immediately after having a pee? If so, are any other members of the family going in there straight after you and all doing the same, each using approximately 9 litres per flush? Is that really necessary?

If you shower daily, is that essential or would a wash be sufficient? I know it is the modern way but it really is quite a recent convention.

If you wash, do you do so with one or both taps running? Why don't you put the plug in and just part-fill the hand basin? If you do that, do you really need so much water in the basin?

If you use separate water for washing and shaving, be it face, legs, armpits or whatever, could you not wash and then use that same water for shaving?

When you have finished, do you simply pull the plug and let the water drain away? If so could you use a plastic bowl and then reuse the water for something else e.g. flushing/rinsing the toilet or watering plants?

When you are cleaning your teeth, do you let the water run while you are brushing? If so, why?

As you consider your daily routine I am sure you will discover many ways in which water is wasted. When instead of it running from the tap on demand you are using a finite supply and obtaining more is going to demand work and possibly danger, you will no longer want to waste a drop.

There are four ways you can reduce your use of water: use something else when possible; make it do double duty; conserve it; or recycle it. Consider these:

Alternatives

Don't shave or if you must, use an electric or battery razor, or moisturiser instead of soap and water

Use baby wipes on vital areas instead of a soap and water wash

Clean your teeth with a chewable toothbrush instead of a normal brush and paste

Use a dry shampoo instead of washing your hair

Buy, make or improvise a composting or chemical toilet instead of wasting water by flushing

Spit roast, fry, or otherwise dry cook foods instead of boiling or steaming

Stock disposable paper plates and cups and plastic cutlery; they can often be used several times before disposal. Don't bin the paper items, save them for fire lighting.

Double duty

Heat cans or packets of food in water and then use it in drinks or for other purposes

Shower or bathe with a friend. Even in the 1950's it wasn't unusual for families to save water and fuel by bathing in turn using the same water, leaving the youngest or dirtiest until last.

Conserve it

Collect rain, snow and ice rather than letting it melt and soak away

Check the root zone of your vegetables before watering. If it's still moist two inches under the soil surface, you don't need to water

Water your plants in the evening when temperatures are cooler, to minimize evaporation. Pour around the base of the plant instead of using a spray or spreader.

Keep down weeds that compete with your food plants for water

Check for leaks, dripping taps, etc. and fix them now

When you shower, use the 'navy shower' method i.e. get wet, turn off the water, soap up, then turn on the water to rinse off, instead of letting the water run constantly

Recycle it

Distil the residue from any other uses to extract pure water

When you give your pet fresh water, use the old water on your vegetables

If you are mopping up, wring the towel into something so you can use it again

Use water in which you washed yourself to water your plants – the soil will remove soap etc before it gets to the roots

Use soapy water from washing to kill insect pests that would eat your food plants

Collect urine in a bucket and pour it into the compost as a valuable additive

Hopefully you can think of many others. If so, please post them on the Facebook page @David E. Crossley Books or for the Twitter followers @TfnsbooksDavid

Hygiene

Mains items: Shower, Toothbrush, Razor, Hair drier, Washing machine, Tumble drier, Vacuum cleaners, Iron, Airers, Dishwasher,

Following on from Water, where various alternatives were examined, it seems appropriate to cover hygiene. Since you might be Bugging In to avoid infection during a pandemic but by reason of that spending much more time than usual in close proximity to other people within your group, there are two important hygiene aspects to consider: environmental and personal.

Environmental hygiene

Without mains electricity and water, in many ways we go back to the late Victorian and Edwardian eras except that our homes are now very different. Despite the fashionable change to laminate, most homes have fitted carpets, rather than rugs that can be taken out and beaten; toilets are indoors; wash basins and baths are plumbed in rather than being a jug and bowl and a tin tub brought in front of the fire once per week on bath night. Yet while Bugging In we will need many of the same facilities, just in simpler forms more akin to those of our ancestors.

For your own comfort and safety you will need toilet provisions for however long the emergency lasts. For the long term you might consider a composting toilet. Otherwise you might have to look to recycling water first used for other things to then use for flushing your usual toilet.

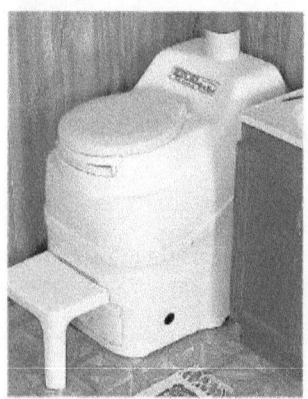

If you don't have enough water for flushing you could fit polythene bags into your house toilet then dispose of the waste in a hole in the ground outside. To keep down offensive odours you can use bleach, garden lime, or chemical disinfectant with a starter layer of shredded newspaper or sawdust in the bag, otherwise a layer of cat litter will do the job as well for you as it does for a tabby.

You might prefer alternative arrangements, such as a portable chemical toilet like one of those made by Thetford or Dometic, used by many families who go tent camping. These contain the waste and make its disposal less unpleasant and the chemicals speed its breakdown while modern variants pose no threat to the environment. At its simplest your emergency fall-back might be a bucket with a lid, but a seat – like the ones on the traditional Elsan toilets - does considerably improve comfort!

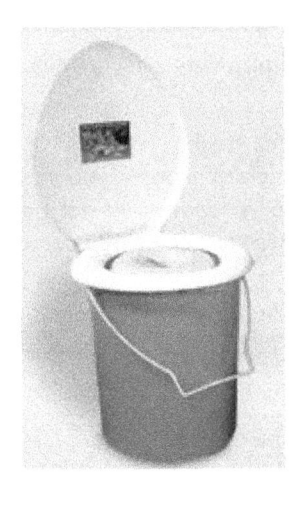

Whichever you choose, think about how you will dispose of the contents. A deep hole outside might be the best that you can do but don't underestimate how quickly it might fill and have to be covered and a new one dug. Otherwise you might choose to burn waste or to mix it with compost. If you bury human waste, ensure that you mark each site with an appropriate notice to prevent nasty surprises at a later date.

Above all do not fail to stock enough toilet paper and cleansing supplies to keep yourself and the loo clean. Check now how long a toilet roll lasts in your household and then stock as many as needed for the time for which you want to prep, plus some extras in case of stomach upsets.

Whatever the form and wherever you place the toilet you will also want to make arrangements for hand washing or a supply of wipes and hand sanitiser.

For your clothes you could revert to washing by hand, or using old-fashioned laundry gear such as the dolly tub and washboard. If you choose this option you might also want an old fashioned mangle for squeezing out most of the water.

Or you could buy a low power-demand washing machine such as a portable twin tub. These have no electronics and no heating element but a good low-power agitator and a reasonably effective spin dryer. We use one extensively while living in the caravan and don't hesitate to recommend them. Cost is around £80. There are fancier models and also single tub washers with no drier but we find the drier invaluable in bad weather.

There are even hand powered washers, consisting of a tub into which you put your clothes, hot water and detergent. The tub is usually mounted on a stand and has a handle on the side that you turn to tumble the container but recently I have seen a treadle powered machine that will both wash and spin. This requires no electricity and price is comparable to the hand turned versions i.e. from £50 upwards. I have put more details, a picture and relevant website details in the 'New ideas and products' chapter near the end of this book.

You will also want to have suitable detergents for washing clothes by hand and at lower temperatures. For some items, such as nappies, you will need a big tub or pot in which you can boil them. You will also need a suitable clothes line, possibly a prop, and clothes pegs to hang clothes out to dry. If you live in a flat, you will have to make a similar arrangement, even if it is a short line in your kitchen or bathroom.

To clean the house you will need suitable brushes, perhaps a non-electric carpet sweeper or maybe a 12v vacuum, together with the usual dusters and so on.

As you live and clean you will generate rubbish and with no bin lorries coming to call you must make your own arrangements. Separating the differing kinds of garbage becomes particularly important and almost everything can be recycled in one way or another. For example:

- Vegetable waste can be fed to animals e.g. rabbits or birds, or added to compost
- Meat scraps can be fed to pets or used as bait in traps
- Food tins can be used as plant pots, bird scarers, candle holders and many other things
- Bottles can hold water or home-made wine or be broken and cemented in place or turned into Molotov cocktails as part of your defences
- Paper and cardboard becomes insulation or firelighters
- Plastic packaging might be used as seed trays

Get into the right mindset and it is amazing what secondary uses you can find for most things you would normally throw away. Excess that you cannot use must be buried or burned if it would present any health hazard by attracting vermin. A purpose made incinerator or one fashioned from a metal dustbin or empty oil drum will contain the fire and raise the efficiency of the burning.

If you are going to burn then make use of the heat. What you are burning might make it unwise to cook in the fumes but you can at least boil water, heat metal, or possibly even generate power if you have a Thermo-Electric Generator (TEG). Non-hazardous waste should be bagged and set aside somewhere for later disposal. Ensure you have plenty of heavy-duty bin liners included in your stores.

To limit the chances of disease being brought in by flies or other insects you should stock and prepare to use appropriate deterrents and killers including: citronella scented candles, mosquito coils, sprays and papers plus sprays or lotions to apply to your skin and antihistamine creams and tablets for those cases where prevention doesn't work. A supply of medication for treating fleas, ticks and lice infestations might also be useful and, of course, suitable products for your pets. Maintain good food hygiene by always covering food to prevent insects contaminating it and immediately clear up splashes, spills and crumbs

You should also keep a plentiful supply of disinfectant and clean cloths with which to wipe down all surfaces, particularly in the kitchen and bathroom but if the Event is a pandemic then all contact points e.g. door and cupboard handles, should be thoroughly cleansed. You will need to include enough supplies to sanitise any materials that might have been contaminated by outside sources but that you have to bring into the home. Note that commercial bleach and some other cleaners have a fairly short storage life before they lose effectiveness so use and replace them regularly.

If you run out of commercial disinfectant then soap and water, vinegar or lemon juice are effective substitutes. You should have lots of soap in store but if the situation becomes really prolonged you can make it from animal or vegetable fat and lye. Vinegar can be made from fruit juice or wine. You will find plenty of recipes online but I suggest that you print them off and keep them in a file for use after the power fails.

For dishes and pans you will need a supply of washing up liquid and suitable dishcloths, tea towels, brushes and scouring pads for your cooking and eating items.

Hygiene in the kitchen

Hygiene in any food preparation area is essential during a Bug In. Nowhere else in the home are the practices and procedures of any one person more likely to have an effect on all other members of the family. Most of you will know the golden rules for safety in the kitchen but hygiene is so important in this context that they are worth repeating.

- Nobody with a stomach bug, cold or other disease should be allowed into the kitchen
- Cooks should keep hair and nails short and hair covered with a net or cap while cooking. There is nothing much more off-putting than finding hair in your food!
- Do not wear watches, jewellery or other loose items that could contain germs or restrict cleanliness procedures

- Wear a clean apron to protect your clothes from food and food from your clothes
- Wash your hands often with soap and water but particularly after handling anything, including your body, hair, mouth or nose, uncooked food, animal carcases, garden produce, waste, chemicals, kitchen implements or surfaces that might pass contamination from one to another
- Either use different surfaces e.g. boards and implements for differing types of food or thoroughly clean and disinfect what you have before using it for something else. This is especially important with any boards that get scratched by knives.
- Clean and cover, with a waterproof dressing that completely seals around the damaged area, any cuts or burns, both for your own safety and that of others
- If reheating food raise the temperature of the whole item to at least 82C
- Keep all food covered to prevent contamination by insects and loose germs e.g. from sneezes and coughs
- In the fridge keep raw foods on shelves below cooked foods so any juices do not drip and carry contamination
- Clean and disinfect all surfaces when you have finished cooking.
- Cleaning cloths should be boiled and dried after use.
- Boil and dry tea towels, do not leave hanging up in the kitchen while damp. Otherwise allow dishes to air dry on a clean surface
- Keep all food waste in a bin with a secure lid and remove from the kitchen at the end of the day.

Personal hygiene

For both physical health and the sensitivity of people around you, personal hygiene is even more important when you are locked down in a confined space than it would normally be.

If the mains water is still running and providing an uncontaminated supply you have a major advantage. If the water is not running and you are making use of an alternate source you could still use your washbasin, but it would be far better in those circumstances to save the grey water for recycling. In that case you might want to use a jug and bowl, rather than a basin with a plug. Include plenty of soap in your Prepping stores.

If water is not in such short supply you might be able to take an occasional shower. Bucket showers go from the most basic i.e. a friend pouring water over you, to the slightly more refined where you pour the water from one bucket into another which is suspended over the shower tray and has holes punched in the bottom to give a multiple stream effect, to the 'sophisticated' bucket with a proper shower rose fitted through a single hole in the base.

For any of these you mix the water to the required temperature first. A tray-shaped waterproof car boot liner, intended to keep the carpet in the boot area free from water and dirt from muddy pets or tools and the like, can be used to collect the water so that it can be recycled.

Slightly more sophisticated is the solar shower. These consist of a black bag into which you usually pour cold water. You then put it out in the sun and wait for the sunlight to heat up the water in the bag. The bag has a length of hose attached to its base with a tap mechanism and a shower rose. You can get a decent shower with these things and if there hasn't been much sun you can always put warm water in and use the shower system anyway.

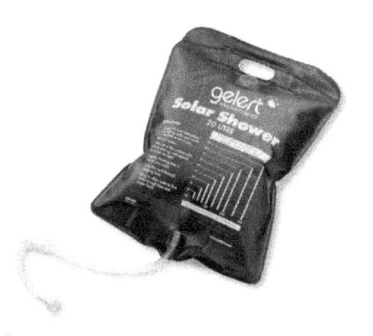

Or you could use a pump-up garden spray. There are some designed for the purpose but any can have a showerhead fitted to the pipe to serve in the same way. They are usually translucent rather than coated or created to absorb sunlight, hold more water and give better pressure but otherwise they work in much the same way as the solar shower.

Fanciest of the alternatives, but still only costing a few pounds, is the 12 volt shower. For this you need a 12v power source – I like to use a small sealed battery or a renewable source such as the Weza with its own recharging system but a jumpstart power pack will work too. You also require a container from which to pump the water; any bucket will do.

With a couple of imaginative adaptations, such as a hanging hook for the pipe or handle, you could use your usual shower stall. If you collect the water in a tray while showering you can reverse the system at the end for recycling by pumping the used water back into the container from which it came. As with all these systems of course there is no heating element so you must mix the water at the required temperature before you start.

While to save water it is not essential that men shave, for maximum effectiveness when washing, to eliminate a cosy home for head or body lice, and to aid decontamination should that be necessary, it is preferable for both men and women to remove as much hair as possible from all areas of the body.

It is also important to maintain dental hygiene. You really do not want to be inviting tooth or gum problems at times when you do not have any access to a dentist. You should include at least 4 new toothbrushes per person, plenty of toothpaste and several bottles of Corsodyl mouth wash, or a similar product, in your stores and use them on a regular basis.

If you are Bugging In with a larger group, you might need to consider sexual hygiene. You should be even more diligent than normal in the precautions that you take and procedures you follow. If appropriate, an adequate stock of condoms and other contraceptives, tampons, and products to prevent and treat yeast infections should be included as part of your stores. If you can access a supply of antibiotics for various STDs then add them to your medical kit.

In general, any time that you are Bugging In, whether with other people or on your own, environmental and personal hygiene is even more important than it is at other times. It is easy to let things slip when you are isolated, on the basis that no-one is going to see you anyway, and in a group children in particular will use the same excuse, but a lack of self-discipline in this regard can easily lead to falling standards in other things too. Becoming ill due to sloppiness is stupid and will do nothing to enhance your chances of survival.

Health and medical care

Mains items: Air purifiers, Nebuliser, Steam machine, Exercise machines, Back massage

The fact that you are Bugging In means something nasty is happening outside the boundaries of your home and very probably aspects of that could threaten your health and welfare.

In any emergency situation, medical help and supplies are likely to become unavailable or at least more difficult to obtain. Doctors, nurses and other medical staff will be affected by the conditions just as much as you are. If there has been major damage to buildings and roads then the equipment and resources that can be obtained by any medics that can function could also be extremely limited. You might be lucky and have a medical professional of some kind among your neighbours but it is more likely, as in so many things, that after a disaster the only people and stocks you can rely on are those you have included in your own preparations.

Everyone interested in Prepping should include taking the highest available level of first aid courses as an essential part of their preps and at least 2 of each group should extend that by studying the subject in more detail. Those extra studies might include expedition first aid and medicine, natural remedies, physiotherapy, survival dentistry, and home nursing among others.

To whet your appetite and give you the basics I will include what guidance I can on those subjects in this chapter but the total amount of information available is extensive and much of it is better demonstrated than explained in print so proper training is invaluable. For the more specialist subjects you will have to search for independent trainers, such as Chris Breen at www.survival-medic.com but for First Aid, St Johns/St Andrews and The British Red Cross are also good sources. Contact them for details of their schedules of courses.

To avoid health issues where possible you will want to maintain a good level of health and fitness on a routine basis. After an Event you must also take exceptional care in many activities, particularly those that involve machinery you currently only use occasionally. You will need to plan for the circumstances under which you will allow contact with outsiders after you have decided to lock down, and that will have to include either group members not present at the time or friends and relatives who arrive asking for help. You might want to consider how you could provide quarantine arrangements for those eventualities. Your plans and preps must take into consideration the care and treatment of members of the group who are present but who become ill after you have all Bugged In.

We will examine all these issues in the next few pages.

Maintaining health

If you are to maintain a good state of health that presupposes that you start with a good state of health, or if not, that at least your efforts are aimed at preventing an emergency from causing you to deteriorate.

As a Prepper, one of the most basic and urgent preps you can make is to develop the highest level of health and physical fitness that is practical for you. How you measure that will depend on your age and any existing conditions you have.

The first step to take is to make a realistic appraisal of your abilities. It is not sensible to plan how you are going to turn your half acre lawn into a vegetable garden if a fused disk makes it all you can do to mow the grass, never mind double digging and cultivating the patch ready for planting. However, if you recognise that and plan ways around it, such as obtaining containers, materials and power tools to achieve the same results but with less physical work, that is simply sensible adaptation. You might not have as big a crop as in raised beds and it might cost you more time or money but it follows the principles of doing what you can with what you've got, or getting what you need in order to do what you must.

There are innumerable examples of people who were older, heavier, or less fit than their companions but who nevertheless survived after a disaster when others did not, but much of that is down to determination, positive mental attitude, and intelligent assessment of and reaction to the situation, while those who died panicked, made stupid decisions or simply gave up. Those less physically abled survived because they overcame their disadvantages rather than using them as excuses.

That is not to say that you can't improve your chances even more by removing disadvantages where that is practical. You can't turn back time or grow a replacement for a missing leg (yet!), but Paralympians show just what can be achieved and thousands of people with disadvantages but who do not get that level of recognition also achieve daily by simply getting on with their lives regardless.

Being overweight, drinking too much alcohol, smoking, or taking non-prescription drugs ARE things you can do something about however and if you have the determination that will be needed to survive then you surely have what it takes to overcome those habits or addictions. You might survive after the event and give up these things because you then have no choice but it will be much easier, free up money for other preps now, and inprove your state of health from the start of a crisis, if you resolve them in advance.

Beyond that, you might have troubling conditions such as arthritis that limit you but with which you press on even though there are potential remedies. You might do so because of stubbornness, or a fear of surgery, or financial problems, or many other reasons, but again, if the reason is something which it is in your power to overcome and you are serious about Prepping then you should push past your objections and get it sorted to give you maximum advantage when things get tough.

Taking all those things into account, you should do your best to develop a functional level of mobility and fitness through regular exercise. That doesn't have to be work outs in the gym or jogging; walking, swimming, horse riding, cycling, gardening, or any other activity that will use your muscles and allow you to push yourself beyond your normal activities will do just as well. Remember to support that increased activity with a healthy diet. We covered that in detail back in the chapter on Food so I won't repeat it here, just make sure you get all the right nutrients in sufficient qunatity.

When you have achieved a level of health and fitness that is satisfactory to you, consider ways to maintain or even improve on that. It might only be a matter of ensuring you continue to get enough exercise and mentally stimulating activity but you may also want to research herbal aids such as Echinacea or the physical and psychological benefits of activities like Tai Chi or Yoga.

Not as interesting perhaps but certainly essential is that you do not ignore the very real routine issues. If you wear spectacles then you should have several pairs in the prescription you use now and also modified for the predicted progress of the condition. For example, if you currently wear simple reading glasses with a +1.5 rating in each lens, stock some at +2, +2.5 and +3 to take account of natural deterioration over time. They are available very cheaply now, usable pairs can be bought in pound shops, so several pairs is not beyond the means of most people. If your prescription is different in either eye you might be able to swap a lens between pairs to produce something that works for you. With cheap spectacles you might need different strengths for differing distances rather than the varifocals you may use now but that is better than being without.

If you use a hearing aid, build a good stock of batteries. If you wear dentures consider getting a spare set. Collect a set of scissors, clippers, files and medications to care for your nails and for bunions or corns. Skin lotions, sun-screen, chap sticks, eye drops, treatment for cold sores and any other minor conditions from which you suffer should also have a place in your stores. You must follow your usual routine and maintain supplies of medication for any more serious condition such as diabetes, asthma, or others; you cannot afford to allow these to deteriorate in an emergency. You should also research alternative methods of dealing with any existing condition for which you take medication, in case your regular prescription is not available.

Emergencies that cause you to Bug In will inevitably be stressful, but to continue to operate effectively and make sensible decisions you need to get sufficient rest and sleep. Standard medication can sometimes leave you sleepy and disorientated next day but there are some herbal and other natural remedies that can help without having the after effects. I find a cup of camomile and peppermint tea before bed is soothing to both spirit and stomach but there are others if those herbs are not to your taste. I know other Preppers who achieve the same things through meditation or prayer.

Potential threats

After an Event occurs, or while it is in progress if it is prolonged, there are likely to be any of several possible threats to your health through injury or illness. These might come about as a result of the effects of the disaster, your own post-Event activities, aggressive or otherwise dangerous animals, or people – either deliberately or through their ignorance.

Since it isn't possible to know exactly what the Event might be, nor therefore what its effects would include, identifying the injuries it could cause is difficult. If you are Bugging In then you might not have sustained any injury but that doesn't mean they couldn't occur later. Either way, you can reduce the risks by applying the safety and security precautions I explain in the next chapter.

Avoiding illness could be down to avoiding contamination by radioactive particles, which I dealt with in Shelter, or chemicals, which will be dealt with in Safety and Security, or biological hazards, be they natural or from an attack.

That latter threat is one of the most likely causes of you having to Bug In and the intent is to avoid infection or contamination by other people or through objects that they have touched. If a potential threat is suspected but it has not yet been identified as local and you are taking the chance to top up your preps, follow these tips to minimise contact with other people:

1. Remember that someone can be infectious for days before they show any symptoms.
2. If you have to shop, remove all surplus packaging from items in your cupboards, empty all your rubbish bins and gather any other

garbage. Bag it and take it with you to dump at a refuse site or in supermarket bins while you are out.
3. If possible use a supermarket that does deliveries. If that is no longer an option, choose somewhere that is open 24 hours and go in the early hours of the morning when there will be few customers.
4. Disinfect your hands before you leave the car
5. Wear disposable gloves and wear a mask or cover your mouth and nose with a scarf
6. Cough loudly so that other people keep away from you
7. Do not buy any unwrapped products e.g. only buy fresh vegetables already packed in bags – the absorbent surface of the veg will have been exposed to fewer people and a plastic bag is easier to decontaminate
8. Pay at a self-service checkout
9. Use bags from further back in the pile rather than those at the front
10. Take the maximum offer of cash back in case you need it later but banks are not operating or cash machines are empty. Take the maximum you can on your debit card from an ATM as well.
11. Take each item from its bag, disinfect the packaging, and then place the item into a clean bag in your car. Leave the shop bags, receipts, etc in the trolley
12. Return the trolley, remove your gloves and leave them in the trolley too
13. Disinfect your hands again
14. Fill up your petrol tank following similar precautions if using a petrol pump or other equipment that could have been handled by an infected person.
15. Pay at the pump if possible.
16. Keep your windows up and air on recycle as you drive home

When you are home and ready to Bug In:
1. Call your work and tell them that your partner, flat mate, or whoever you live with is showing symptoms of the disease. The chances are they will order you not to come in to work. Arrange to work from home if possible and confirm that they will still pay you. If the event is not too prolonged you might need the money.
2. Instigate most of your security precautions. Leave the front door accessible but seal the letter box.
3. Set up an intercom with a notice telling any caller to use it to speak to you.

4. Place a plastic box with a lid outside your door and attach a notice saying that it is to be used for any mail for which you don't have to sign

5. If someone is making a delivery that requires a signature have them leave the signature device on the step and back off. Put on a mask and gloves, open the door and sign the device. Put the package in a bin liner and close it up. Take it in and shut the door before allowing the courier to retrieve their device.

6. After they have gone: take the parcel back outside, thoroughly decontaminate your gloves, remove the parcel from the bin bag, decontaminate the outer layer, remove all packaging and put it in the bin bag, decontaminate the contents and put them aside, tie and secure the bin bag, decontaminate your gloves then take your delivery inside.

7. If the caller is anyone other than a delivery person, tell them you think someone in the house might have the illness and for their safety you don't want to open the door.

8. Prepare facilities to dispose of rubbish and human waste

9. Top up all water containers

10. Do a thorough clean of the house

11. Start taking any preventive medicine

In case the survival demands of an Event do require that you need to expose yourself to some form of biological or radioactive contamination, you should have appropriate protective equipment including:

a. Hooded Tyvek Suits
b. Safety goggles
c. 3M quality N95 particulate respirators
d. 5mil Nitrile gloves
e. Disposable shoe covers
f. Anti-microbial wipes.

Chemical events could require military-type charcoal lined suits and respirators with activated charcoal filters.

After Bugging In you will be shielded form most minor illnesses that you might normally catch from other people, unless one of you already contracted something before the lock down. Stomach problems will hopefully be avoided by good kitchen and bathroom hygiene.

There are, however, other illnesses that might affect you after you are isolated and the ability to identify and if possible treat them will be essential. Some conditions are so serious you would not be able to do anything to resolve them and that might force you to consider trying to get outside help. Being able to tell whether an illness falls into that category or is less serious could save you from unnecessary exposure.

The same applies to injuries; with some knowledge, skills and equipment there are many things you can successfully treat yourself but for which you might routinely go to the doctor, mainly just to be on the safe side. Finding a doctor might not be possible so the more you know and can do the better your chances.

You should be aware, however, that in a disaster, as millions of people inevitably discover, there are times when the best that you can do is not enough and you will lose people. Don't get into blaming yourself; even the most skilled, highly qualified and best equipped teams of doctors can't save all patients and nor will you. I have tended to friends hurt in battle, applied first aid and dressings for horrendous wounds and burns, inserted catheters and fixed up drips, and given morphine where appropriate. I've seen some die where they lay, some were evacuated and I met them later for a drink, others I heard had died during evacuation or after reaching the medics. That is part of the reality of these situations. It might be for you too. Accept it and move on.

Whether from loss in those circumstances or more at a distance or simply because of the situation you are experiencing, grief, stress, fear, and withdrawal can cause emotional and psychological issues in you and other members of the group. Part of your responsibilities may be to deal with those issues. We will look at the psychological effects of disaster, and effective responses to them, later in this chapter.

Preparation for medical care

Being in any sort of survival situation will inevitably see you undertaking tasks that are not part of your everyday routine or that have to be done in a different way e.g. with hand tools rather than power equipment. While making your preps you should have identified most of these tasks and gained at least some familiarity with them and the equipment needed in performing them but mix a lack of practise with a demand to perform under stress and the chance of an accident is significantly increased.

In addition to accidental injury in the kitchen, garden or during DIY in the house, things go wrong with our bodies at times. These are not necessarily infectious diseases contracted from other people; they can come from contact with plants, animals or insects, through something we have eaten or drunk, or life factors that affect our organs at various stages.

Whoever is responsible for health within the group should have a medical record for each group member that is as complete and current as possible. They should definitely know of any long term illnesses or other conditions and any medication routinely being taken. These records don't need to be as comprehensive as those held by your GP but they should cover all the salient facts.

Medical stores should include a minimum of 3 months supply of the essential medication for any group member and this should be rotated regularly by the member exchanging their latest prescription supply for the oldest in the store. Stocks should also include emergency supplies for irregular but known vulnerabilities such as allergies to bee or wasp stings, certain food types, pollen, etc. or to asthma attacks or angina.

Stores should also include a wide range and substantial amount of standard first aid supplies and non-prescription medicines plus non-standard equipment such as suture sets, transfusion equipment and much else. If you cannot use all this equipment currently then you should develop the skills to do so where possible. I'm not suggesting that you try your hand at DIY surgery but you might be surprised at how much you can do with appropriate training. Even if you believe some things are beyond you there is the chance you could get access to someone that has the skills if they had the equipment to apply them.

To help in that you will also want diagnostic equipment such as thermometers, stethoscope, blood pressure monitor, watch with second hand and, essentially, reference books. For the latter I particularly recommend:

Wilderness & Survival Medicine – Chris Breen & Dr Craig Ellis

International medical guide for ships – W.H.O

Where there is no doctor – David Werner

Where there is no dentist – Murray Dickson

Before you call the doctor – Dr Hilary Jones

Blacks Medical Dictionary

The complete home guide to medication – Dr Warwick Carter

First Aid Manual – authorised by the voluntary aid societies (BRC, St Johns, St Andrews)

Diagnosing illness and injury

If you do not consider it safe to go out to seek medical help but some hospitals and local surgeries are still operating, you might be able to talk to a doctor on the telephone to seek advice on whether you can treat an injury or illness yourself. In some cases of suspected pandemic the NHS sets up emergency help lines you can call for advice or to arrange to get medication. If either of those facilities is available then by all means use it.

If you have to make your own diagnosis then when someone comes to you with an injury or as feeling ill, the first thing to do is LOOK at them. Some signs or symptoms might seem obvious; bloodied skin or clothing, ashen face, or deformation of a limb are definitely signs that something is wrong and you should take note of them but bear in mind that they can be deceptive. A lot of blood might mask an injury that is not as bad as it first seems, a pale complexion might be a result of shock as opposed to a direct effect of the injury or illness, and a deformation could be a dislocation rather than a fracture, so acknowledge them but then investigate further.

Look for other initial indications too, such as the way the casualty is moving and holding their body, any signs of weakness or pain, sweating, breathlessness, or anxiety. Assess their level of alertness i.e. are they fully awake and clear; able to answer your questions, confused or only making unintelligible sounds; responsive to pain; unconscious?

After that first survey ask the patient, or if they cannot respond anyone who was with them when they became injured or ill: what happened, where they are hurting. If it is an illness or something like a muscle injury find out if they have had anything similar before. Combine this with your knowledge of the person and their medical record. If you don't know, ask them if they are on any medication and if so what and whether they have taken it as they should. Have they missed a dose or perhaps accidentally take too much?

After gathering as much information as you can then start a physical examination. Use all your senses and, as appropriate, any diagnostic equipment that you have.

Look for any signs. If you are dealing with an injury then clean it and the surrounding area so that you can properly assess the damage. If the wound isn't open check for bruising, deformation or pain if touched. If the injury is on a limb, has circulation to points beyond the injury been affected? If there is no bleeding is there any other type of discharge, especially from the nose, ears or eyes if a head injury is involved? If lips are pale and the person is sweating then they might be in shock. If the lips are blue then breathing or circulation could be affected. Check for odours, the heat of their skin, any odd noises when they breathe.

If the person is conscious ask how they feel; establish if they are hot or cold, nauseous, anxious, etc. Always use open questions rather than making suggestions e.g. 'How do you feel?' rather than 'Are you feeling hot/cold/nauseous/dizzy?' Even if they weren't feeling that way patients will sometimes report that they are after you have suggested it. Then check their pulse, temperature, blood pressure, and breathing, as appropriate.

A thorough interrogation and examination can provide most of the information that you need in order to make a diagnosis, if not from your existing knowledge then with the help of reference books. Doctors say that further testing is only needed in about 10% of cases to make the initial judgement, though clinical tests and advanced equipment might be used to confirm that judgement or provide more detailed information. What I have provided above is only a brief introduction to the process; you will gain far more from proper training and the books listed above, but it is important that you realise that much of this knowledge and many of the skills are available to you if you study them.

Some diagnoses are simple; a headache combined with a runny nose and a slightly raised temperature is probably a common cold, unless it develops into something more serious. A cut finger or a burn on someone who has been working in the kitchen and knows exactly what they have done requires no real investigation, only treatment. But determining whether someone who comes in from working in the garden and is complaining of pain in their knee has pulled a muscle, twisted the joint or torn a ligament can be more difficult. Do your best with what you have, accept that as a lay-person with limited resources you aren't always going to get it right, particularly on first examination, and arrange the most effective treatment your knowledge and stores will allow.

Treating disease and injury

After you have made a diagnosis the next stage is to start treatment. For either illness or injury you should first consider whether it is necessary or advisable to isolate your patient to prevent them being infected or infecting others. If that is the case, you will need to think about the factors covered in the next section: Home nursing.

I am assuming here that you only have one casualty to consider. If you have more than one and especially if you have several, then considering your limited resources you might be faced with the daunting task of applying triage in prioritising who to treat first, or at all.

There are official triage systems and then there are your own instincts. Instinct will drive you to want to treat the person most important to you – on a personal basis – first, or perhaps to treat children first. Official systems generally work on the basis of the condition of the casualty and whether they have a realistic chance of recovery, treating the most serious casualties as Immediate, the next most serious as Urgent, and finally the Walking Wounded after the others have been stabilised.

In a survival situation you also need to consider who is most important to the group. If you have one of your most intensively medically trained people among the walking wounded for example it might make sense to first spend a few minutes making them fit enough to help in working on the others. If you have two people with equally serious levels of injury but one has knowledge or abilities that are critical to the group and the other is less essential, then whatever the self-sacrificing wishes of the more-able one might be, that decision might not make sense for the good of everyone.

What decision would you make? Really? If the fitter person was someone you didn't like much and the other was your mother? Thinking now about the hard decisions involved in Prepping and survival can help develop your mindset so that you make the right ones when the time comes.

A similar but less critical issue to prepare for is the general use of resources. For example you might have a limited supply of some standard or prescription medicines but the alternative for some conditions of using natural remedies. You could decide to use the modern drugs until they are gone and then fall back on herbs when you have nothing else or you could try using the herbs on less serious cases and save the pills for when they are really needed. Many of our modern remedies have been produced on the basis of cures used for centuries and you should not overlook the original forms.

One of the medical needs of your group that might be considered urgent, and in normal times may even be classed as an emergency but that is rarely life threatening, is a toothache. In some cases this is due to a cavity that exposes the root and nerves to cold or heat, or a broken section that does the same, or sometimes it isn't actually the tooth that is the problem but the gum.

A dentist would usually remove any infected tissue or decayed tooth and perhaps apply a filling. If you don't have any specialised dental skills or equipment then a pain killer such as oil of cloves and a temporary filling will often give some relief. If there is infection then I have found that Corsodyl used over a few days can work wonders. Eventually you might have to resort to more desperate measures and then proper equipment such as a tooth extractor and even minimal skills can make a horrendous experience a bit more bearable than a pure amateur with a pair of pliers!

For less serious wounds and illnesses of any type, first aid and basic care will usually suffice and hopefully that will be the case for most of those who need treatment. Doctors say that upwards of 80% of the people they see in their surgery come with conditions that over time the body would heal without intervention and that most prescriptions are palliative, relieving symptoms rather than aiding cure. For the other cases, and further information on identifying which are which, I will refer you to the specialist books listed earlier that are written by doctors and other medical professionals.

Home nursing

The sick room

Very few Preppers will have the luxury of a spare room that they can set aside purely for use as a sick room when needed but you might have a room that would be suitable to adapt for the purpose. There will probably be some cost involved in the initial modification of the room but after that nothing that has been done will detract from its normal use and most will make it more convenient and pleasant. If you don't have a room you can modify in advance then at least identify somewhere that you will use if necessary and be ready to apply as many as possible of the items below.

The important features are:

Easy to clean

Big enough for easy movement all around the bed

Has bright lighting when needed and subdued levels when preferred

Well ventilated but draught-free

Capable of providing isolation

Safe to access with a patient who is being carried

Bathroom facilities en-suite or close by

Able to provide quiet and privacy

The flooring should be an easily cleaned surface such as laminate or cushion flooring that will withstand being mopped and scrubbed or disinfected daily, as it must be when in use for a patient. Rugs should be small and easily removed.

The walls should be painted in a light colour with bio-resistant or washable paint. The floor-to-wall joint should be sealed and if possible curved to eliminate dust-collecting corners. Any pictures or other wall decorations should be in simple frames that are easy to clean or remove.

Furniture should be kept to a minimum and the bed, bedside table and other items should be strong but light, of simple design and washable materials. The bed should be raised on legs so that the floor underneath it can be brushed and mopped. The bedside table/cabinet should also be on legs for the same reason and the top surface should be high enough to prevent the patient accidentally knocking things over but low enough that they can easily access a water tumbler and jug. It should have a drawer or cupboard for personal items, magazines, etc.

There should be a wall mounted clock positioned where the patient can easily see it from the bed, and a chair for visitors. Waist-height mains sockets are easier for patients and carers to access and safer for wet cleaning. A plastic bucket or bin, with a lid fitted with a disposable rubbish bag, should be available for clinical waste. A smaller bin beside the bed, also with a removable bag, is useful for tissues, etc.

Lights should be ceiling and wall mounted with cleanable covers. Dimmer switches for each light are ideal. A socket-mounted emergency/night light that provides enough illumination to check on the patient during the night without disturbing them is very useful. However it might be that you have no electricity and the lights have to be solar, dynamo or battery operated.

Ventilation and heating should provide a stable temperature within two or three degrees either side of 19C, with a regular change of air but no draught blowing directly onto the patient.

If the patient is infectious or highly vulnerable to infection apply what arrangements you can to provide isolation around the bed and at the entrance to the room and provide/follow strict hygiene procedures.

A room on the ground floor is ideal, so that neither a patient who cannot walk nor their helpers are put at risk by carrying up or downstairs.

En-suite bathroom facilities or a plumbed-in hand basin and mirror, or a washstand with jug and bowl are necessary for both patient and carer hygiene. If there is no toilet nearby then a commode or as a minimum a urinal and bedpan/chamber pot will be required. For the sake of all, the patient and carers must have access to facilities that are not used by other people.

Because the patient will need rest through the day due to nights disturbed by discomfort from their condition, a room that will provide quiet, and privacy during examinations, washing and toilet needs, is preferable and will also avoid inconvenience to other group members who might otherwise be regularly prompted to keep quiet.

Cleanliness and hygiene

We must all know that a major complaint against many of our hospitals is that they are unacceptably dirty and unhygienic. In a Bug In situation you simply cannot allow the same to be true of your home and especially not of a sick room.

The room should be dusted, swept and disinfected at least daily. Facilities within the room or used by the patient must be kept spotless and should not be used by anyone else. Any clinical and body waste must be incinerated.

Bedding, towels, flannels, clothes worn in bed, bathrobe, and any other items used by a patient must also be for sick room use only. You should have 3 sets of these items. When they are washed they should be placed in a sealed bag for transport to where they are laundered, processed separately from other materials and then returned in a clean bag to the sick room.

Items brought into the room should similarly be sanitised to prevent infection of the patient. Be especially careful of anything brought by well - meaning visitors, if they are allowed.

Clothing for carers

Carers must wear clean, easily laundered outer clothing protected by a gown or apron. Clean sip-on canvas shoes that are only worn indoors, and preferably only in the area of the sick room, are an important part of the outfit. Something similar to the uniform worn by regular medical staff might be reassuring to some patients and a boost to morale for others!

Surgical masks that protect the patient from the wearer or, if required, a level 3 mask that works both ways, plus disposable gloves should be used when appropriate.

Skills and responsibilities

The main responsibilities of a carer are to keep the patient clean, comfortable, properly fed and hydrated, medicated as required and motivated, plus to keep accurate records of their bodily functions, diagnostic readings, and progress.

Patients should be encouraged to wash themselves daily and to practice good hygiene after using the toilet. If they cannot clean themselves then you might have to wash or bed bath them. Tooth cleaning, whether of the persons own teeth or dentures, is also important and men who do not usually have a beard should shave or be shaved.

If the patient can get up and move about, even if only from the bed to a chair, they should be encouraged to do so.

If they are confined to bed then the patient must be turned at least every 2 hours and checked for bed sores, which should be treated by gentle washing with soap and water or saline solution, soothed with antiseptic cream and covered with a dressing. If the condition prevents easily turning the casualty then special attention must be paid to checking and early treatment of pressure sores. Bedding should be straightened and smoothed whenever the patient is moved and must be changed daily or as soon as possible if soiled.

If the illness causes urinary or faecal incontinence, a waterproof sheet should be fitted to the bed under the sheet and the patient must be cleaned and absorbent pants and fresh clothes provided before they are returned to bed. If you don't have absorbent pants, make a nappy from a towel.

Nutrition and hydration

Ensuring that the patient drinks enough water, or if necessary a Rehydration fluid, is vital. Dehydration causes weakness, lack of elasticity in the skin and various other signs but one of the easiest to look for is reduced urination and very dark, strong smelling urine. Don't underestimate the effects; it is a common cause of death in patients with serious diseases. A suitable Rehydration fluid can be made with a pint of water to half a teaspoon of salt and a teaspoon of sugar.

The patient should be provided with a jug that is calibrated so that consumption can be checked and have a separate jug so that to measure urine output too. A record of how much has been drunk and passed should be kept and the patient's water refreshed regularly. If they have a cup of tea or other drink record that as part of the total. If they are not drinking enough then encourage them to do so. If they cannot drink then the fluid must be administered. You can do this by use of a jug or a bottle with a spout or even a baby's bottle with a teat. If they cannot swallow 'you can administer fluids through an enema.

Proper nutrition is also essential to maintain and build strength. If the patient can eat normally then that is good, though their appetite will probably be less due to lack of physical activity. If they cannot take solids then a nutritious chicken soup is easily swallowed and digested and will provide energy. Otherwise try something like scrambled eggs.

Alternatively nutritional drinks such as those designed for dieters and athletes might tempt them and go down more easily.

What the casualty needs is much the same nutritional elements as a healthy person, less calories but more protein if they need to rebuild muscle and strength. Some conditions demand more of one type of food than another and in other cases it might be necessary to limit a certain class, such as carbohydrates or fats. The medical guides should give information on those things for differing illnesses.

As the patient recovers you can gradually move them back to a more normal mixed diet. One good thing is that many of the storage type foods that should form part of your preps work very well for feeding sick people and a multivitamin will be a valuable addition too.

Medicines and other treatment

If you have suitable medicines and skills for treating the patient's condition, be it in the form of pills, herbal infusions, physiotherapy, acupuncture or whatever, these must be given at the appropriate intervals. Stay with the patient and ensure that they take their medicine or complete their treatment.

Maintaining morale

Injury or illness affects different people in differing ways. They might be angry, frustrated, frightened, or depressed. Some are good patients who will co-operate and others will fight everything that you try to do for them. Some will be compliant or resigned to their fate, some will enjoy the attention and others will just want to be out of the sickroom as soon as possible.

Many will be worried about the potential outcome of their problem or about how they will be affected once they move back into the group, if they survive. Listening to and reassuring them can make a big difference to the outcome of their treatment and the time it takes them to recover.

Patience, understanding, humour or assertiveness will all be demanded of you at one time or another. Extremely sick patients are relatively easy from this point of view, but as they get better some can become a right P.I.T.A.!

Many patients report that one of the worst aspects of having been sick but starting to recover is the boredom. Giving them something to keep them occupied can be a great help. Books, magazines, a TV and DVD or a computer (if you have electricity) can all help. So can a visit from someone close to them if their condition makes that safe. Some will want to do something constructive and if they are capable then information and minor tasks related to their usual responsibilities within the group might help.

Records

At regular intervals through the day take and record the patient's pulse and temperature and if appropriate their blood pressure too. Keep records of what they drink and eat and of when they go to the toilet. Record the dosage of medicines taken and the results of other treatments. Add notes about their general condition and any changes you observe.

These records will not only be of use in monitoring this patient's progress but also valuable for analysing what apparently did or did not work, in case the same happens again either to them or someone else and they will add to your own gradually growing knowledge and experience. Maintaining a regular routine is also reassuring for the patient, even if they do moan about it.

Medical kit

A list of suggestions for first aid, surgical and nursing equipment, supplies and medicines for Preppers is included in the kit lists near the end of this book.

Dealing with bodies

Despite all your best efforts there might be nothing you can do to save some patients. For normal times, the law in the UK is very specific about what is and is not allowed in regards to the disposal of bodies. In Events involving large numbers of deaths nation-wide the national or local government might issue emergency instructions and make relevant arrangements including collection and mass burials or cremations. In these cases they should also provide information as to amendments to the other normal procedures and suspension of or changes to the law. However, while confusion and lack of organisation persist it might take some time to sort out such niceties.

You should be prepared to follow the usual procedures in so far as possible or keep a record of what you had to do instead in case anyone requires those details at a later date.

If there are no arrangements for official disposal of remains then you will have to do the best you can as at least a temporary measure.

    Wrap the body in a sheet or other cover.

Wrap it in polythene or place in poly bags or a bivvy bag – be prepared that if disposal is delayed as the body starts to decay it will give off gasses that will cause any sealed cover to swell. Venting these is not a pleasant task.

Keep the body in a cool place until you can deal with it and then either:
bury it under at least 3 feet (1 metre), preferably up to 6 feet (2 metres), of soil with a layer of rocks or other hard material on top of that

Or cremate the body. Note that it is not easy to do this completely. It requires a considerable amount of material that will burn at a high temperature. It is best if it is done in an enclosed container to facilitate that but an open fire maintained for long enough can achieve destruction of all soft tissue though at least the larger parts of the skeleton might remain. In any event, you might then want to bury or otherwise dispose of the ashes or other remains.

Whatever method you choose, by all means then follow or apply any religious or other ceremony that you feel is appropriate. The fact that you are having to do these things yourself will not make the grief any easier to deal with so any familiar processes that help will be all to the good.

Psychological problems

It is said that no-one who is involved in a disaster, either at first hand or by contact with those who were there, is ever totally unaffected. That is certainly supported by my own experiences and observations. It is, however, possible to mitigate some of those effects by being able to recognise them in yourself and others and being ready to deal with them.

The effects you or others might suffer could include: Anxiety, Fear, Fatigue, Grief, Self doubt, Guilt, Depression, Loss of faith, or Boredom. These effects might be short term or prolonged and might arise almost immediately or as PTSD only years after the cause of the trauma

You also need to understand that some people are particularly vulnerable to the trauma caused by disastrous events. Those people will include: the elderly, people with existing mental illness particularly depression, those who have previously experienced trauma or to whom it is new but whose coping mechanisms are simply overwhelmed, and women, especially though nor confined to, those with young children. Your family or group might include people from any of those categories.

The resulting effects might include any or several of the following: Insomnia, nightmares, hallucinations, flashbacks, Obsessive Compulsive

Disorder, dependency, addiction, withdrawal, anger and violence, and eventually suicide.

How you deal with the effects and their results will necessarily differ. Over all, what a therapist will tell you is that people need to talk, about their experiences, their feelings, their fears, what they want, what they hate, what their plans are, what can they give to others, how they have coped in the past and why they aren't now, and many other things. Some people will find talking is easy and an immense release, some will find that revealing such personal things is traumatic or even impossible for them. For some it is easier to do in a group, for others it will only happen one-to-one and in the most strictly agreed privacy.

People who will not talk will sometimes write it down and doing so can help them to put their feelings into perspective and bring them clarity and understanding. Drawing, listening to or making music, reading or looking at photographs can also sometimes be of help. Often memories only half realised will take shape and, where denial or confusion was twisting them, can be brought into much sharper focus and reality.

Sometimes, listening to other people talking and helping them to identify their issues and the solutions to them can help people who share those feelings but can't express them to come to terms with their own problems. Often, sharing and being willing to accept physical help with tasks can develop into a greater willingness to share thoughts too, even if only with a work buddy, but it takes time to build that level of trust.

For some of the effects behavioural therapy or exposure can help; thinking about what is truly causing fear or anger and examining whether that is valid and if not exploring ways to overcome those feelings. After a hurricane hit Central America in 1982, I was trapped when part of a building from which we were recovering injured people collapsed. Colleagues got me out about an hour later, but it felt like a lifetime. After I got home from that tour of duty I took up pot holing. I hated it but decided it might be useful therapy. Now I control the fear when it arises by deep breathing and examining the situation and my feelings logically and in detail, but it hasn't gone away, and can be particularly bad just as I'm falling asleep. I've learned to deal with that by directing my thoughts elsewhere. Hopefully similar techniques will help you.

Psychological trauma, its effects and potential resolutions can be as great a threat to Prepper groups as the physical dangers that cause you to Bug In. It is something of which you need to be aware and to gain a firm understanding. When someone is suffering, simply telling them to 'get a grip' or 'pull their socks up' won't always cut it, and with some of your group it could make the situation worse.

Safety and Security

Mains items: External lights, Cameras, Alarm system

In the previous chapter I tried to cover the preps you might need to make in order to give your group a decent chance of survival when ambulances, doctors, nurses and pharmacies are no longer available to you. In this chapter I want to do the same for those times when the police and fire services are not going to be able to respond, even though the threat level is substantially higher.

In both cases the measures are divided into Passive and Active defences. The Passive defences include all the protective preps and actions you can take to reduce the likelihood of a danger becoming a reality. The Active defences are what you can do if the passive measures fail.

WARNING: many of the active measures I am going to outline will be in conflict with the normal advice of the emergency services. These measures are ONLY for survival situations when those services are not available to you within a timescale when they would be able to help.

The conflicts are, unfortunately, inevitable. The standard advice is centred on the concept of you taking immediate action to protect yourself until the professionals arrive. In some situations after an Event the only survivable option might be to follow the usual advice and then deal with the consequences of no help arriving; in others not taking action beyond what you should normally consider could put you in greater danger than simply getting out and staying out or hunkering down and waiting for rescue that might never come.

I understand that some readers will be happy to take the passive defence actions that follow but for reasons of belief or health will not be willing to take, or even prepare for, the active measures in relation to security. If reading those sections would offend you, please pass them by but I feel obliged to include them for those who believe they will be willing to use the information.

Following some of the advice offered will not only put you at risk of immediate injury but for some situations might also require you to use weapons and cause injury to other people. Consider carefully if you are really willing to do that; it is not something to be taken lightly and you might later suffer psychologically if you do so. I suggest only that what you or members of your family/group might suffer if you do not defend yourselves, will make that defence both morally and legally justifiable and that the physical and emotional trauma that would result from your doing nothing would be far worse. If you won't defend, prep to leave.

Fire – passive measures

As many of you might remember from fire safety lectures at work, a fire requires 3 things in order to start and continue burning: Fuel, Oxygen, and Heat. Your home is going to be full of fuel in the form of furniture, bedding, etc. as it always is but almost certainly more so while you are Bugging In. Even so, there are some things you can do to lessen that issue. There isn't much you can do about the initial supply of oxygen but you can make preps and take action to cut down its resupply to the fire if one starts. However, most of your preps will be based around preventing the source of heat that will provide the initial ignition for the accidental fire and there is quite a lot you must do in that regard.

When you Bug In you will inevitably introduce additional potential threats:

Much of the time there will probably be more people in the house than usual and more to a room, whether awake or sleeping

Some of those people might be elderly, ill, or otherwise less-mobile, presenting additional challenges if you have to evacuate

At first, most of the additional people will not know the layout of your home nor be familiar with your emergency and evacuation plans

You will be using different stoves and cooking arrangements, with which some volunteers will be even less practised than you are

You might be using different sources of heating, including open fires and portable heaters

You could be using lighting that generates heat such as oil or pressure lamps or candles

You might be using self-installed untested electrical systems from alternative power sources

There might be external threats from fires caused by the Event, or people in the same circumstances as you but less well prepared and informed, or from a direct attack including arson

Any of these could present a danger from flame, smoke and other fumes or delays to you escaping from them.

You can take positive steps to reduce the risk from most of the internal hazards but for the external sources you might only be able to reduce the possible impact rather than their likelihood.

I have mentioned above the most common risks and having identified them you should do what you can to minimise them. Firstly examine and test all equipment that might cause a fire to ensure that it is fully and safely functional. Check seals and pipes if they are fitted and renew or lubricate them as appropriate. Ensure electrical wiring is of the correct gauge; connections are secure and fuses of the right size. Make sure no wiring is run under furniture or floor coverings and that sockets are not overloaded. Have chimneys swept and inspected.

Doors and windows that are designated as fire exits must be tested for easy opening and if they are usually locked the key must be immediately available. Any lights or warning devices must be tested regularly and batteries replaced as required.

For reducing the Threat, the first precautionary step I am going to urge you to take actually applies equally to fire and security and I'll sum it up in one word – caches. The proverb, 'Don't put all your eggs in one basket' dates back to at least the 17th century and possibly the 16th; you would have thought we might have learnt the lesson by now!

In Bugging In situations we are assuming that you will not have access to your usual sources of resupply, so if you lose everything you have then basically you are stuffed! Whether that might be due to a fire or a raid by looters one of the easiest ways to avoid losing everything is to hide some of your preps separate from the rest and in a place where they are less likely to be found or destroyed.

In the book Bugging Out I dedicated a chapter to creating caches: in your place of work, differing Bug Out Locations (BOLs), and along the way on routes you might have to travel. If you are Bugging In we have to suppose that most caches to which you will have access will be on or very close to your own property. The type of property in which you are Bugging In will affect what options you have in that regard. If you have a large garden, perhaps with outbuildings, then you have a myriad of opportunities but if you live in a terrace with just a small back yard, or worse still in a flat, then you will have to be a lot more inventive.

If you have a garden then the ideal answer is to seal a variety of your preps in some of the ubiquitous blue barrels, complete with desiccants and deoxygenators where appropriate, and bury them somewhere raiders will be less inclined to search e.g. under the compost heap. Even if you have been driven out by looters, the chances are that they will move on after stealing everything that they can find that looks useful or attractive to them and you can then return to recover items from your caches. If a fire has forced you to flee from the house you certainly won't have gone far and you can access your caches even more quickly.

If burying the caches isn't practical but you have any outbuildings, even a small shed in the yard, then you can seal items in flatter containers and hide them either under the floor or between the rafters or wall studs, which you then cover with other boards as if for insulation. If you have an area of decking or slabs then you can place a cache under there. The base of a garden parasol can be filled with water or with small bags of supplies. Smaller items could go into well sealed bags or boxes and then be hidden at the bottom of plant containers, a water barrel, or something disguised to appear like a container of waste oil or other noxious substance. If necessary, place a tool that will aid your recovery of a cache somewhere that it will appear to have been abandoned or forgotten. It might eventually become so rusted that you need to replace it but at a car boot sale you should be able to find something already suitably battered for a pound or two. Hiding things isn't necessary if the threat is only fire, of course, but placing the caches outside the main residence is.

If your home is in a block of flats and you are prepping for being confined to the building then caching supplies for after a fire is a definite challenge. The fire could be one started in your own home or it could come from another family. Either way, because fire principally burns outwards and upwards, the stash should definitely be on a lower level than your home and the further down it is the less chance of it being destroyed from below. It has to be somewhere that other residents don't access and where even a janitor or utilities engineer is unlikely to go or look. If the building has a basement or garage, that might offer possibilities.

It might be that you have to accept the risk of moving outside your own building to a nearby garage or lockup that will both contain your cache and offer temporary accommodation. There are no easy answers; investigate all possibilities and try to find a solution that fits your individual location and circumstances.

When you identify somewhere to hide your cache, what should you put in it? Basically, these caches are a subset of all the things that you include in your main preps but possibly with some additions. For example you are going to need food, water, medical supplies, tools and all the rest, but unless you have an outbuilding that will provide shelter you might also want to include tarpaulins and cordage. These can be used to construct a quick refuge and then later to provide temporary cover for damaged roofing or windows.

Evacuating from your home due to fire means that you are moving from Bugging In to Bugging Out and you will want all the facilities that demands even if you go no further than the end of your garden or across the street. Your Bug Out Bags (BOBs) should cover this eventuality and are a limited form of mobile cache. If you are forced out by looters hopefully you will at least be able to grab those as you go. When you can return, the BOBs will then be extended by your static Bug In caches.

Having reduced the threat from loss, you should next look at the reducing or eliminating the threats of harm. I said earlier that the major causes of harm will be heat or fumes but if you are using liquid fuel or gas appliances there is also the risk of an explosion. You cannot avoid having the in-use fuel container connected to the device but wherever possible spare containers should be stored outside any occupied building; even in a garage or workshop accessible from the main part of the residence without going outside is better than near to living areas. If that is not possible, store spare containers on the ground floor (or in the cellar if you have one) in a room that isn't normally occupied e.g. a cupboard or storeroom.

Remove any non-essential flammable materials, and ones that could emit noxious fumes, to a store well away from the main building. That might include: paint, thinners, oils, spare insulation, cardboard boxes, and rubbish. While you are at it, ensure all hallways or other routes to fire exits are cleared of any obstructions or hazards that might cause a slip, trip or fall.

Clear all flammable materials from around the walls of the home, including balconies. This preferably includes decking (go for a concrete patio instead), plants, wooden door arches, garden tool lockers, logs or other solid fuel, etc.

Store all flammable liquids, gas cylinders, etc, in a secure and hidden location well away from the main building.

Remove and replace any materials or objects containing materials that are not treated to be fire resistant or which are non-essential but could emit poisonous fumes. This includes older furniture and wall coverings but by all means get rid of those horrible old polystyrene ceiling tiles; in the event of a fire the gases they release are lethal.

Fire – active measures

Apart from the physical precautions you also need procedural ones:

> Create a fire safety checklist including all of the points in this chapter and any others that are specifically applicable to your home and situation then carry out an audit on a regular basis e.g. every 6 months or if there are any changes to the buildings or residents. Immediately institute any corrective measure that you find are needed.
>
> Make a fire safety and evacuation plan that clearly explains the potential risks and threats and the measures required to minimise and if necessary deal with them. Ensure everyone knows the plan and

make it a priority that anyone new to the home is fully familiar with it and their part in it.

Have an agreed verbal or other audible alarm e.g. bell or triangle, to alert people even before smoke alarms activate.

PRACTISE your fire drills!

Establish safe working practices, such as:

Nobody is to smoke in a building

Nobody is to try to use any equipment with which they are unfamiliar unless they are first fully trained and supervised. Children especially will be keen to help and show their capability but a confident cry of, 'I can do it!' is not acceptable in these circumstances.

Candles must only be used in proper holders or lanterns and may only be lit by an adult.

Liquid and gas appliances must only be refuelled outside in a designated safe area and must be tested before bringing them back inside.

Fires and lamps must be positioned at a safe distance from any flammable materials and where appropriate guards must be sited to protect children or others from contact with them.

There must always be someone awake in a room where a portable heater or hot lighting is in use.

People must know the exits, places of safety, appropriate actions and their responsibilities, including for others.

Each night, someone must have the responsibility of going around ensuring all electrical equipment; lights; fires; etc. are extinguished, disconnected, and otherwise safe in all rooms including bedrooms.

If there is an external threat you may have a designated sentry/safety watch and if so they should also perform regular patrols to ensure that internal safety procedures have been followed.

Equipment

A smoke alarm must be fitted at each level. If the dwelling is large and has long corridors consider fitting more than one at appropriate distances. The smoke alarms should all be tested and new batteries fitted on a regular, established basis e.g. we do ours every 4th November, the day before Bonfire Night in the UK. Batteries should be changed even if apparently still holding a working charge – finish using them in something that serves a less critical function.

Carbon Monoxide alarms should be fitted anywhere that open flame appliances are used.

At least one fire blanket must be fitted in the kitchen and any room where liquid fuel or open flame is used. In a large room, one at each end is not excessive. Learn how to open, carry and use the blanket.

A 2Kg dry powder extinguisher must be fitted near to the door to the kitchen. Carbon dioxide extinguishers should be fitted in or immediately outside rooms where electrical devices are in use and especially by the battery room.

Water or foam extinguishers can be positioned for use in areas where solid materials might be involved but must not be used for electrical or in the case of water extinguishers on liquid fuel fires.

Having obtained suitable extinguishers it is absolutely essential that you learn to use them properly! All are designed to be simple to operate but differ depending on the type of fire and extinguisher as to whether you direct them at the base of the fire or above it. This is because the extinguishers work in different ways e.g. water and foam cool materials, removing heat from the triangle; dry powder, CO2 and to some extent foam, smother the fire, denying it oxygen. The wrong type of extinguisher or using it in the wrong way can actually make the situation worse or cause injury to the user. Enquire about a course at your workplace or the local fire station or search for an independent safety trainer.

For upstairs rooms have an appropriate exit and provide an escape ladder or other means of getting to the ground without jumping or dropping.

If you have group members with mobility problems, identify suitable equipment and procedures for getting them out, even if it is a case of 2 people picking them up in a blanket or one using a fireman's lift.

Smoke hoods – will help you to evacuate or deal with a fire with less risk of inhalation injury

Flame proof clothing – an NBC suit or even the jacket or hood, while not giving the same protection from heat that a fireman's outfit does, will give you protection from flame and radiated heat and is relatively cheap from surplus stores, though you might decide to go for more specialist gear such as Nomex

Pre-wetting hoses – hoses that you can fit along the apex of the roof and under your guttering, which are drilled along their length and connected to a water supply inside can be used to reduce the flammability of the outside of your building(s)when there is an external fire threat

Anti-arson letterboxes and doors – although after a major event when no mail is likely to be delivered, or you don't want it coming into the house before you have sorted and disinfected/decontaminated it, you might decide simply to bolt or superglue the letterbox shut. Anti-arson doors are usually made of double-skin metal with a fireproof insulation layer inside. They also offer good general security against forced entry.

Window film/shutters/boards/grids – prevent petrol bombs being thrown through windows or them being broken and fire introduced. These also help with resisting or delaying any other entry by attackers but also reduce the number of escape routes you might have.

Because fires often spread very quickly and the smoke and fumes present such a major hazard, the conventional advice is to get everyone out of the affected building as quickly as possible and to stay out until the fire service arrives. However, in a wider emergency when you are Bugging In it might be that without your shelter and preps your situation might be equally untenable.

For that reason, designated group members might be trained and equipped to do whatever they can to fight the fire and/or rescue designated supplies. If you have an alternative shelter – even if less suitable – and supplies in caches, that might be less urgent. This is a decision you should make in advance of need, based on the people, equipment, and alternative preps you have available.

If the fire comes from an external threat your actions will depend on whether it is direct i.e. an attack, or indirect i.e. fire spreading from elsewhere.

If you face a direct attack you need 2 teams to deal with it:

1) Defence team

2) Fire fighters

Your response should be:

Begin prep for fighting retreat and a move to your back-up location

Deploy the defence team to repel and deter the attackers.

As soon as it is safe, deploy the fire fighters to extinguish the fire.

The fire fighters then return to the house

The defence team return when they believe the threat is lowered to the point they can safely do so.

If the attack cannot be defeated, and there is no other option, evacuate!

If the threat is indirect but heading your way:
Raise the alarm

Begin pre-wetting and check that all other inflammables are clear of the building

Prep for evacuation and a move to your back-up location

Monitor the situation - watching for progress of the fire, and any other threats e.g. rioters/looters

Fight the fire at a distance from your home if you can

Evacuate if it becomes clear that it is the only viable option

Flats (Apartments), Hotels and other Multi-occupancy buildings (MOBs)

If you live above ground level or one higher in a MOB most of the passive defence measures outlined above will still apply, but if you have to evacuate you might face some serious challenges and the higher you are the more difficult your situation becomes.

If the fire begins at a level higher than yours the situation might not be so grave. MOBs are built to take account of fire and to provide protective features. The fire might travel upwards but lower levels and the escape routes from them should remain viable. Afterwards you might find you have lost some facilities e.g. water, electricity, if they were previously still working, and even if the fire didn't reach the roof but upper level windows were broken you might get some rain seeping down, but despite that you might be able to stay in your home. If the fire starts in your rooms, or rooms below you. that is less certain, so having alternatives is definitely a good plan.

You must get to know the evacuation plan for your building and practise it for yourself, including in the dark. Count the stairs at each level and the number of doors between you and the fire exits. Locate alternative exits e.g. to flat roofs in case the main exits are blocked. Know where fire hoses, extinguishers, axes, alarms, etc. are located. Extra equipment like a smoke hood is definitely a good investment. The cheapest I found in the UK is the Xcaper at around £48. This covers the mouth and nose and is designed to give at least 15 minutes of breathing protection.

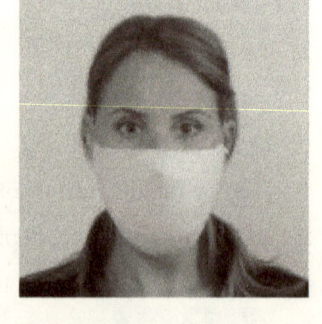

Otherwise you can go for a hood with filter such as the Draeger Parat C Fire Escape Hood which protects the whole face and head but costs £118. There are quite a few alternatives available with differing designs, specifications and prices.

You might also want to investigate, and if you buy then train with, alternative exit methods, such as abseiling kit. There are fire specific kits, such as the Davy Descender Descent controlled escape system (£500+) but standard abseiling gear will work provided you have the relevant skills and a strong fixing point. Don't forget appropriate gear for infants and pets too. These mainly consist of a strong bag you can use for lowering them so you might be able to improvise something as effective as the commercial products.

Flats have advantages and disadvantages when it comes to safety and security. The disadvantages can be overcome but will need some different procedures and possibly different equipment to deal with them. On the good side, you are saving money and work in other aspects of Prepping.

Security – passive measures

Many passive defence measures either depend on or involve the concept of not looking like a productive target.

Undoubtedly, the first measure to implement is Operational Security (OpSec) i.e. learning and teaching others to keep their mouth shut about your preps. Remember the wartime slogan, "Careless talk costs lives". In this case, it could be the lives of you and your family!

Even if your default option is to initially Bug Out to some other location where you will then Bug In and that second location is where you keep your preps and you don't talk about it, what happens if you have talked to neighbours about the need to prep but circumstances then force you to stay where you are rather than heading for your intended BOL? What will happen is that before too long they will be on your doorstep, possibly asking for help that you might be happy to provide if it is in the form of advice, but more likely they will be asking for some of your supplies. If you are lucky and you do get away, when you eventually return you are liable to find your home ransacked by people looking for things you 'might' have left behind.

A community of like-minded, independent-natured mutually-supportive individuals or families is a very valuable survival resource but if you are the one trying to build that community you need to be extremely careful who you talk to and how you approach the subject. Basically you need to be confident that the people to whom you are talking will be receptive.

That is easier if you know the general approach to life of the target and if they have interests or hobbies, perhaps ones you share, that give you an indication of an independent approach e.g. if they are a vegetable gardener, angler, camper, shooter, or enjoy making or fixing things rather than buying new or hiring someone else to do jobs they can do for themselves.

If this is something you want to test with a neighbour, look for an indirect way to raise the subject. After a power cut or when there is the threat of a strike by tanker drivers or another topical issue arises, lead the conversation to what they are doing to avoid disruption or inconvenience or ask for advice on what they think you should do. Watch their body language as closely as you listen to their words to make a judgement about their response and where or whether to take the discussion from there. This applies equally, if not more, to family members who don't usually live with you unless you already intend to prep for them as part of your group.

If the response is dismissive or otherwise does not encourage you to expand it in the direction you would like, then simply drop it, don't raise it with them again, and look elsewhere for potential allies.

Related to what you say, but in fact a part of what people see, is what you and other members of the group write and these days that is particularly important in relation to the Internet. Even though I use the Internet extensively, am a member of some online discussion sites, use LinkedIn, Facebook and Twitter for professional and publicity purposes, I am constantly amazed at how much people are prepared to reveal about themselves. I know some of that is exaggerated or even false but even so the information that can quickly be gained is frightening.

A couple of weeks ago I had an email from one of my sisters. She lives in Australia and has recently moved house. Within seconds I had entered the address in Google maps and was looking at a satellite image of the property and its surrounds (that isn't it in the picture by the way!). The imagery is a little out of date of course and I was simply curious but I couldn't help but notice that the amount of tactical data on approaches, potential obstacles, entry points, and the like is more detailed than I would have had available from military reconnaissance photographs taken for a specific mission during most of my time in the forces. The internet might or might not be down in a situation where you are Bugging In, especially in the early stages, but that doesn't stop people looking and making plans now for what they might do in the future.

We know that there are predators out there whose intended method of survival after The Fall is to prey on others and particularly on Preppers. If they know what area you are in, and perhaps have photographs of the layout of your home and garden from proud posts you have made of how your restoration and cultivation efforts are coming along, then together with web searches, the electoral role, etc. it wouldn't be too difficult to find you. Add to that the information children will casually reveal to their 'friends' and 'followers' online and Big Brother might be the least of your worries. Don't become paranoid but do be careful in the lands of the wild wild web, there are injuns and bandits out there and they don't all identify themselves by wearing war paint or a black hat.

Closer to home, you also need to restrict what others see going on around you. If movement between your car and house is visible to others and you have been out to stock up you might want to use bags or boxes that hide what you have bought and transfer it in batches rather than all at once. If a nosey neighbour makes comment, quip that it won't last long the way your family eats or about big discounts at a local supermarket or that a friend is ill so you have been shopping for them. When you are moving items that you particularly want to conceal, put them in bags that disguise the size and shape.

In and around the garden there are some things that are not so easy to conceal. In the chapter on Food I suggested using irregular and companion planting rather than rows but you are still going to be out there working. If you have a solid fuel stove, large stocks of logs are not easy to hide - coal is more compact – but you can surround your store with trees or put it between outbuildings so that it is not so visible to anyone passing.

If you have a generator that you will not use regularly, test it somewhere away from home or at times when you know neighbours are out. They will certainly know it is there when you first start it up in an emergency but at least they won't have thought about it in advance. To limit the range at which it can be heard, build a box or make a place in a shed, put noise insulation around it and create a safe outlet for the exhaust. Extend the exhaust outside the enclosure and bury it. Only run the generator, or other noisy power tools, during the daytime when other things will be going on so the noise will not be as noticeable.

If you are planning to cook outdoors then make the most of it during the early stages after an Event, when the fact that you have food and fuel is not so surprising. If you have more in the freezer than you can otherwise process for storage you might even want to share some of it but do advise the recipients to enjoy it because 'once its gone, its gone!'

One of the disadvantages of either outside cooking or solid fuel fires indoors can be that they advertise your presence by the smoke and smell that they give off. You might not have many alternatives but it is certainly something of which you should be aware if the effects of an emergency become prolonged.

If rubbish removal services have stopped and you cannot go out to dispose of your rubbish elsewhere then compact and hide it whenever possible so that you are not seen to be producing lots of empty tins and packets when other people are on short rations.

Other than using solar tile rather than panels on the roof there is not much you can do to hide an array but they are becoming more common and therefore less noticeable. Also, many have been installed for cost savings and are tied in to the grid so they don't necessarily offer any advantage when mains power is out. Yours might be connected to a battery bank of course and if you are not using the output for lighting then you will have other arrangements. Fit efficient blackout boards or curtains to all windows so that the lights don't bring unwanted attention.

In all these matters, become security conscious and evaluate the impact and possible consequences of what you do. Some might be unavoidable, some you might be able to turn to your advantage but those should be conscious decisions not the result of a lack of forethought. Your aim should be to blend with the appearance of your surroundings and reveal as few as possible of the advantages your preps provide. Whenever you can, don't make it obvious you are there at all.

Some of the passive defences you implement can be passed off as general security measures to deter burglars and with them being overt can actually be an advantage. If neighbours believe you are applying these precautions because you tell them you are concerned due to a friend/family member having been robbed and assaulted in their own home, **even though that victim did not have anything of great value to tempt the criminals,** they are unlikely to suspect you of doing so to protect specific valuables. Of course you will probably implement other measures that they don't see, or don't particularly associate with security, but what they don't see they won't wonder about.

Although it is not the 'first point of contact' with an intruder when you are Bugging In, I suggest that you begin your security preps with your main building and then roll out from there. That will give you the best value for money on your preps as most of the measures on your house or flat will also be of benefit for normal anti-burglar protection and might save you money on your home contents insurance. In particular you should look at reinforcing all potential entry points to your home.

Begin with your doors and if you have more than one then apply the same level of security to all of them, not just the front door. As an ex-police associate of mine always emphasises, 'Your security is only as good as its weakest point'. The door itself should be robust and not include any glass panels – many are not much sturdier than an internal door. Either solid wood or metal plated on the inside and out is best. This might cost you but it is a sound investment. The door must be mounted in a solid frame that is securely bolted to surrounding stone, brick or concrete – a door and frame that shakes in the wind or when a bus goes past is not going to keep out anyone that has ill intent!

If you cannot fit a suitable door or frame, consider a reinforcing bar across the door and bracing struts for the frame.

Your main lock should be a 5, 6 or 7 lever mortice deadlock with anti-drill and anti-pick features and the bolt should slide into a solid keep mounted in the frame – rim sash locks and keeps offer very poor security and most can be overcome by a hard kick.. The lock should be supplemented with mortice bolts that slide up and down into the frame above and below the door rather than into the frame on the side where the lock is situated. The bolts should be positioned about one third of the way back from the open edge of the door. The hinges, which should also be robust, should be supported by 2 hinge bolts spaced one third from the top and one third from the bottom of the door.

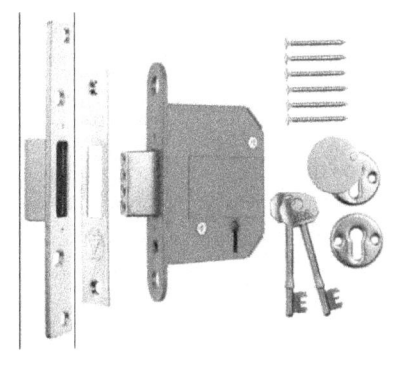

If the door has a letterbox its outer cover should be coated steel not brass, fitted with a waterproof rubber seal and lockable from the inside – that will help prevent entry of unwanted/contaminated mail, airborne contamination, or fuel. If there is a viewer in the door it should be covered so that people outside do not know it is being used.

All windows should lock and starting with those at ground level if you cannot afford to do all at once, should be coated outside and then inside with clear safety and security anti-shatter window film. Protek films make a good one. 76cm wide film will cost about £5 per metre length (3m £15, 4m £20, 5m £25) 50cm width will cost just over £3 per metre. The film is fitted using a solution of one pint of water to one teaspoon of washing up liquid, a sharp knife, glass scraper, squeegee and a lint free cloth. This isn't completely impervious to attack but it will substantially deter and delay anyone attempting to break through.

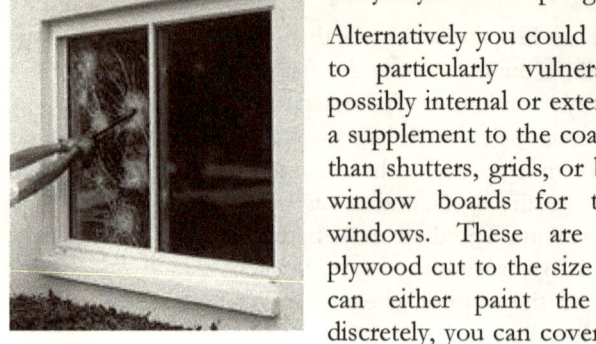

Alternatively you could fit strengthened glass to particularly vulnerable windows and possibly internal or external grids or bars. As a supplement to the coating but less obvious than shutters, grids, or bars you could make window boards for the inside of your windows. These are made from thick plywood cut to the size of the window. You can either paint the outside or, more discretely, you can cover it with material that matches your usual curtains or blinds. Paint the inside of the boards white to keep things light when you are using off-grid lighting, or you could fit a poster showing pleasant outdoors scenery, it might even be an improvement on the real view. If properly fitted, these will serve for blackout too.

On the inside of where the board fits, drill the frame top, bottom and sides and mount strong door bolts onto the board so that the bolt will slide into the hole in the frame. Depending on the height and width of the window you might have to use more than one bolt to a side or even several widths of board. You might also want to fit one or two handles to the inside of each board, to assist when you are lifting and positioning it. Together, the safety film and boards will give good protection against anyone entering or throwing a petrol bomb through the glass.

French windows should be similarly coated and fitted with locks in the tracks but, because this might be one of your designated fire exits, you should consider a sliding or folding grille and blackout curtains rather than boards. Skylights and dormer windows should be reinforced in the same way as any other window.

Every possible entrance to the building should be covered by a PIR activated sensor that is either connected to a central control board that shows the location of the breech or with a localised alarm that gives an audible warning from that area.

Externally you might want to fit solar-charged PIR security lights. They can be a deterrent to thieves that want to remain undetected but when the grid is down and the whole area is dark their sudden glare can attract attention to your home or make them a target for theft.

I use these lights for normal times but intend to switch them off in a major emergency and rely instead on a 12v CCTV system. The cameras are small, so as not to attract attention and mounted high so that they cannot easily be tampered with. They have infra-red capability and an associated microphone so that we might be able to hear what people sneaking around are plotting. Both lights and cameras cover all sides of the building plus the front and back garden and are sited so as to prevent any dead spots or hiding places for intruders. External buildings are also alarmed and covered by lights and cameras. There are many systems available. Maplin or Amazon is always a good place to start your search.

Progressing into the garden area, the boundaries should be protected by thick hedges of spiky bushes with deeply set concrete pillars hidden among them no further than 3ft (1m) apart. Large boulders can be used as decorative features inside the hedge instead of or in addition to the pillars if you prefer. Gates should be tall, made from or reinforced with metal and locked and bolted. The frame of the gate should have a spiked design that makes it difficult to climb.

If you have walls or fences rather than hedges, they should be strong, designed to be difficult to climb, and have anti-cat spikes along the top. If you prefer, you can leave the top clear in normal times and cement broken glass or fit nail boards in place when things turn rough. Wooden fences should be backed with wire netting to hinder attempts to saw through them; thick wire can wreck even a chainsaw. Ensure no scaleable structures or objects are sited near fences where they might aid intruders getting in or out.

More spiky plants, ponds and other structures can be used to funnel any intruders into the approach lines you want them to take but beware of providing hiding places. I have mentioned PIR activated lights but for more covert observation you might want to consider an Infra-red night sight. Some are very expensive but serviceable ones for relatively close use are sometimes available on special offer from outlets such as Lidl or Aldi. My Bresser model came from Lidl and cost under £100 and provides a good clear picture out to about 150 yards. Alarm mines that fire a blank shotgun cartridge, or other audible warning devices can be useful if they can only be triggered by an intruder rather than someone passing by. Dogs that will bark or growl when they detect an intruder outside are also a great help and can be a deterrent even if they are not trained or inclined to attack physically.

Security - Active Defence

The law in the UK is somewhat strange. You are not allowed to possess anything with the intention of using it as a weapon but you can use anything you've got for the defence of yourself or anyone else against a third party or parties who you have reason to believe intend to hurt or kill you or those you are defending, provided that what you do in your defence is reasonable and proportionate to the threat posed. You can even use reasonable force in the protection of your property.

The Crown prosecution advice on their web site states:

http://www.cps.gov.uk/legal/s_to_u/self_defence/#Principle

>>In the context of cases involving the use of violence, the guiding principle is the preservation of the Rule of Law and the Queen's Peace.

However, it is important to ensure that all those acting reasonably and in good faith to defend themselves, their family, their property or in the prevention of crime or the apprehension of offenders are not prosecuted for such action. The CPS have published a joint leaflet with ACPO for members of the public making clear that if householders have acted honestly and instinctively and in the heat of the moment, that this will be the strongest evidence for them having acted lawfully and in self-defence. Prosecutors should refer to joint the CPS-ACPO leaflet - Householders and the Use of Force Against Intruders. <<

http://www.cps.gov.uk/publications/prosecution/householders.html

>> In explaining the purpose of the leaflet, the CPS and the Association of Chief Police Officers (Acpo) said it was a "rare and frightening prospect to be confronted by an intruder in your own home".

They were responding to "public concern over the support offered by the law and confusion about householders defending themselves.

"We want a criminal justice system that reaches fair decisions, has the confidence of law-abiding citizens and encourages them to support the police and prosecutors in the fight against crime."

The leaflet says that "wherever possible you should call the police" but summarises the position when one is faced with an intruder in the home, and provides a brief overview of how the police and CPS will deal with any such events.

The leaflet does not specify which forms of force or violence, or which weapons, used in self-defence at home are sanctioned by law.

The six questions and answers in the leaflet are:

Does the law protect me? What is 'reasonable force'?

"Anyone can use reasonable force to protect themselves or others, or to carry out an arrest or to prevent crime.

"You are not expected to make fine judgments over the level of force.

"So long as you only do what you honestly and instinctively believe is necessary in the heat of the moment, that would be the strongest evidence of you acting lawfully and in self-defence. This is still the case if you use something to hand as a weapon.

"As a general rule, the more extreme the circumstances and the fear felt, the more force you can lawfully use."

Do I have to wait to be attacked?

"No, not if you are in your own home and in fear for yourself or others. In those circumstances the law does not require you to wait to be attacked before using defensive force yourself."

What if the intruder dies?

"If you have acted in reasonable self-defence. . . and the intruder dies you will still have acted lawfully. Indeed, there are several such cases where the householder has not been prosecuted."

But it gives examples of cases where "you would be acting with very excessive and gratuitous force and could be prosecuted".

These include when a householder knocked someone unconscious then "decided to further hurt or kill them to punish them", or "if you knew of an intended intruder and set a trap to hurt or to kill them rather than involve the police".

What if I chase them as they run off?

The situation is different "as you are no longer acting in self-defence and so the same degree of force may not be reasonable".

However, "you are still allowed to use reasonable force to recover your property and make a citizen's arrest. You should consider your own safety and whether the police have been called.

"A rugby tackle or a single blow would probably be reasonable. Acting out of malice and revenge with the intent of inflicting punishment through injury or death would not."<<

Section 1 of the Prevention of Crime Act 1953 prohibits the possession **in any public place** of an offensive weapon without lawful authority or excuse. (Archbold 24-106a.)

The term 'offensive weapon' is defined as: **"any article made or adapted for use to causing injury to the person, or intended by the person having it with him for such use"**.

However note that only applies to a **public** place; your own home and garden or other property where you have permission to be and to which the public does not is not a public place. There are some exceptions e.g. to possess a firearm you need an appropriate certificate, and some items such as flick knives and sword sticks are specifically prohibited unless a special waver has been granted e.g. to a museum and use of an offensive weapon is different from possession of it e.g. if you have a walking stick to help you walk that isn't an offensive weapon but use it to hit someone and it could then be classed as such.

Threatening someone with a weapon could bring other charges such as common assault but you could have legal defences such as the right to self-defence. How all this would turn out in a situation where you couldn't contact the police to ask for help or they couldn't get to you and especially if the intruders were mob handed and armed, we would have to wait to see.

Just be aware that you do have the right to defend yourself and yours, including by use of a weapon, provided it really is necessary and you don't go beyond what is 'reasonable' in the circumstances. Read up on the references above and **please note: I am NOT a lawyer, I am NOT giving you specific legal advice,** I am merely trying to refute the impression that I know some people have, that in the UK you are not allowed to defend yourself and must pretty much let the trash do whatever they want!

Having accepted that if your life is threatened you have the right to defend yourself and to do so robustly, including by the use of weapons if that is proportionate to the attack, let's examine some scenarios with which you might be confronted and then how can deal with them in an effective manner. In the situations we are considering, people are only going to attack you if they suspect that you have something they want. That could be any of the goods necessary for survival, or people for sex or labour or entertainment.

The people who threaten you might be: Troops or police, Predators, Passing evacuees/looters, or Neighbours.

Police and troops

I don't consider officials raiding you for stores to be a probable scenario in the UK but if due to the disaster some emergency legislation is passed, troops or police who come to the house are likely to first request or demand entry and then confiscate whatever portion of your stores is authorised or they see fit to take. Only if you refuse or try to oppose them will it degenerate into an actual attack. Let's be clear here, if it comes to that you are not going to win! If you repel them once they will call in reinforcements and come again until they get their way, doing whatever damage is required to property or people in the process and probably dragging the rest of you away to prison or some other secure facility. They could not allow somebody to successfully oppose them and word of that to get around.

If they are simply going door to door and have no reason to suspect that you are Preppers, and you appear compliant, they will search the house, outbuildings and garden and take what they want, but are unlikely to start tearing the walls apart. This is one of the benefits of good OpSec. If you have secure caches hidden in the house e.g. under the stairs, under the floorboards, etc. and in places outside, then you are going to lose some or most of what is in cupboards ready for use but you will have some left to replace it.

Do be aware that not all who present themselves as officials will necessarily be who or as they seem. They might have been official but now be acting on their own behalf or they might be impostors in stolen uniforms. If you decide either of those is the case, treat them as thieves in accordance with their and your numbers and capabilities.

Predators

Predators will tear the place apart; leave you with nothing they like or can use; rape, torture, mutilate and/or kill whoever they see fit including women of any age, children, men, and animals; and then possibly burn the house down on the way out. I've seen it in Africa, South America, Asia and the Middle East and none of them were any better than the others. You oppose predators to the utmost of your ability; if necessary until you either go down or make a fighting withdrawal, or you prepare to take the consequences. I do not recommend the latter!

People think that this type of attack is unlikely in the UK because there aren't many guns here, not that these scumbags always rely on guns, but that isn't true. There are millions of guns in the onshore armouries of regular and reserve military forces; navy ships in harbour; police armouries and some vehicles; arms manufacturers; gun shops; some gun clubs; embassies; some foreign ships and aircraft; zoos, wildlife parks and some vets; museums; the private homes of certificated shooters; and the caches of criminals and terrorists. Predator groups will have their own and know where to go if they want more.

They will use reconnaissance and observation of likely targets and then, depending on the strength of their group, choose either the easiest target or the one they decide will probably be the most rewarding. Once again, OpSec and an appearance of being neither an easy target nor any better off than people around you will help to focus their attention on someone else. That might sound cynical but if you then want to help your neighbour and believe you might be able to do so, you will be in a far better position to attack from a flank than you would have been had you been the target. If you decide the predators are too strong to confront successfully, keep your heads down. If they decide to try other targets close by and come to you then since they will already have got some of what they want from their earlier raids they will be less inclined to push an attack on someone that presents a strong defence.

If they do attack you first, they will employ subterfuge and basic military tactics of deception, distraction and ambush; they might try a diversionary attack on one point and a main assault on another; perhaps try to get you to open up to give help to a child, elderly or injured person; or have someone come into your garden to steal vegetables in order tempt you to send one of yours out to confront them; or start a fire that you will go out to extinguish. The main gang will then either take hostage whoever is outside and order those inside to open up, or attack the point where you have opened or left the building and storm inside, forcing any opposition to surrender by using further hostages taken as they burst in.

The only good thing I can tell you about these groups is that current reports say the numbers of gangs that have organised in advance are few and currently quite low in membership numbers. Some members will almost certainly be lost to their group by whatever disaster is affecting you. Unfortunately, in the aftermath those who do remain always seem to find willing volunteers to join them and new groups will form. Considering the size of the UK you would be unlucky to have to face one of these gangs but you should know about them and their tactics and recognise them in your preps.

Evacuees/Looters

Most looters and desperate evacuees will attack obvious targets such as shops or apparently vulnerable ones such as a house that is isolated from others. They will not be going from house to house in a suburban street looking for what tins they can find; at least not until the situation is really desperate and all the easier and more productive targets have been emptied. Even then, if one place is more difficult than others or if some are empty of living people while others are still inhabited, they will raid the easier ones first.

Although there are generally more avaricious and aggressive individuals and groups per square mile in the city than there are in rural areas, there are also more targets and a much greater concentration of protective resources such as police, fire, medical, relief and military personnel and equipment gets deployed there. This is why, even when resources are scarce everywhere, bandits often roam the countryside where they will face less opposition, while regular people move to, rather than from, the cities; exactly the opposite of what many Preppers who haven't had any experience of the reality of disasters believe will happen.

Only when people believe their death is inevitable if they stay, such as when a city is being bombarded to destruction in war or threatened by an approaching hurricane, will many inhabitants move out and even then some will stay to take their chances where they are. Remember our own cities and those of other European countries during WW2 or Beirut during the civil war in Lebanon; many fled but many stayed.

In the UK, even given that many cottages and village houses are being bought up by city folk willing to commute or as weekend retreats, the saving grace might be that people in rural areas are still much more likely to know their neighbours and to band together with them in times of trouble. It is also probable that a higher percentage will have guns of various sorts, usually used for pest control and game shooting but that can be equally effective for defence when needed. To take advantage of those country mindsets, however, you must have neighbours within a reasonable distance and if you were not born and brought up there you must establish good relationships, and/or have a large group that can look after itself in most circumstances.

Before, or instead of an attack, what you will face are people at your gate or door asking for help. Sometimes it might be a surly looking bunch that are easy to ignore or turn away, at others it will be people with children or other dependents asking for something as simple as a drink of water. As part of your practical and psychological prepping you must consider these situations and decide in advance how you will respond to them. If you refuse to answer or turn down their requests, some refugees will accept it and move on, some will try to steal from you, others will vandalise your property and a minority will become aggressive.

Neighbours

The response of your neighbours is largely going to be decided by your relationship with them but if they become desperate even people that are usually friendly and helpful can behave in ways you never thought possible. Fellow soldiers who will guard your back and if necessary take a bullet while defending you will at other times steal the chocolate from your ration pack and justify it by saying you should take better care of your stuff. People are weird and often unpredictable.

Unless you have developed a Prepping relationship with your neighbours and work together as a team, maintain OpSec with regards to them and even then you don't necessarily have to tell them everything. Need to Know is as good a security policy for Prepper groups as it is for the armed forces or security organisations.

How you respond to a neighbour who is trying to steal your cabbages is up to you. You might confront and shame them by telling them that if they were that desperate they only had to ask, or you might shoot them on the spot; it depends on how you feel about them, how severe your situation is, and the potential wider consequences of what you do or don't do.

Strategy and Tactics

Your strategy is your overall plan and principles. Tactics are the measures you take to achieve that plan. Your strategy in this regard might be to survive by denying any outsiders unacceptable access to your people or preps. Your tactics will involve all the passive and active defensive measures that you take. What these consist of will depend on the cause and effects of the situation that has you Bugging In.

However else you organise and manage yourselves in relation to Preparedness activities, active defence demands that you have a commander. That commander must be prepared and ready to co-ordinate all activity and other people must respond immediately. Hesitation and confusion in defence will lead to your defeat. If you want to go back to committee management and group hugs afterwards then fine, but when you are fighting you must have a leader. Choose him or her carefully, test and if necessary replace them in time of peace, but when under attack be ready to obey.

The basic principles of defence are summed up by the acronym DAMROD which stands for: Depth; All round defence; Mutual support; Reserve; Offensive action; Deception

Depth

The basis of this principle is that the further away you keep an enemy the less harm they will do to your core resources. How far away you need to keep them depends on the resources they have available. In your case it might extend to your village/area, street, garden, or house. As a minimum it should cover the latter two. Each level of depth should reduce the motivation or ability of the enemy to advance any further in your direction.

I have covered some of the tactics in the section on passive defence, with suggestions for fences, barriers, gates, reinforced windows, etc. For after the Event happens there are more ideas for that and further out later in this section when we consider deception.

It is taking Bugging In to its extremes but if there has been a complete loss of law and order then measures for depth could include layers of barriers, booby traps, and defenders at various distances from your centre.

All round defence

Remember, 'Your security is only as good as its weakest point'? I emphasised that all your doors and windows should be as strong as those at the front of the house and also that fences and gates at the rear should provide at least as much security as those facing the road. Your ability to see what is going on all around you is also as important, as is remembering that a basic tactic of attackers is to divert your attention to one direction while they make their main assault from another.

If you have only one gun or golf club in the house then it can only be pointing in one direction at a time but you must do what you can with what you have got or can improvise to cover all likely approaches and make a logical assessment of what you have heard or seen and whether it is a ruse.

If you are locked down and/or suspect an attack do NOT open your door for anyone. If someone is outside trying to steal from the garden or an outbuilding 'dissuade' them from inside. If it is someone you recognise, remember that they could be a pawn for other people hiding nearby. You only have to read the papers or watch the television news to know that there are people in the UK who are as bad as any of those I have encountered in other parts of the world; desperate times and the reduced presence of police will only embolden them.

Mutual Support

Mutual support is based on one fighting position being able to give help to another when needed. You are not going to have unlimited resources and this might come down to the few people present retreating to one final refuge where they can all support one another, even if that means leaving the rest of the property open to the intruders. If you can cover more positions then good communications between them are important, whether you do that by intercom, radio, whistles or shouts.

Reserve

The reserve is related to both mutual support and offensive action but is really only for large groups. The concept is that you deploy people in positions where they can give all round observation and warning if not defence and then if an attack comes from any direction, all or part of the reserve can respond as required to act as reinforcements. Also if you have enough people, a reserve can be used to mount a counter attack without weakening the standing defences.

Offensive action

To the military this equates to, 'taking the fight to the enemy', part of the concept that 'the best defence is a good offence'. Well, I'm going to assume neither that you are soldiers nor that you are trained or equipped like them. If you are, then you don't need my advice on this subject. For those of you that aren't, a few words might be in order.

In any Bugging In situation, where you do not have access to outside facilities or supplies and your life and that of members of your family depends on the stores which you have gathered, anyone who tries to take those stores from you is trying to kill you as surely as if they were trying to take the blood from your veins or the air from your lungs.

If someone is trying to kill you then you have the right to defend yourself with whatever force is required to stop their attack, including if necessary lethal force.

Weapons have developed in the way they have, from a club to a spear, to a bow and arrow, to a crossbow, to a flintlock, and finally to modern firearms because each development gives the user a longer reach and more accuracy, which allows you to strike your attacker while they are too far away to strike you.

I am not going to get into the relative merits of the AR15 versus the AK74 nor semi-auto pistols versus revolvers because it is irrelevant to most people in the UK who will read this book. All I will say is that a weapon that gives you parity with an attacker who also has one, or an advantage over an attacker who doesn't have one, is a major defensive improvement over a baseball bat or a broom handle with a kitchen knife tied on the end.

If you do not have need for a gun other than for personal defence you will not get a licence to possess one. If you have one regularly used for target shooting, pest control or game then you might want to investigate appropriate ammunition for defensive purposes and include a couple of boxes in your stocks. Do NOT under any circumstances try to obtain a firearm or ammunition illegally; the potential penalties are simply not worth the advantage in a situation that might not ever arise.

If you do not have good reason to apply for a firearms or shotgun certificate and don't want to take up a hobby that would give you that reason, then consider taking up one that will develop your skill with older weapons. In the UK the ownership of crossbows and longbows is only restricted to adults, you do not need any sort of licence to buy, posses or use them. Their use is restricted to target shooting i.e. it is not now legal to use them in the pursuit of live prey whether it is classed as game or a pest species and as with any weapon you need good reason for having them in public e.g. travelling to and from a club, while engaged in target shooting or historical displays, etc. You can also use them in your own garden or home provided that you do not endanger anyone else while doing so.

The principle is, if you do not have a weapon, then work your way back through history and equip yourself with the most modern that is available to you, whether that is an effective commercial model or one you have to make yourself. A broom handle certainly becomes an offensive weapon if you tie a kitchen knife to it but it has a longer reach than a knife or a club and if that is what your attacker has then it gives you an advantage, but not as much as a crossbow would. Whether it is by learning a martial art, or having a weapon and learning to use it effectively, or having the most people with the greatest determination or the best weapons, the outcome of defence is decided by who has the most advantage in one way or another.

Determination can sometimes overcome skills, technology or numbers, but having determination and a big gun can go a long way to reducing the odds. So however can tactics. From jungles to castles and alleyways in cities, trapping an enemy where they have limited room for manoeuvre and then hitting them by surprise has always given defenders a big advantage. If you allow attackers to crowd into a narrow passageway that is blocked by a barrier, from beyond which you can stab them with spears, squirt them with bleach, or shoot them, you can reduce their numbers and capability and destroy their confidence and resolve but you must follow that up by driving them away before they can recover and regroup.

I don't want to get into some gung-ho fantasy here. I have fought enough wars and other engagements to want never to have to do it again. At the time it can provide a tremendous adrenalin rush but the physical, psychological and emotional results can be and often are horrendous, whether you win or lose. Nevertheless, we are looking at the defence of your life. That is why you prep. Mental and physical prep for defence against violent attack is a part of Prepping. Keep it legal before anything happens and remember that you might have to justify your actions if it does, but do not neglect it.

Deception

Part of deception involves concealment, something that you are doing by your maintenance of OpSec, concealing piles of fuel and rubbish, minimising noise, smoke, and smells, etc. but it can also include specific measures such as putting up signs that warn of a biological hazard or other form of contamination in your house. If troops are checking houses for bodies and resources and marking them as they go, identify the symbols that would show your house to be of no interest or use and then put that mark on your door.

A few dead animals scattered around, bags of rotting rubbish, and human-shaped, fly-infested, sheet-wrapped packages at the roadside could also provide a disincentive to people who might otherwise investigate the area more closely.

If you can get out into your local area, you might block off approach roads with an apparent accident using a lorry with its front against a tree and a punctured wheel in a ditch, or a barrier and sign warning of disease, flood, fallen trees or road works, but do it where travellers have an alternative route so that it is easier for them to go that way than investigate a route that might be impassable. Or instead of/in addition to warning them you can tempt them by putting up a pointer to a relief centre 5 miles down the other road; if they find nothing they will probably assume they have either missed it or it was there but has gone; either way they are unlikely to waste the fuel or shoe leather they've used to get there by coming back to investigate a road that might be blocked anyway.

Active defence isn't an easy subject. Preparation for it is fraught with problems and the more so because you can never be sure exactly what the situation is going to be at the time. I can only offer advice based on my own experiences and even in those there have always been differences. Beyond this chapter, if you want to learn more I suggest you read up on accounts from battles and engagements in various wars or other strife in situations nearest to your own and then try to mentally compare them to your location and people. If you decide that the only realistic option for you would be to retreat rather than fight, then I refer you to my book, Bugging Out.

If it comes to it, may all that is good be with you and care for you.

Chemical Biological Radiological (CBR) protection and procedures

Many of these measures are complimentary with and additional to the passive defence measures against fire and intruders and with those of health and medical care, but there are also some that are specific to these particular threats.

The best known industrial disaster involving chemicals has to be the 1984 Bhopal tragedy in India. The release of Methyl Isocyanate gas and other chemicals from the Union Carbide pesticide plant caused over 2200 immediate deaths and, depending on whose figures you accept, between 3787 and 8000 deaths in total plus 558,125 temporary and permanently disabling injuries. Modern industrial processes are far safer in all countries than those that were in place during that disaster but there are still a lot of dangerous chemicals being produced, transported and used and always the chance of another major incident.

Chemical attacks by terrorists have been far fewer in number. The worst were undoubtedly the Sarin nerve agent attacks by Aum Shinrikyo on the Tokyo underground system in 1995, which killed 13 people and severely injured 50 others, with up to a thousand suffering temporary effects. Under normal circumstances a chemical attack requires quite a sustained artillery bombardment or other release of large quantities of gas. The area affected is usually limited but within that zone the effects are devastating.

I remember when I completed the NBC Defence instructors' course at Winterbourne Gunner we were visited by a representative from the research establishment at Porton Down. He was asking for volunteers to undergo testing at PD, during which you would be exposed to limited amounts of various agents in order for the scientists to observe and record the effects. After weeks of study on the horrendous injuries these agents can cause and how to avoid and deal with them, the reaction from the whole course was an initial stunned silence followed by deafening laughter. The man from the ministry was quite taken aback and offended that we wouldn't trust ourselves into their hands but considering what we had seen and learnt he really shouldn't have been surprised at all; chemical warfare agents are nasty stuff!

There are basically two types of delivery, liquid and gas. Liquid can kill or injure through absorption if it gets on your skin or in your eyes or is ingested, or through inhalation as it vaporises. Gas usually kills through inhalation but can also be absorbed. The three main classes are the nerve agents, blood agents, and blister agents. Nerve agents are killers though they can leave you alive but with permanent nerve injury. Blood agents affect the ability of the blood to absorb or transmit oxygen and can kill or cause brain damage. Blister agents are mainly used as a damaging agent and cause exactly the sort of effects the name implies but do kill if they are inhaled and damage the lungs. Blister gas was the type of agent responsible for the terrible injuries and blindness caused to so many soldiers during the First World War.

To be protected from the contact hazards of liquid agents you need to be wearing an impermeable suit such as the charcoal lined NBC suits issued to the armed forces, or you need to be under cover so it doesn't get on your skin. Protection from inhaling gases requires either a respirator with a chemical filter or a closed breathing system with oxygen tanks.

There are technical monitors and simple colour reactive papers that will detect various types of agent, and decontamination powders to remove them from your skin or equipment, or medicines for the immediate treatment of the blood and nerve agents. However, unlike soldiers on the battlefield, it is doubtful we will be in a situation where we have notice of any attack with a chemical agent so unfortunately the chances of you being able to detect them or be in a position to get suited and masked up to avoid being affected are remote at best.

The forces' training slogan for masking drill is 'Be in time, mask in nine.' That means that from the time an attack starts or warning is received, you have 9 seconds to get your mask on and hood back up if you are to avoid becoming a casualty. Having done that you then take cover and begin immediate decontamination procedures. And that assumes you are already in NBC kit, with your respirator and other gear immediately available, not when they are in a box in the attic with the filters still in their foil wrappers.

Biological agents can be even worse, though so far the only known deliberate attacks in modern times have involved Anthrax spores being sent through the post in the US. I say in modern times because biological warfare is as old as Mongol hordes catapulting decaying animals and infected human bodies over the walls of places under siege, or both British and US officials giving disease infected blankets to Native Americans during the 17 and 1800s. Various diseases were also used by the Japanese against Chinese troops and civilians during the 1937-1945 Sino-Japanese war.

More worrying is the potential for a pandemic on the scale of the 1918 Spanish Flu outbreak, which is believed to have infected a third of the world's population and killed between 50 and 100 million people worldwide. Another threat is a possible agricultural biological attack by terrorists. This would be used to cause damage to supplies of food staples, causing starvation. A secondary effect would be financial damage to industry and individuals due to soaring prices, which might bring further starvation.

The procedures I outline in the Health and Medical Care chapter should provide some protection against the direct effects of these diseases and your food storage preps would give you a buffer against the agricultural attacks but we will also consider some other measures here. You can get more information on the diseases that might be involved and their symptoms and treatment in the section by Chris Breen in the Ludlow Survivors Group book, Streetcraft, much of which I wrote, which is available in print from Lulu and for Kindle from Amazon.

Nasty as these agents are, there are some measures you can take to protect yourself if you Bug In. Firstly, if you receive warning of a biological threat while away from home, get there as quickly as you can by a method that keeps you away from other people as much as possible. If you are affected by a chemical agent don't worry about how to get home, you won't make it that far. What you need is a hazmat team and an ambulance!

When you arrive home, remove all your outer clothing at the door and bag them. If possible just leave them outside but if you have to take them in then seal the bag and deal with them later. If possible, ignore the cold and the fascinated stares of your neighbours and thoroughly hose yourself down and shower with soap or antibacterial washing up liquid and then rinse off before entering the building.

Once indoors immediately take a thorough hot shower and wash your hair again while somebody else dons a protective mask and gloves, turns off all fans and ventilators and then ensures all openings such as windows, doors, letter box, etc. are sealed. Where an opening can be locked that should be done. You can use duct tape to seal around any edges that aren't draught proof and polythene sheeting to cover any larger openings such as cat flaps.

If the cat comes home later you have two choices, leave it outside or don protective clothing, then go outside, catch it and thoroughly bathe it in disinfectant solution until you are sure it is decontaminated before you carry it in; either way it isn't going to like you much for a while.

As soon as possible begin a thorough cleaning and disinfection of the home, starting around the door. If you are on your own, shower first then put on protective gear before you start the cleaning. Anyone involved in cleaning can then have another shower. Hopefully, this early in the situation both water and electricity will be unaffected.

If anyone is at home and likely to be uninfected then they should be fully protected before anyone else is allowed in and should stay that way as much as possible. If most are at home and only one or two arrive later consider putting them in isolation or quarantine.

If clothes were admitted in a sealed bag, a protected person should empty them from the bag into the washing machine, without touching them, add detergent and antiseptic solution and then wash them on the highest heat setting available. If they aren't wearable afterwards, so be it!

After that, Bug In and stay safe.

Communications

Mains items: Telephone, Radios, Computers, Modem, Back up drive, Printer, Mobile phone chargers, label printer

When you talk to people who have been in Bug In situations for an extended period, or even to Preppers who have tried it for a week, one of the factors that comes across strongly is the sense of isolation.

Most of us live in a highly interconnected world and with the popularisation of the Internet it has become even more so. Web sites, newsgroups, discussion forums, chat rooms, email, Twitter, Facebook and the rest, plus the advent of mobiles phones for talk and text put us in contact with other people almost all the time we are awake. Many people thought the introduction of the public telephone was the beginning of a new world but the communications revolution has taken off in ways those early pioneers could never have imagined.

I must admit that I enjoy times when I am on my own, away from the computer and with my mobile phone switched off. My wife prefers me to keep the phone switched on so that she can call to make sure I am OK if I haven't been in contact for a while. Unfortunately having it ring, or even buzz, when you are in the final stages of a long stalk that would put rabbit or venison on the dinner table is not conducive to good marital relations, so there are times when it is on and times when it isn't!

But it isn't surprising that many people, and especially younger ones who have never known life any other way, miss having contact with others when systems fail or are otherwise denied to them. If non-personal information media, such as radio, TV, and newspaper deliveries are also down then the frustration and boredom can quickly grow to nervousness, fear and paranoia. If the cause is related to a genuine emergency, the lack of information can be especially worrying.

There are three things you can do to counter this situation:

1. Develop alternative information and communication systems
2. Keep people busy with other things
3. Develop familiarity with isolation at times when there is no external danger. You can stop the session if someone becomes genuinely distressed and resume later; building tolerance gradually.

If your local power goes off that doesn't mean that it is off everywhere, of course. If you have alternative power systems for your television, or batteries or a dynamo for your radio, and power is still available to any local transmitters or repeaters, then you should be able to get a signal from somewhere even if it is not from the station you prefer. If you are on cable TV then you might need to switch to a terrestrial aerial but if you pay for satellite download then you will probably be OK, depending on the cause of the power loss.

You should have at least one battery or dynamo powered radio that will pick up MW, FM and SW channels and that has manual tuning, so that you can accept transmission on frequencies that a scanner might skip over as too low powered but that you find comprehensible. Try local and community channels as well as national ones; they might have access to alternative power even if they can only be heard over a limited distance. At the other end of the scale, you might receive a foreign station and if you have the relevant language skills might even understand what they say.

If your telephone is a cordless model, or has an answering machine and other features, it might rely on mains power. If so, on one socket or in your stores, you should have a basic handset that plugs directly into the telephone line and doesn't require any other power. Often the telephone system will be operational despite the power being off.

Otherwise, if you are willing to leave your property albeit only at a time when you are unlikely to meet anyone else, it would be worth trying a public phone. Don't forget to carefully clean the door handle, phone and any other parts you touch if necessary. You could also post letters to relatives or friends, just in case any mail service is still running.

Whether a mobile phone service will still be available depends on the extent of the outage and the back up arrangements at your local masts. Sometimes civilian services are closed down during an emergency if the channels are required for other use or the authorities fear they could be misused, and power backups are rarely for more than 24 hours.

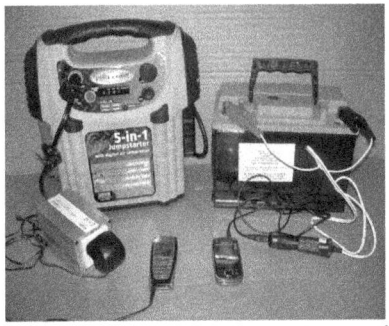

In case the service is still up, ensure you have off-grid charging arrangements for your phone, even if that is from the car, or an adapter or inverter connected to a 12v battery, or one of the small emergency chargers with a dynamo or battery system. If you have one of the more recent models of phone you might get an Internet or text connection although you can't get one to another telephone number.

Getting access to the Internet through your computer could be limited by any of the factors above but even if you normally use a wireless connection to a cable modem, your computer might still have the option for a plug in connection to the telephone line, or an infrared or wireless connection via your mobile phone or if, like us, you are often away from home you might have a USB mobile broadband dongle. That relies on a working mobile phone provider and possibly on the same masts as your phone so we use 3 for our dongle and Vodafone for the mobile to increase the chances of a connection to one or the other. In the UK the best data connection by far is undoubtedly provided by 3 but I'm not enough of a phone geek to discuss the relative merits of phone services.

If you access the Internet through your satellite provider you might or might not have more luck than through a totally terrestrial system, it depends on the situation wherever the gateways and network operations center that relay the Internet signal to and from the satellite are located and how they are affected.

To make best use of restricted battery power and recharging facilities, you might want to have a netbook, tablet or other low draw device as one of your computers, should you have the luxury of more than one. If you are buying one, do consider the various communication connections it offers as well as its other features. For the chance that you get a brief restoration of power, have emails to family and friends written and in your outbox ready to go automatically. They might get through at some time and offer comfort to those who receive them. For when you can get an Internet connection but not a phone line, install Skype as an alternative.

Radio - CB

If none of these more normal services are available then there is the possibility of using Radio. For short to medium ranges you could use either CB or maritime VHF. The popularity of CB has been badly affected for people on the move by the cheapness, easy availability and reliability of mobile phones and for those at home it has been replaced by the internet. It still has some fans, however, especially among truckers and farmers.

The advantage for Preppers is that CB does not rely on any outside facilities; you don't need mains power and there is no network. The main disadvantages are that your range is restricted to a maximum of about 30 miles if you have a base station, a good antenna and a high, open site – less if you are using a handheld or vehicle mounted system or are among buildings or hills – and because of the falling number of users you might actually never find anybody online with whom to talk.

Although it would certainly be worth scanning through the frequencies in search of anyone with information, these sets are of most use for communication between Preppers who are either part of a network or operating from a home base but talking with a group who have had to go outside the property. Sets cost £60 upwards including a decent antenna and no licence is required.

Maritime band

Under normal circumstances the marine band radios can only be used at sea and using them requires a licence which costs around one hundred pounds. For that reason many boat owners have the radio but not the licence and keep them only for transmitting in an emergency, though they can of course listen in at any time. The emergency channel, which is monitored by the coast guard, is channel 16. The advantage of these radios over CB is that with a good set and aerial you can get up to 60 miles range. Many boat owners have them, even on inland waterways, so you might get to exchange information with someone who is Bugging In or Bugging Out on their boat. Cost is £60 upwards for hand-held sets and £100 up for base stations.

HF/SW/Ham (amateur) radio

For long range two-way communication the only practical option is Short Wave i.e. 'Ham' radio. To transmit you do require a licence and you do have to pass an exam to get that licence. A short course of instruction or a few hours of reading will give you the information you need to get started and from there it is remarkably easy to develop the knowledge you need to pass the Foundation exam.

You will then be able to apply for a licence and a callsign, although at Foundation level there will be some restrictions including a limit on the power at which you can transmit. That will not prevent you from communicating world-wide. If you become keen, further study and exams will give you access to higher classes of licence and fewer restrictions.

Depending on where you live, the main obstacle you might face is finding a club or other venue where you can get the training and take the exam.

However, although a training course or other instruction from a qualified callsign would be invaluable in selecting the most suitable equipment and a much faster way of developing the knowledge required, you don't need the licence before you buy the gear, nor to operate a receiver and it need not be expensive, especially if you buy second hand. That will give you the chance to learn how to set up and use the radio and by listening in you will become familiar with the culture and terminology used by the callsigns as they connect with others throughout the UK and beyond. Then you can go on to get a licence when a course and exam becomes available.

If you are only interested in SW for use after an Event then a licence and authorised callsign might not be absolutely necessary but as with anything, the more you use the radio and try various things the more competent you will become and the more use to you it is likely to be. The only way to really know that you are getting it right is to establish a connection and talk with another callsign.

One of the early things you will learn is that which transmitter/receiver (Tx/Rx) you buy will not have nearly as much impact on your success in contacting other users as will your antenna. There are several types and formats ranging from a simple omni-directional dipole to a fancy directional Yagi. In the forces we were even taught how to improvise by calculating the length of antenna we needed to match the frequency we wanted to use and then isolate a stretch of wire fencing to act as the antenna.

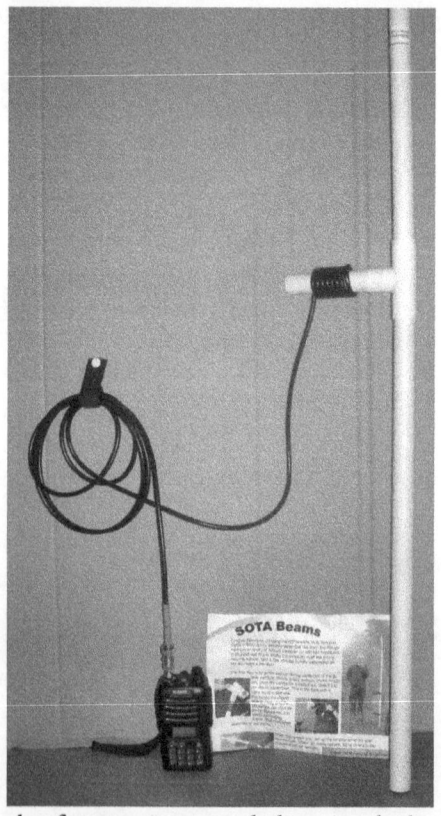

The type and length of antenna you use will – in the main, there are other factors – determine the distance over which you can transmit or receive and the quality of the signal, so it is a vital part of your equipment. For example, you can use a cheap (£30+) handheld radio and by use of an adapter connect it to a better antenna to give you both portability and range of operation.

The Internet has undoubtedly dethroned Ham radio as the only affordable way of talking with strangers world wide but despite that, rather than decreasing as you might expect, the number of callsigns has increased by around 60% over the past 30 years. There are many resources for further information but the best starting point is the Radio Society of Great Britain http://www.rsgb.org/ RSGB can provide books, guidance, contacts for equipment, and much more.

Short range communication

Whether it is TV, radio, mail, telephone, internet or longer range radio, the purpose of the systems I have outlined so far is principally to maintain contact and exchange information with people outside your Bug In group. However, there are times when communication within the group but beyond normal talking distance is also required. That might be for defence or safety purposes and the bigger your Bug In location the more useful it becomes.

An intercom system can be used to talk to people outside the home while you are inside or to people in differing parts of the house or outbuildings. These systems sometimes need their own wiring but increasingly work by using the mains circuits or a wireless network. For some purposes you could use a two way baby alarm.

Alternatively, to maintain connectivity while not restricting movement, you could opt for short range radios based on the Personal Management Radio (PMR) 446 system. These are the walkie talkies often available from supermarkets for a few pounds per pair, though you can pay much more.

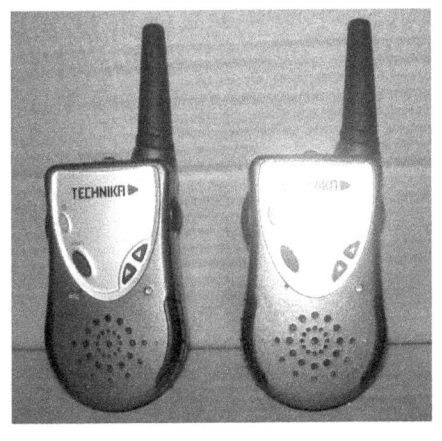

The maximum range of these sets is a few kilometres but for short range they are ideal. They are light and cheap and models are available that are powered by replaceable AA batteries rather than a mains charger. The short range

242

makes them relatively secure even though they have a limited number of frequencies. Very handy for while people are around the house or garden.

If you want or need something less technical then you can devise your own system of shouts, whistle blasts, bells, light flashes or, more covertly, hand signals. When Bugging In it isn't likely that you will need to make use of flags, heliographs (signal mirrors), smoke, drums or bugles, or carrier pigeons but for longer ranges they are all proven methods from the past!

Whatever system you choose, maintaining reliable short range and if at all possible long range communications is an essential part of Preparedness. Be aware of the options available to you and set up whatever arrangements you believe are relevant for you and your family/group. When you need them, you will always be glad that you did!

Family/Group meetings

An aspect of communication you really must not neglect is talk among members of the family or group. People are going to be tense, frightened, angry, confused, worrying about the fate of people they can't contact, and a gamut of other emotions. Some will want to withdraw, some will want to talk, but all will benefit from having time together and it is an essential part of the bonding and team building that will be so important to the survival of you all.

I'm not a psychotherapist or a social worker but my military and Red Cross service did include studying and applying skills in negotiation, intervention, mediation, anger management, and psychological responses to disaster, so maybe I can pass on some of what I learnt.

Group meetings are also times for learning about the skills and interests of group members, for discussion and planning of tasks, for finding out what people are doing, if they need help and who can provide it, for resolving disputes and behavioural issues, and for relaxing and having fun. We will look at that latter function in more detail in the next chapter, Education and Entertainment.

Perhaps the most important 'technique' applied to these meetings is allowing and encouraging people to talk. You want them to talk about their feelings and concerns, to help them and others understand the causes of those feelings and concerns, and to identify ways of overcoming them or redirecting them into productive rather than destructive modes of thought and response.

Some group members won't want to talk about their feelings, only about 'practical' issues, but once you have them talking about something they care about you can sometimes glean information about the deeper motivation behind those concerns and suggestions of how they want to deal with them. After getting involved in that discussion they might also relax and open up about additional topics.

For example someone who wants to discuss how to raise plants indoors may express frustration or anger about the lack of space and light available and their failure to get things to grow, but in the process reveal – whether they realise it or not – that they are really being affected by claustrophobia or general feelings of inadequacy. Some gentle and oblique probing might then help you to formulate ways to resolve or lessen both the stated and background issues.

In many cases people within the group will want to offer advice, not all of it sound or appropriate for the person expressing their concern, but a more constructive approach is to use open questions to help the speaker develop their own solutions. When the reasons for perceptions and feelings are understood, alternative ways to look at and direct them are often accepted or welcomed. Sometimes, of course, simply aiding the person to resolve what they say are their concerns will help too, by helping them to realise that people do understand their concerns, problems can be overcome, and support is at hand if and when they need it.

These discussions might also indicate a need to arrange for someone to work with another group member who will be empathetic and constructive in their approach to the one who is suffering.

When you are tackling conflicts, allowing each individual to express their side of the argument can be therapeutic but you should ensure that others present listen to both viewpoints and only express moderated suggestions for resolving the issue, rather than taking sides. That is easier said than done at times but it is essential if you are to bond the group rather than split it and if there is that possibility you should consider carefully whether the conflict should be discussed in public or in private, with only the opposing parties and a mediator present. Similarly, sometimes unacceptable behaviour is best dealt with in public, 'for the encouragement of others' and at others in private, depending on the nature of both the offender and the offence.

Planning practical tasks and finding ways of dealing with the problems involved is usually so much easier than dealing with these troublesome human traits of feelings and emotions but it will be an unavoidable part of Bugging In.

Education and Entertainment

Mains items: TV, Cable TV box, Radios, Games machine, Computers,

If an emergency arises suddenly then boredom is not going to be a problem when you first Bug In. Cleaning, setting up security, recovering stores, adapting the house to meet the situation and attending to all the other tasks covered in this book will keep you well occupied. After the equipment lists you will find a checklist of the tasks that you might need to complete before, as, or after you Bug In depending on the Event and the situation it is presenting.

Immediately afterwards you will undoubtedly spend a lot of time watching the television or listening to the radio to keep track of how the situation is developing but after all the immediate tasks are completed and you have time to take a deep breath, how do you keep people occupied and motivated?

While you have mains power, TV, radio, Internet and other utilities available make full use of them for recharging batteries, downloading music, films, and books, and getting any other jobs done that you can. You might be lucky and retain those facilities throughout the emergency or they might be lost without warning. If you do lose them be ready to take advantage of any resumption for as long as it lasts.

If you have children or other students in the group their studies should continue as much as possible inline with their normal itinerary. If you can put those studies into context with your current circumstances it will both emphasise the importance of their past learning and use what has been learnt to inform the development of knowledge and skills relevant to your survival. If the situation becomes prolonged the slant of their learning will inevitably change, with the practical, survival-related aspects of subjects assuming priority over the academic.

In a Preppers online discussion forum someone posed the question, 'In preparing our children for life After The S*** Hits The Fan (ATSHTF) what should we teach them?' This was my response:

Teach them to think for themselves, not to reject what they are told to but to question and test it.
Teach them to value and enjoy learning, to try new things.
Teach them to strive for success, to never fear failure but to learn from it.
Teach them to value and enjoy meeting new people, but never to take them at face value.
Teach them to read with an open mind.
Teach them that strength comes not from others but from inside themselves.

Teach them that strength is not following the trend but leading the trend. Teach them to recognise danger but face it with courage; to understand that fear is a creation of the mind, that it gives warning that should be heeded but can be overcome and should never in itself prevent them from doing something they need and want to do.
Teach them WHY they should learn old and new ways, and then do not teach them but help them to learn what they come to realise they must know.
Teach them that they are valuable, that they are the future, and that that future will be what they make it.
Teach them that life is good, that it should be treasured and fought for, and never surrendered, nor taken, lightly.
Teach them that as good, as valuable, as treasured as it is, sometimes it is right that life is surrendered for the good, and the love, of others, and that if the time comes they should do it as ONLY the last resort but then without fear, and teach them to honour those before them who have done likewise for them

You might think that is rather corny or 'new age' but I stand by the concepts it includes, and no, I never did put it to music. Maybe I could have made the lines rhyme and got Whitney to sing it!

Nevertheless, it won't only be people who regarded themselves as students who will be learning or developing their skills. There should be no task that has to be done, no area of knowledge that is needed for survival that isn't the domain of at least two members of the group. If you have one expert in any subject they should have at least one apprentice and preferably two. If there are any areas of expertise that you don't have covered, somebody who is interested should make it their own and then later share that knowledge with others.

A part of that knowledge, and a good deal of relaxation and entertainment as well, will come from reading, particularly if you are on off-grid power sources. A substantial and varied library of both reference books and novels for all ages represented in your group should form a valuable part of your preps. Although paper is more durable, you can build a huge library in very little space and at little cost from online resources. It will only be available if you have power to at least the battery of a laptop computer or e-reader but it is a way to have more information on hand than you could perhaps ever afford or have room for in the form of printed books.

Other than basic and advanced survival skills, one of the areas in which you might want to do some reading and then apply what you have learnt is that of traditional crafts. You might not need these unless the situation becomes very long term indeed, but many Preppers find them interesting and enjoyable activities regardless of their practical applications. Spinning and weaving, knitting, tanning and dyeing, leatherwork, pottery, wood carving, blacksmithing, making rush lights and candles, and newer crafts such as making greetings cards, can provide recreation and as we will consider in the next chapter possible sources of trade as well.

Time will certainly be spent scanning the commercial, CB and SW channels in search of news, information and contacts. If you make contacts that can be maintained, you might be able to set up scheduled discussions so that the operator and maybe the whole group have something to look forward to on a regular basis.

To most people a routine is reassuring, although children might whinge about it. Having regular times for work or study, meals, leisure and rest – possibly adapted to include the need for safety and security duties – will give some sense of normality and reduce the likelihood of people taking to their bed and sinking into depression. Anyone who seems to be succumbing to that temptation should be pulled out of it both physically and mentally if necessary.

During the leisure time there might sometimes be an opportunity for those who like it to play on consoles but activities where people within the group interact are more constructive. This might include board games, cards, indoor bowls or soft-air shooting games, family games like charades, a 'your town' version of Mornington Crescent, Just a Minute, story telling ('one-liner' where one person starts a story or poem and then the next takes it over can be hilarious), or many more. The Victorians were great creators and players of parlour games so check out your bookshop or library for details of their games. Singing and playing musical instruments will appeal to the talented and creating instruments from household objects or people writing their own songs can add an extra dimension and creative outlets. The great thing about these activities is that they rarely require any electricity and often no equipment of any kind or only a pencil and a sheet of paper.

One way and another, between work, study, communication and interactive games, you should be able to find enough to take people's minds off the trauma and fears for at least some of the time. They might not prevent all the nightmares but together with group or individual discussions they can give people who suffer from them something else to think about and that can be a great help.

Finances

Mains items: Computers, Sewing machine

Although writers and some Preppers like to fantasize over and discuss the causes, effects, and after-life of an apocalypse, in reality few disasters throughout history have resulted in a total loss of society and a requirement to completely start from scratch. While it is important that we prepare for the long-term consequences of some Events that could cause major disruptions to our lifestyle, your financial responsibilities will remain for some time after you Bug In and will probably never go away.

If the reason for you Bugging In is temporary e.g. severe weather and power failure, transport strikes, or riots on the streets, or even rather longer such as a pandemic or financial collapse, your life might be changed but the computers in the banks and tax offices will keep ticking along.

I am writing this chapter in April 2013 and one of the recent big news stories has been the financial collapse of the Greek section of Cyprus. Cyprus is a member or the EU and uses the Euro. The government debt and financial instability of the banks resulted in an application for a loan from the International Monetary Fund and Central European Bank. An agreement was reached but with some devastating consequences and huge disruption for residents and visitors on the island.

To help finance the debt and prevent the collapse of the banks, the Cypriot government demanded that depositors with over €100,000 (£85,000) in the Bank of Cyprus forfeit between 40% and 60% of their savings. Those in the smaller Laiki bank could lose 100%. Any money under £85,000 is protected, though in the original proposal the EU wanted 6.7% from bank customers in that bracket and a lower percentage from the higher levels. Despite trying to reassure people in other countries that this is a deal specific to Cyprus, it has later emerged that in fact the IMF, CEB, and EU finance committees consider it a sound concept for future loan agreements.

Several southern European states, Ireland, and not so long ago Iceland have severe fiscal troubles and few of the countries of Europe or elsewhere are unaffected by the current world financial difficulties caused by fiat money, uncontrolled printing of bank notes, and massive international debt. Keeping your money in the bank, and the fate of peoples' money savings in general, are no longer the safe option they were once considered to be. Considering other options therefore seems only sensible.

One of the first things to happen in Cyprus, and a reflection of previous situations elsewhere, was an extended 'bank holiday' during which the banks were closed, all electronic transfers frozen, and withdrawals from cash machines first restricted, then stopped, then eventually reopened but again with restrictions. Financial controls on withdrawals and both internal and international transfers were also imposed.

An almost immediate result was that shops and other retail outlets, including those selling basic groceries, medicines and household goods, stopped taking credit or debit card payments, either because their machines wouldn't work or they no longer trusted them, and would take payment in cash only. Unfortunately many people then found that they could not get cash, either because they didn't have a debit or credit card or even if they did the cash machines were closed. Both import and export were affected, shortages of many goods became rife and shops, cafes and bars closed due to lack of customers. Before too long, people were running out of food and other basics and there were demonstrations and riots.

Because those who did manage to find a machine that was working tended to get notes of relatively large value, shops that did have goods to sell found that they were unable to give change because the banks were shut so they were running out of both small denomination notes and coins. Sometimes they rounded prices up or down, sometimes people could buy a selection of items to the value of a note they had, but customers who only wanted a bottle of milk or a few vegetables were stuck. Businesses that usually work on small amounts, such as public transport, newspaper sellers, and the like were badly affected for the same reason.

Although things are now more stable in Cyprus and daily life has resumed some normality, some people have lost their life savings, others have had debts foreclosed and lost their home, up to 10,000 businesses of varying size have closed or are expected to do so, with a consequent loss of jobs and income for their workers, and many who are retired have lost their pensions. The government is laying-off employees, services will be reduced or delayed and various utilities will become less reliable. People will continue to suffer for years to come.

While many UK Preppers find it difficult to relate to the misery of people in Syria, Somalia, even Greece and Spain, the popularity of Cyprus as a holiday destination, our military presence there, and the large number of British Ex-pats who live on the Island, plus the way people's savings have been stolen, makes the happenings in Cyprus strike home. It has served as an excellent reminder of the various potential outcomes of all sorts of major crises and provides both a sound affirmation of the measures recommended in earlier chapters and very real and contemporary basis for the subjects and suggestions I will cover in this one.

Hopefully you will have read the earlier chapters, given great thought to the information provided and suggestions proposed, and then begun or continued to stock up with the resources you will need in an emergency. Those preps will give you a buffer against the fiscal consequences of either a financial or other national or international crisis because you won't be short of food or water or fuel or medicines and will therefore be unaffected if the banks are shut or shops have no change.

For convenience in many situations, however, a stash of cash on hand, mainly in small denomination notes and coins will be useful. If you use local shops and tradesmen regularly, continue to do so for small quantities of supplies and services during hard times and are ready to pay in cash with low value notes and the right change – counted out carefully to show you are watching every penny - when others are unable to do so, you will be recognised as a valuable customer without appearing to be either cash rich or able to do without the things they sell. That gets noticed and can help build useful relationships while supporting your OpSec measures.

For the longer term and larger amounts, you need to keep sufficient money in the bank to pay your basic outgoings. If you can build that to cover the important bills usually paid by direct Debit or Standing Order (but not regular shopping which can be paid for with cash) for 3 months you have a sound hedge against many personal or wider emergencies. That will reduce stress by giving you time to make other arrangements if necessary. Keep the money in a savings account, just in case they ever resume interest payments, but easily available if needed. Beyond that banks are no longer the place of safety they were originally intended to be.

Along with putting aside some cash and bank deposits for bills, the most important fiscal prep you can make is to get and stay out of debt. Debt costs you and a disaster can destroy your usual sources of income while making your creditors desperate to recover what you owe them. All your preps will do no good if they are taken by bailiffs and you find yourself on the street looking for a cardboard box big enough to shelter you and the kids. If ever this does look like a possibility, get everything but the basic furniture and immediate needs out of the home and hidden away in storage long before they knock at your door.

To prevent those sorts of problems, when any emergency does loom one of your early tasks should be to contact your bank and any creditors to discuss the situation and make arrangements for what you can do if things turn bad. Most organisations will be far more constructive with a customer who talks to them and who they see is making an effort than with those who are apparently burying their head in the sand. I say 'most' organisations but do be aware of the reputation of anyone with whom you do business; some government agencies in particular are well known for pursuing those who are doing something but who they think they can squeeze for more rather than chasing those who are avoiding their responsibilities altogether.

There are various things you can do with any cash beyond that required for immediate needs. You might want to keep some in cash for large unexpected bills and more for last-minute prepping purchases. That can be split up for security, with some in your grab bag, some hidden in the car, some in a cache or a fireproof box under the floorboards on the ground floor of your home, etc.

If your physical or training preps are not yet complete then extending them would be a sound investment and insurance policy. Precious metals are plummeting in value this week but that is due to manipulation of the share and commodity markets. Demand for physical gold, silver and platinum has never been higher, they are a form of savings you can build a little at a time and wise investors recognise them as the safe bet they have been for centuries.

Stocks and shares go up and down and can be lost completely if a business collapses; most artworks and antiques are subject to investor fashion, can be a good fallback if you can sell them at a formal auction but don't bring much if you are hawking them at the roadside; If you have tens of thousands to invest, property is subject to fluctuations but a suitable piece of land can be useful for all sorts of prepping purposes; vehicles and caravans depreciate in value but a static caravan or a touring model on a good site or a boat in a nice location can be a good BOL or alternative Bug In Location (BIL) that will serve you well for holidays for years. There are many alternatives but, to me, banks and the stock market are the least attractive for most Preppers.

Alternative systems

Even if there is a total political, social and/or economic collapse, whatever the cause, at some stage you will be able to come out of isolation and begin to interact with your neighbours and eventually beyond that. The situation you then face, however, may be very different.

Even now there are alternative financial systems in operation. Online for example there is Bitcoin about which Wikipedia says: "Bitcoin is accepted in trade by various merchants and individuals in many parts of the world. Although bitcoin was initially promoted as a virtual currency, many commentators currently reject that claim due to bitcoin's volatile market value, relatively inflexible supply, and minimal use in trade". Considering that the Internet might not be available in a Bugging In situation and there are already recognised issues with its viability, Bitcoin probably wouldn't be particularly useful but it is an interesting example of a different way of doing trade.

There are, however, some long established systems that have proved to be viable on a relatively small scale. One of these is the Local Exchange Trading System (LETS), known elsewhere as Local Employment Trading System (or Scheme). The concept is that someone who has goods or service/labour to offer registers with the local scheme and agrees a value in LETS credits for those goods or services.

This value is sometimes based on an equivalent in the national currency but may also be on a completely different but agreed value system, which allows a local scheme to value physical labour at the same or a higher credit level than IT skills, for example.

If someone employs them or accepts their goods the 'provider' is then credited and the 'buyer' debited with the agreed value in LETS. If the original provider then finds someone in the scheme who is offering something they want they can pay that provider in LETS credits. The original buyer must then provide something to pay off their debt in the system and earn credits before they are allowed to make another purchase.

The credits and debits are usually recorded in a central register, which also acts as a sort of Yellow Pages for anyone looking for particular goods or services, but individuals sometimes have a notebook that serves like a bankbook in which the buyer records and signs to acknowledge their purchase and the agreed value. Fraud is not unknown in the larger schemes but is easily exposed at local level.

LETS has the advantage over traditional Barter in that there doesn't have to be a direct exchange between the provider and the buyer, but that doesn't stop barter working in parallel with a LETS system if 2 or more people can arrange a mutually agreeable swap. In the past, barter between people not known to one another was usually done at a market place or trading post and involved some negotiation and trading skills to reach agreement on the exchange value.

Value will often be based on the scarcity or desirability of what is offered. If you have a roll of soft toilet paper for trade and they are both rare and desired, you will get a better trade than for a bar of soap that people might be able to make for themselves, for example. In skills the same is true; the work of the one doctor in the county would almost certainly be valued more highly than that of one of the dozen carpenters offering their labour.

As a Prepper you will have more skills and potentially more goods to offer in trade than most. Advertising that you are rich in trade goods would not be sensible but your skills and knowledge are not so easy to steal and might be even more valuable. Skills also have the advantage of taking up no room except for your tools and materials and only being restricted by your fitness and ability to work.

The goods you can offer fall into the categories of basics and luxuries and might be things you have stored or things you produce. Some Preppers actually buy and store items specifically as trade goods. I tend to put aside things I have bought and that work but that I have later replaced with a more effective or efficient version, or things I have collected over the years such as soap, shampoo and books of matches from my many stays in hotels while working away from home.

Small containers of consumables make good trade goods because the buyer will probably be back for another trade before too long but sometimes what you want to trade for justifies a bigger item such as a wind-up radio or lamp that will be better than anything the trading partner has but that you no longer need. What will people want to trade for? Basically all the same things that you need or want. Ideas on what are essentials and what are luxuries will differ but I offer the following ideas.

Essentials might include:

Food basics – vegetables, meat, fish, eggs, fat/oil, grain/flour, salt, hand tin openers and kitchen appliances, seeds,
Clean water – Water containers, filters/purifiers/chemicals, gathering systems
Hygiene supplies - Soap, detergent, nappies, sanitary goods, buckets, rubbish bags, clothes line and pegs, insect and vermin killers
Medical - Commercial medicines and herbal remedies, plasters, bandages,
Fuel - for heat/cooking/light, containers
Fire starters - Matches, lighters, lighter fuel, 'flint' kits,
Light – candles/holders, oil lamps, liquid fuel lamps, wicks, mantles, globes, batteries, wind-up or solar lamps, gas lamps and cylinders, etc
Food gathering and defence - Guns, Ammunition, Knives, other defensive devices, fishing gear
Maintenance - Hand tools and supplies (nails, screws, tape, glues, etc), sewing supplies,
Transport – bicycles and equipment, baggage trolleys/carts, bags and packs
Camping gear - especially if the Event has caused widespread destruction of residential property - tents, kip mats, sleeping bags, cookers, lamps, etc
Reference books

Luxuries might include:

Food extras – Fruit (fresh and dried), sweet preserves, tinned/bottled and dried goods, herbs and spices, flavourings, yeast, milk, deserts, vitamin pills, cooking foil, zip-lock bags, bottling jars/lids/seals
Drink flavourings – coffee, tea, fruit and herbal teas, cocoa, fruit juice, sweeteners (sugar/honey/saccharine), vinegar,
Hygiene - Scented soap, Shampoo, toothpaste, razor blades, soft toilet paper, tissues, cosmetics, hand washing machines, washboards, tubs, mangles,
Fuel - for vehicles or generators
Power - Generators, batteries, solar panels and devices, wind/water/dynamo turbines, lamps and torches
Communications – wind-up radios, paper, notebooks, pens/pencils/erasers/etc
Drugs – alcohol, cigarettes, tobacco and supplies
Entertainment – books, board games, dominoes, cards, musical instruments
Precious metals – particularly gold/silver coins, marked bars, jewellery

Skills you could offer might include:

Medical specialities – Doctor, Dentist, Vet, Nurse, Midwife, Pharmacist, Physiotherapist, Psychologist, First Aid worker, Acupuncturist, Herbalist, Masseur/Reflexologist, Carer, Undertaker
Food provider – Farmer, Gardener, Stockbreeder (chickens, rabbits, goats, etc), Hunter, Wild plant expert, Fisherman, Pest controller, Bee Keeper, Butcher, Cook – specialist in making and using stoves burning wood/coke/coal and cooking wild edibles, Brewer, Wine maker, Distiller, Salter
Water specialist – Distiller, Filter Maker, Diviner, Well Driller/Digger, Drainer
Energy Provider – Battery Charger, Renewable Energy Specialist, Candle/lamp Maker, Chimney sweep, charcoal maker
Clothier – Cobbler, Seamstress, Knitter, Spinner, Weaver, Tanner/Dyer, Leather Maker
Makers – Blacksmith, Mechanic, Engineer, Builder, Carpenter, Cooper, Tinker, Wheelwright, Boat builder, Soap maker, Chemist, Gunsmith, Ammunition reloader
Knowledge and skills – Teacher, Librarian, Researcher
Security – Guard, Soldier, Messenger, Communications expert (Radio, Morse code, flags, etc)
Luxuries – Gold/silversmith, Jeweller, card maker, wreath maker
Entertainer – Musician, Singer, Poet, Story Writer/Teller

Bug In Kit and Supplies

This is a list of equipment and supplies that you might need for a Bug In scenario. It doesn't cover everything you will have, such as ordinary household items, but includes as many as I could bring to mind of the essential extras that you might need for emergencies. Not everyone will want everything on the list and some people will have some of these items for their everyday activities, and I might have missed something that you consider important for you, but hopefully the list will serve as a guide and a memory prompt.

Shelter:

Hand tools:

Wood saw, tennon saw, and hack saw

Hammers - claw and tack

Screw drivers – Flat, Phillips, Posidrive, in various sizes

Pliers

Wire cutters

Metal file

Sand or glass paper and emery paper

Craft knife with replaceable blades

Heavy duty scissors

Mole grips and adjustable spanners

Measuring tape

Supplies – nails, screws, nuts and bolts, brass wire, fuses, gaffer tape, insulating tape, string, nylon cord, cable ties,

Plywood (minimum 5 ply, thicker preferable but heavy) for window boards and emergency repairs

Rolls of heavy duty sheet polythene - Opaque polythene (blackouts) and some clear (dust traps / seals but allows light in)

Brace and bit / Hand drill - Variety of wood, masonry and metal drill bits

Glue (CA for fixing, epoxy)

Mastic gun and mastic (for sealing air gaps, waterproofing rain harvesting etc.)

Plastic pipe and push fit joints

Electrical cable

Plane

Wood rasps

Steel rule

Carpenter's pencils

Wire strippers

Glass cutter

Putty

Chisels

Post rammer

Post Hole digger

Wire tensioner

Work Gloves

Electrical Multimeter

Self-amalgamating tape

Vice and work bench

Bricklayers Trowel

Mortar

Cable ties

Temperature control:

Solid fuel stove

Fuel – wood, coke, coal,

Axes, hatchets, saws, shovel, etc

Chain saw and safety clothing

Log splitter, wedges

Butane/Propane heaters + cylinders of gas

Solar charged or other 12v fans

Lighters, matches, ferro rods, tinder items

Matt black paint, aluminium foil (for reflectors)

Hot water bottles

Water:

Water butts – with down-pipe diverters

Water containers

 Hand and/or battery water pumps

Hoses

British Berkefeld (or other) water filter

Bleach or other chemical purifier

Poly sheeting for rain collection

Still

Food:

Stored food – tins, packets; dried basics e.g. corn, flour, pasta, rice; salt and other seasonings; oil, honey, milk powder; beverages – plus paper coffee filters if you store coffee ground or beans; treats

Multivitamins

Gardening tools, equipment, and supplies – Spade, fork, rake, hoe, shovel, trowel, hand fork, dibber, yard brush, pocket knife, gloves, goggles, wheelbarrow; seeds; pots for seedlings; watering can and/or hose and water butts; compost bin(s); Incinerator; shears, croppers, pruning shears and saw, sledge hammer, pick, twine, wire, canes, netting, cable ties, buckets, cloches, greenhouse, sieve, fertiliser, insecticide, anti-fungus, soil improvers, and more according to your skills, space and needs.

Guns, bows, catapult, and associated ammunition, equipment and supplies

Snares and traps

Fishing kit – rods, line, hooks, flies, yoyo reels, spring hooks, nets, etc

Wild plant identification guide

Storage tubs/jars, and mylar bags, bag sealer, oxygen excluders

Dehydrator

Bottling equipment and supplies

Grain mill

Wine/beer making kit

Cooking:

Wood/multi-fuel burners

Butane/Propane cooker(s)

Other fuelled cookers – meths, paraffin, petrol, hexamine, etc

Fuel for cookers

Barbeque and supplies

Dutch oven

Kelley Kettle

Trivet, chain and pots

Lighters and matches

Power:

Generator(s) + fuel and oil

Solar panels

Wind or water turbine

Dynamo chargers and devices

Battery chargers – various power sources

Rechargeable batteries AAA/AA/C/D/9v

Battery adaptors – to allow use of smaller batteries e.g. AA in things intended to use larger ones e.g. D cell

Leisure batteries

Top up water, and funnel

Inverters

Charge controllers

Cables, connectors and adapters

Portable power kits

Light:

Solar-charged lighting systems - including PIR switched solar security lights

Gas/dynamo/paraffin/oil/petrol/battery lamps, with fuel, batteries, etc

Candles, holders, lamps, snuffer

Long neck lighter and gas

Torches

Rechargeable batteries and chargers

Health and Hygiene:

Toiletries: soap, shampoo, toothpaste, toothbrushes, floss, mouthwash, denture fixative, razors and blades, toilet paper, wipes, hand sanitiser, tissues

Spectacles and fixing kit

Chiropody equipment and supplies

Chemical/composting toilet/bucket with lid + liners and chemicals or kitty litter as required

Wash bowl and jug

Solar and hand pumped showers

Disinfectant and cleaning supplies

Bin bags

Washing up liquid, hand wash for clothes

Boiling bucket/pan

Low power twin tub or dolly and washboard

Clothes line and pegs

NBCR kit and detectors inc. biohazard suits/masks/gloves/etc

Vermin traps and poisons

Insect killers

Medical: (adapted from various references – does not include prescription drugs)

Surgical gloves and masks

Hand cleanser

Resuscitation face shields

Antiseptic wipes

Cotton wool pads

Standard bandages – various sizes

Wound dressings – various sizes

Low-adhesive wound dressings

Adhesive dressings (plasters)

Liquid dressing – with applicator or spray

Burn dressings

Crepe bandages – various sizes

Elastic bandages

Joint supports – wrist, elbow, knee, and ankle

Heat patches

Cold patches

Surgical tape, safety pins

Triangular bandages

Bandage scissors

Clotting agents

Eye pads/patches

Nasal plugs

Surgical spirit

Antiseptic cream

Antihistamine cream

Calamine lotion

Iodine

Potassium permanganate

External muscle relaxants e.g. ibuprofen cream

Eye wash

Eye drops – lubricating, soothing

Chap sticks

Vaseline

Haemorrhoidal cream

Ventolin inhalers

Wart and Verruca remover

Athletes foot lotion

Cold sore cream

Canestan oral and cream

Emergency dental kit

Surgical and nursing equipment:

Charts: temperature, pulse, blood pressure, medication, water/food intake, urination/defecation, other notes + pens

Antibiotic soap

Nail brushes

Paper towels

Gowns

Aprons

Surgical masks

Surgical gloves

Hand cleanser

Pen torch

Thermometer

Heart rate meter or watch with second hand for taking pulse

Blood pressure monitor

Stethoscope

Blood testing kit – glucose, blood, ketone, protein, bilirubin, and pH.

Pulse oximeter

Metal basins for instruments

Steriliser

Airways

Scalpels

Forceps

Scissors

Clamps

Needle holder

Sutures

Wound closure – butterfly and area

Suture adhesive

Syringes

Needles – hypodermic, intramuscular, intravenous

Catheters and administration sets

Dental instruments

Oxygen set

Enema kit

Medical saline solution

Neck support

Splints

Plaster bandages

Walking stick

Crutches

Wheelchair

Midwifery supplies if appropriate

Sheets, pillow cases, pillows, blankets for sick bay use only

Water jug with level markings and tumbler

Water bottle with spout, babies' bottles and teats

Tissues

Cutlery and crockery – disposable or for sick bay use only

Bed pan, urinal (male and female), and commode

Toilet rolls

Baby wipes

Waterproof sheets

Bowls for washing

Soap

Flannels

Towels

Razors

Disinfectant liquid and wipes

Scrubbing brushes

Mop and bucket

Disposable cleaning cloths

Yellow bin liners for surgical/body waste

Body bags

Medicines:

Aspirin

Paracetamol

Ibuprofen

Codeine

Antibiotics – as available

Cough medicines – tickly and chesty

Antacids

Activated charcoal powder

Antihistamine

Laxative

Imodium (or similar loperamide drug)

Antiemetic

Oil of cloves

Corsodyl or similar antibiotic mouthwash

Oral Rehydration salts

Safety and Security:

Window boards

Door wedges/bracing struts

CCTV (to see what is happening outside when the window boards are up – powered from 12v leisure battery with inverter)

Fixed and mobile alarm systems

Solar charged security lights

High power lamp

Night vision scope or binoculars

Barbed/razor wire, fence-top spikes, mortar for setting broken glass in wall tops,

Smoke and CO2 alarms

Fire extinguishers and blanket, hose.

Sand and rubble bags

'Other security equipment and supplies'

Communications:

Emergency charger (battery/dynamo/solar) for mobile phone – just in case the network is working

Plug in phone – may be operational without electricity at your location and for longer than a mobile

SW, CB, PMR, radios, antennae, batteries/chargers, accessories

Solar/battery/wind-up radios/mini TV/laptop computer

Signalling equipment e.g. marker pens, high-visibility vests or other items, flares, whistles, heliograph,

EMP protection for electronic kit

Transport:

Urban vehicle + associated kit and tools

Fuel in cans.

Fuel preservative

Hand and battery fuel pumps.

Bikes – motor and/or pedal

Protective clothing

Tools

Boat and paddle/oars

Other:

Spinning wheel, carders, needles and thread, hand sewing machine, supplies

Leather working kit

Stationery supplies – including an A4 pad for your log/diary

Books, cards, board games, music media, films, computer games

Trade items and goods

Reference books

Paper towels, plastic cups and cutlery (for when water is too scarce to use for washing up)

Local area maps and Yellow pages (reference for efficient foraging)

Bugging In task list

What you need to do prior to or immediately after a major emergency and in what order or priority will depend on the nature of that emergency and its probable and potential effects. Many of the items in the following list will be appropriate to some situations but not to others. Pick, choose, and add to the items as you see fit but if in doubt do it anyway; more will rarely be wrong or irreversible if it proves not to be needed.

First actions

Contact members of your family and group to ensure they know about the situation and what you are intending to do

Do any final bank withdrawals, shopping, and vehicle refuelling - if safe to do so

Move to your Bug In location

Keep monitoring the news about the situation

Just in case

Prepare or check your kits in case you have to Bug Out

Prepare and pack your vehicle or other forms of transport then secure them

Confirm that intended BOLs are still viable by calling the occupants or considering the news, as appropriate

Check news, Internet, etc. to confirm, in so far as possible, whether Bug Out routes are still viable

Set up any coded message systems ready to put in place if you have to go

While you can still go outside

Move animals inside or otherwise provide for those that will stay out

Move flammable materials away from the house and outbuildings

Position and prepare fire suppressant measures e.g. spray hoses under gutters and window ledges

Position and if appropriate activate any warning and deterrent signs and devices

Check fences, walls and hedges. Repair or reinforce as required

Finish any external security precautions e.g. apply security film, replace blown light bulbs, fit intercom by door or gate, etc

Check alarms on outbuildings are working, replace batteries as required

Seal the letterbox and by the door provide a large plastic box with a lid, marked as for post, papers, etc.

Top up or empty and refill water barrels

Clear gutters and pipes whether leading to drains or water barrels

Install alternative water pumping arrangements

Prepare and position other water collection measures

Take out and dispose of all rubbish

Prepare incinerator and dig pits for disposal of human and other waste

Move any supplies normally kept outside to safe indoor storage

Harvest any crops that are ready and move them into appropriate storage arrangements or prepare them for preservation.

Trim or prune any plants that could provide concealment for intruders

Weed and tidy the rest of the vegetable garden

Prepare and test generators

Deploy any additional solar panels, etc

Apply fallout shielding if required

Whitewash the outside of windows to reflect light and heat flash

Close or remove down pipes leading to water barrels

Clean paving slabs or concrete to ease removal of contamination

Prepare a place and materials for temporary storage of bodies

Once all tasks are done and everyone is in, secure all outbuildings, gates, etc.

Indoors

Carry out a thorough clean and disinfect of the house

Check and prepare alternative power arrangements ready for use

Review and prepare warmth and cooling arrangements

Prepare, test and position alternative lighting, cooking, heating equipment

Unpack and prepare other emergency equipment and clothing

Apply security precautions e.g. lock all windows and doors other than main access, fit window boards and door bracing struts

Replace or position batteries for powering security and devices instead of from mains e.g. lights, intruder/smoke/CO/CO2 alarms, etc

Clean, prepare and position weapons

Fit any additional blackout curtains or tape

Seal gaps and openings against chemical, biological, radiation ingress

Clear all fire escape routes

Check and position fire extinguishers and escape equipment

Issue or position smoke masks and other clothing

Recharge all batteries

Prepare isolation/quarantine/sick rooms

Begin issue and monitoring of preventive medicine

Prepare alternative toilet arrangements

Wash and dry all laundry including only recently worn items, while water and electricity are still available

Have a shower and wash hair while water and electricity are still available

Review food supplies and decide on order and routine of usage

Begin preparation and preservation of frozen and fresh foods

Refresh water supplies

Institute food and water saving or rationing methods when required

Check alternative comms arrangements

Establish comms with external contacts and agree codes, contact times, frequencies, etc

Contact work, bank, creditors, etc. to discuss the situation and alternative arrangements if required

Position internal radiation shielding materials

Begin radiation monitoring and recording

Monitor all news channels

Review all lists and arrangements

Have a family/group meeting to discuss next steps, provide reassurance, review responsibilities and tasks, etc.

New products, ideas and information

Here are some examples of new and upcoming technology and ideas I have come across since writing the main parts of this book. Since they are new, unlike the other items in the book I haven't tested them so I include them for information and interest rather than as a recommendation.

The Tellurex tea light powered lamp

http://www.buytpod.com/products-page

Powered by a tea light candle heating a thermoelectric generator, or TEG, the compact Tellurex tPOD1™ (Patent Pending) provides four hours of continuous bright light for 3p. Or, it can charge a battery pack to provide minimal power for limited smartphone GPS rescue signal use. 1 tea light will provide up to 4 hours of bright light from 24 LEDs. Price is currently $69 plus shipping.

Indiegogo gravity powered lamp

A recent and very interesting dynamo-type system is the gravity powered lamp project being run through Indiegogo.

http://www.indiegogo.com/projects/282006

The purpose of the project is to provide free or very cheap lighting to parts of Asia and Africa where the people have no electricity or none to their homes. The intent is to develop a reliable source of lighting that is low-cost to make and zero-cost to run to replace paraffin or expensive solar projects

The result is an LED lamp that is run from a dynamo wound by a gradually descending weight. The weight is simply a bag of earth, sand or other suitable material, so only the bag needs to be included in the kit.

The expected cost to users in remote places should be less than £3 which will quickly be recovered from the savings on paraffin.

The lamp/generator contains no battery, so there is nothing to replace, and lifting then releasing the bag takes seconds but produces light for up to 30 minutes. You might not want one of these in your living room – though it would be a fantastic conversation point - but for the garage, workshop, shed, cellar, etc. it has great promise.

The only way to get one of these lights at the moment is to become a sponsor of the project at a minimum of $50, which will not only get you a kit but provide one free to a villager and help to fund further development.

Camping Gaz oven

Camping Gaz have launched a new camping stove with oven.

http://www.campingaz.com/uk/p-26652-camp-stove-oven.aspx

The stove has Piezo ignition, two burners, plus an oven large enough to take a 30cm pizza. Boil time on the rings is given as 7 minutes. Run time using the rings is nearly 12 hours or 46 hours using the oven on an R907 2.75Kg Butane cylinder. Oven temperature is adjustable up to 250C. RRP is £250

External size is : 69 x 47 x 38 cm
Oven size is 37 x 34 x 14 cm
Weight: 18.5kg

Solar Kettle

http://www.contemporaryenergy.co.uk/solarkettle.htm

Another off-grid idea. To me the kettle looks big for carrying around but it is an idea for Bugging In. It would give you hot water with no use of fuel or generating smoke or smells in the process.

From Contemporary Energy: Our solar kettle, which we have been developing for several years, is now in full production. This version was developed from our T45 prototype. It is extremely portable and very stylish. In use, its reflectors are folded out to gather three times more energy than with only a plain tube. During transit the reflectors are folded in to protect the tube and assist with its portability. The solar kettle looks and feels just like a large thermos.

The Solar Kettle is ideal for any outdoor activity - camping, bird watching, fishing, hiking, picnics, etc £35.00 + £8.00 P&P UK airmail to other countries varies (max £12 Europe, £22/23.00 elsewhere)

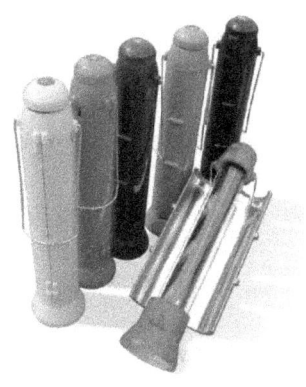

Pedal powered washing machine

http://www.norwichcamping.co.uk/products/ventus-twister-self-powered-washing-machine/

This is a recent product and Norwich Camping offers it at the lowest price I could find at £49.99. Price from other sellers varies up to £65 plus delivery. The machine is lightweight and portable, requires no electricity and has a capacity of 13 litres of water. It will both wash and spin the clothes. It is most suited to lightweight materials and underwear. The website above has more details and a video of the main features and use.

Summary

I have written Bugging In to explain and emphasise the need for Preparedness and provide information and advice on how to be prepared to survive in many differing situations where you have to batten down the hatches.

The concept is based on the fact that to prevent you and your family or group suffering the effects of a failure of normal facilities and to maintain your freedom of self-determination, you have to be self-reliant.

Despite, and sometimes because of, all our modern technology and advances in scientific knowledge, our world remains a fragile place with many potential dangers. We still see war; terrorism; human, animal and plant diseases; drought, floods, long cold winters and unexpected heat waves; global financial failures; resource shortages; industrial accidents and so much more.

We complain about our governments and their seeming inability to respond as they should when disaster strikes and yet we increasingly surrender our fate to them when all our history and experience should scream the futility and wrongfulness of relying totally on other people rather than being prepared to care for ourselves and one another. To survive you need to reject any sense of entitlement and fully accept responsibility for the welfare of yourself and those who depend on you.

To survive you will require supplies, skills, knowledge and an appropriately positive, determined and resourceful mindset. In this book I have attempted to share some of the knowledge you will need and to direct you to where and how you can obtain more and if appropriate to sources of relevant training so you can develop the skills; gathering the supplies and developing the mindset is up to you!

I hope you never need it but I pray that if you do what I have written in these pages will be of help to you.

Acknowledgements

My sincerest thanks go to: my wife Pat, for her constant support and her knowledge on many subjects in this book, especially those dealing with food storage, preservation, and cooking, Tim for his most welcome proof reading, Hugh and Dave D for advice on many items, Chris Breen for his medical knowledge, Jan for her advice on psychological issues, and members of Ludlow Survivors Group for their suggestions for the Bug In kit list.

Thank you all

Reading list and links

More information on various subjects included in this book can be gained from:

Ludlow Survival Group: http://www.ludlowsurvivors.com

Chris Breen, Survival Medic http://www.survival-medic.com

The Energy Saving Trust:
http://www.energysavingtrust.org.uk/Take-action/Start-saving-money

Gravity light project: http://www.indiegogo.com/projects/282006

Fenix torches: http://www.fenixtorch.co.uk/

Tellurex tea light powered lamp: http://www.buytpod.com/products-page

Building regulations for fires and stoves:
http://www.planningportal.gov.uk/buildingregulations/approveddocuments/partj/approved

Portable wood burners: http://www.campingsolutions.co.uk/

Wood burners, multi-fuel stoves and related advice:
http://www.stovesonline.co.uk

Urban Aquaculture – raising fish and plants for food at home
http://www.webofcreation.org/BuildingGrounds/aqua/TOC.html

Streetcraft – David E Crossley and LSG members

The Off-grid energy handbook – Alan and Gill Bridgewater

LDS Preparedness manual – compiled by Brother Christopher M. Parrett

How to store your garden produce – Piers Warren

Wilderness & Survival Medicine – Chris Breen & Dr Craig Ellis

International medical guide for ships – W.H.O

Where there is no doctor – David Werner

Where there is no dentist – Murray Dickson

Before you call the doctor – Dr Hilary Jones

Parlour Games for Modern Families – Myfanwy Jones

About the author

Son of a Scottish mother and Yorkshire father, David Eric Crossley was raised in Yorkshire. After a number of unsatisfying jobs, he joined the forces in 1970 and was a soldier for over 20 years.

Qualified as an instructor in Nuclear Biological and Chemical Warfare, Combat Survival, Urban and Counter-revolutionary Warfare, Signals, Advanced First Aid, Light Rescue and Fire fighting, among other things, he served in Africa, Asia, the Gulf, Central and South America and Europe. He has lived through the reality and aftermath of wars and counter-terrorist operations, and as an advisor and rescuer during Aid to the Civil Powers missions after major disasters overseas.

After leaving the forces, David settled in Scotland. He worked as Training Manager Scotland for the British Red Cross for 4 years including training overseas service and emergency response volunteers, and now works as an independent training consultant and writer.

David has been writing professionally since the 1980s and has had over 80 magazine articles and short stories published in outdoors, survival, military, business and general interest magazines. He has also published the companion to this book – Bugging In, plus There Falls No Shadow - the first novel of a post-apocalyptic series, is working on the second, Slow the Shadow Creeps, and compiled, edited and wrote much of an urban survival reference, published as Streetcraft, for Ludlow Survivors Group.

Check out David's website at: http://www.tfns.co.uk/index2.html

David welcomes feedback from readers of his work. Please email him at: books@decrossley.co.uk

Twitter @TfnsbooksDavid

Facebook David E. Crossley Books